I0606136

The Artful Pie Project

A SWEET *and* SAVOURY BOOK *of* RECIPES

Written by DENISE MARCHESSAULT

Artwork and Photography by DEB GARLICK

The Artful Pie Project

A SWEET *and* SAVOURY BOOK *of* RECIPES

whitecap

EDITED BY Patrick Geraghty
PROOFREAD BY Patrick Geraghty
DESIGNED BY Andrew Bagatella
PHOTOGRAPHY BY Deb Garlick

Library and Archives Canada Cataloguing in Publication

TITLE: The artful pie project : a sweet and savoury book of recipes/ written by Denise Marchessault ; artwork and photography by Deb Garlick.
NAMES: Marchessault, Denise, 1959- author. | Garlick, Deb, artist, photographer.
DESCRIPTION: First edition. | Includes index.
IDENTIFIERS: Canadiana 20220140960 | ISBN 9781770503601 (hardcover)
SUBJECTS: LCSH: Pies. | LCGFT: Cookbooks.
CLASSIFICATION: LCC TX773 .M36 2022 | DDC 641.86/52—dc23

Whitecap Books acknowledges the financial support of the Government of Canada through the Canada Book Fund (CBF) for our publishing activities and the Province of British Columbia through the Book Publishing Tax Credit.

Printed in China

whitecap.ca

THANK YOU

In a world where recipes are as close as your keyboard, and cookbooks are plentiful, it seems a little magical that our book has made its way to you. Thank you for choosing *The Artful Pie Project*.

For my sweetie pies, Lucie and Elise Marchessault

For Elizabeth and David Garlick who would have laughed, and been delighted.

TABLE OF CONTENTS

INTRODUCTION

ARTFUL PIE

If pastry is an art, then bakers and artists would seem a natural fit.

I first met artist Deb Garlick when she attended one of my cooking classes in Victoria, BC. I marvelled at the breadth of her creativity, her striking photography and the playful whimsy reflected in all of her art.

Baking is my first love and I'd been dreaming of a pastry-themed project for years, but it took running into Deb at a book store to set the wheels in motion. When I suggested we team up to create a book where pastry and art intersect, Deb was all in. We took a deep dive into handcrafted pies with a shared vision—to create a cookbook as beautiful as it is practical.

Few things in life are as comforting as homemade pie, and we hope this book inspires you to discover, or rediscover, the art of pastry.

GETTING STARTED

Like all crafty projects, pies take a bit of planning. They're not difficult, but they involve a number of steps. New bakers tend to underestimate the amount of time required, but with a game plan, pastry is easy to master—even if you've had a few false starts.

If you've ever baked a pie that fell short of expectations, you'll appreciate the handy tips in the Practicalities section (page 5). And you'll find straightforward strategies for avoiding Soggy Bottoms and Other Pie Pitfalls (page 11).

A pie is only as good as its crust, and there are plenty of options for fail-proof pastry made by hand or machine. Bakers enjoy sampling new doughs, so these have been bundled together, allowing you to easily swap one for another. For example, if you love the Chocolate Walnut Dough featured in the Triple-Chocolate Tart recipe (page 232), you may want to try the dough in other tart recipes. Baking is all about creativity, so feel free to mix and match doughs.

Recipes have been sorted by ingredient (fruits and nuts, vegetables, etc.) so you can jump to your favourites and bake in-season when fruits and vegetables are most flavourful.

Beyond pie, you'll find plenty of creative ideas for using up those precious scraps of leftover dough (and surplus egg whites). And because pies love company, there's a selection of sweet and savoury accompaniments to partner with your favourite recipes.

Whatever your skill level or baking temperament, *The Artful Pie Project* has a recipe that's just right for you!

COLD PASTRY
HOT OVEN!!

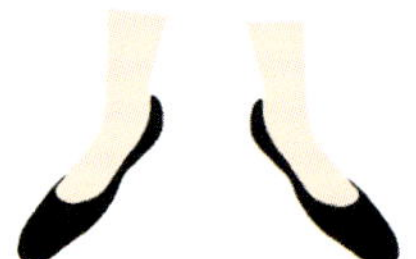

PRACTICALITIES

(THINGS I WISH I'D KNOWN WHEN I WAS STARTING OUT)

I've been baking for decades, but seldom make a pie in one sitting. I prefer to prepare my pastry and filling a day or two in advance and leave the assembly for later. This is because pastry, and often the filling, need considerable time in the fridge to firm. When pastry is parsed out in manageable steps it can be made at your leisure, and if you consider that pastry can be refrigerated up to three days before using, or frozen up to two months, it's easy to fit into your schedule.

FILLINGS

It makes good sense to prepare fillings in advance, as most need to be chilled *before* they're added to the pastry. Savoury fillings, such as chicken or beef pot pies, taste even better after they've lingered in the fridge a few days. Custard and cream fillings can be prepared days in advance, too.

If that's not reason enough to plan ahead, consider that most pies need a resting period after they're baked. Some fruit pies, for example, take up to four hours to firm.

HOW I ROLL

I prefer to roll my dough between parchment paper and plastic wrap. This prevents the dough from sticking to my rolling pin and my work surface. (Periodically, I lift a portion of the dough to smooth the parchment which tends to scrunch-up as the dough is rolled.) It's a technique noted throughout the book, but it's not the only way to roll. Some bakers prefer to roll their dough directly onto a floured work surface. Or a non-stick baking mat or floured pastry cloth. All these methods work, the key is to find a method that works best for you.

Dough is always rolled from the centre to a pastry's edge in all directions. With parchment beneath your pastry, you can reposition the pastry easily, turning the dough in all directions, while keeping your rolling pin in the same comfortable position. Some bakers, however, dislike the way parchment can slide on the countertop when the dough is rolled. You can prevent this by placing a damp paper towel or dish towel beneath the parchment. I don't bother with this extra step, but every baker finds their own way to roll.

WHEN TO ROLL

Dough taken directly from the fridge is too firm to easily roll out. Allow your dough to rest on your counter (still covered) until pliable but still cool. Doughs containing lard and shortening need little rest, but butter-based doughs, such as the Sweet Tart Dough (page 38), need at least 30 minutes to come to their ideal rolling temperature. When in doubt, press the dough with your finger—if it leaves a slight imprint, you're ready to roll.

If your dough becomes too soft at any point, wrap it in plastic and return it to the fridge to firm. Moving your dough between the fridge and counter allows you to work with the pastry at its most malleable temperature.

COLD PASTRY, HOT OVEN

Pastry is chilled throughout the baking process—after the dough is made, after it's rolled and transferred to a pie plate and again after it's assembled. It helps to make space in the fridge before you get started. If you're making tarts, for example, you'll need enough room to chill the tarts on a baking tray or platter before they're baked. If space is limited, you can stack the tarts, but be mindful that space is still needed.

Chilling dough is important for several reasons. It allows the moisture in the pastry to diffuse, the fat to firm and the gluten to relax, which prevents your pastry from drawing back when you roll it out or shrinking during baking.

Pastry doesn't behave well in warm conditions. The fat in the dough melts too quickly, making the dough difficult to manage. If you're making a berry pie on a warm summer's day, for example, plan to make the pastry when your kitchen's at its coolest, either early in the morning or late at night. Be mindful of your kitchen's subtle temperature nuances. If your countertop has a dishwasher tucked beneath it, as mine does, your counter will heat up when the machine is running. Marble and granite countertops are nice to work on, as they keep things cool, but I've rolled dough on everything from steel counters to wooden benches. The key is not so much the counter's surface, but the temperature of your dough. Some bakers refrigerate their flour and mixing bowl (some go as far as cooling their countertops with ice), but I find these steps unnecessary when working with chilled butter and lard.

Chilled unbaked pastries should be transferred to a preheated pan or pizza stone for baking. The heated base sets the pastry before the filling has a chance to seep in, preventing a sad, soggy crust. When in doubt, follow the baker's mantra: "Cold Pastry, Hot Oven."

A GOLDEN CRUST

Pastry is more flavourful and has a better texture when it's well browned. Some bakers make the mistake of removing their pastries from the oven just before they're about to take on a rich, golden crust. Keep a watchful eye on your pies and tarts, and tent them with foil as necessary, but allow them to take on colour.

LEFTOVER DOUGH

There are plenty of ways to use up any precious scraps of leftover dough (see pages 62–65 for a number of examples). However, if you don't plan to bake within two to three days, it's best to roll the dough into a circle (large or small) about ⅛–¼ inch (3–6 mm) thick and transfer it to a reusable freezer bag. If you have more than one portion of rolled dough, separate the dough between sheets of parchment. You're more apt to use frozen pastry when it's rolled out and ready to go.

STORAGE

Pies are at their optimum flavour and texture on the day they're baked. However, fruit pies do keep well at room temperature in a domed cake container (or covered with plastic wrap or foil) up to two days. Pies containing eggs, cream or meat should be refrigerated.

Pastry can be frozen up to two months in plastic wrap or reusable freezer bags (foil and parchment do not protect pastry as well as plastic). Fruit pies, mousse tarts and meat pies will freeze well up to two months stored in reusable freezer bags. Fillings made of custards and cheese do not freeze well.

SEE

SENSE & SENSIBILITY

Making a great pie involves more than following a recipe blindly and turning on your oven. It's a mindful practice that engages all your senses.

TOUCH—Trust your hands to know when a pastry is too warm and needs firming in the fridge, or when it's too cool and needs to rest on the counter until it's malleable enough to roll out.

SMELL—The scent of toasted almonds and spices lets you know when they're perfectly roasted. Hold a nectarine or strawberry to your nose and the fragrance will reveal if it's ripe or not.

HEAR—The sizzle and sputter of onions as they hit the pan tells you whether your skillet is the right (or wrong) temperature. Keep your ears attuned to your kitchen—a custard simmering gently sounds different from one boiling madly.

TASTE—Sample your pie filling *before* it's baked and you'll know if it needs an extra pinch of sugar or salt, or a squeeze of lemon juice. Tomatoes and berries may be tart or sweet; taste them first and you'll fine-tune your baking.

SEE—Keep a watchful eye on your ingredients—meringue is beautifully glossy and billowy before it collapses and turns grainy from overwhipping. Likewise, pies are always perfect just before they burn.

SOGGY BOTTOMS & OTHER PIE PITFALLS

When I was a fledging baker, an acquaintance tasted one of my pies and asked me to show her how to make pastry. Flattered, I jumped at the opportunity to show off my pastry skills. It didn't go well. The dough wouldn't stick together and I became flustered and added too much water. I still recall the unsalvageable, sticky mess I created—and the sting of embarrassment. It was a long while before I picked up a rolling pin again.

Pastry trauma is real. And sometimes it's inherited. My friend Pamela's baking reticence comes from a critical mother who set the bar sky-high (a consequence of *her* mother's incontestable pastry skills). My colleague Carolyn, who shies from baking, recalls how distressed she felt as a child watching her usually stalwart mother dissolve into tears over a fallen cake or a less-than-perfect pie.

Perhaps you've made a pie with a soggy crust. Or a pastry so tough you needed a steak knife to cut through it. Maybe your crust was so fragile that it crumbled in your hands. Perhaps you've baked up a soupy pie or your filling overflowed in the oven and set off the smoke detector. I've made all these mistakes, and plenty more!

But every blunder comes with a lesson. Knowing what not to do is as important as knowing what to do. If you've had a pie fail or two, consider yourself ahead of the curve. With time, you'll adapt to the nuances of baking and discover that the process is as pleasurable as the end result.

PREVENTING SOGGY PASTRY

There are a number of reasons pastry can end up soggy. Here are a few ways to prevent it.

Bake chilled pies on a preheated baking tray or pizza stone—the base firms faster, preventing the filling from seeping into the crust and rendering it soggy. Ensure your oven is hot (425°F/220°C) before the pastry is added. Not all ovens are trustworthy, but an inexpensive oven thermometer will allow you to adjust your oven's temperature if necessary.

A soggy crust is often a result of underbaking. Sometimes an extra few minutes in the oven will solve the problem. Tent with foil as necessary to prevent burning.

Blind baking (prebaking a pastry crust) is another way to prevent a soggy bottom. This is useful when a filling is especially moist, such as a juicy plum pie, or when a filling is baked at a lower temperature than the crust requires, as with a custardy quiche. Blind baking is also necessary when a filling requires little or no baking, such as a mousse filling.

Blind baking involves covering an unbaked pastry shell with parchment or foil, then filling it with pie weights (or dried beans or rice) to prevent the pastry from buckling in the oven. Once the pastry is sufficiently cooked, the pie weights (and parchment and foil) are removed.

Coating a blind-baked crust with Parmesan cheese or egg white before it's baked helps create a barrier from the filling, thereby keeping the pastry firm. Lining a pastry with breadcrumbs also helps absorb excess moisture, keeping the crust firm.

Cooling racks help prevent soggy bottoms by lifting the pastry off the counter and allowing air to circulate and cool it. If you don't have a cooling rack, you can improvise with a trivet, a rack from a toaster oven or just about anything that lifts your pastry.

PREVENTING PASTRIES FROM SHRINKING

Pastry dough tends to shrink during baking if not chilled for a sufficient period of time after the dough is made, after it's rolled and shaped and after the pie is assembled. Properly chilling also prevents the dough from springing back when it's rolled out.

Blind-baked crusts can shrink during baking if the pie weights do not come all the way to the top of the pastry.

If pastry is stretched when it's transferred to your pie plate, it can shrink during baking.

UNEVEN BROWNING

Most ovens have hotspots, so you'll need to turn your baking tray midway during baking to ensure the pastry has browned evenly. Tent with foil as necessary. Edges tend to burn faster, so fashion a foil ring around the pie to protect the edges, or use silicone pie shields. To make a handy foil ring that doesn't fall off your pastry during baking, cover an entire oven-ready pie or tart with foil, secure the edges in place and cut out the centre with scissors, leaving only a 1-inch (2.5 cm) border of foil.

TARTS STUCK IN TART MOLDS

If you've ever had a tart crumble in your hands while you try to pry it from its mold, you'll remember to line your tart pans with parchment paper *before* adding the pastry. For small tarts between 2½ and 4 inches (6–10 cm), line the molds with parchment baking cups. The baked tarts will slip away from the molds with ease. Parchment can be cut to fit any size of tart mold.

TOUGH PASTRY

If pie dough is tough, it has likely been overworked. Pastry takes a delicate hand and should be mixed just until the ingredients come together in a cohesive but somewhat shaggy mass. Adding too much flour to your work surface can result in a tough pastry (which is why I prefer to roll my dough onto parchment paper). Temperature also plays a role—in a flaky pastry dough, for example, butter must be cold, otherwise it can result in a tough crust (the water in melting butter is to blame as it can bind with the flour and activate the gluten).

DIFFICULT TO ROLL

When dough is difficult to roll, it's often too cold or too warm. Pastry direct from the fridge is often too firm to roll and needs time on the counter to come to a more manageable temperature. Conversely, when dough is handled for too long, it becomes too warm and soft to work with, and needs firming in the fridge. Moving your dough between the fridge and counter is key to a successful pastry.

If your dough is sticking to the counter and your rolling pin, you're likely not rolling it between parchment and plastic wrap. Although some experienced bakers prefer to roll their dough directly onto a flour-dusted counter, it's easier to manage soft sweet doughs between parchment dusted with flour and plastic wrap.

TEARS, CRACKS AND KROBLEES

Fragile doughs tear easily, particularly sweet and nutty doughs, but they can be pressed directly into a pan with your fingers and patched easily with excess pastry.

Cracked or dry pastry dough is often a result of exposure to air. Wrap doughs tightly in plastic wrap before refrigerating.

If all else fails, you can always reclaim and rename. I have, on occasion, poured a delicious mess of a pie into dessert cups, added a dollop of whipped cream and a jaunty cookie and christened it a "kroblee" (a name as improvised as the dessert itself).

PARCHMENT PAPER

EQUIPMENT

In addition to standard cooking utensils you'll need a few baking tools to get started.

The following list is meant to make the process as enjoyable as possible, but keep in mind that pies have been around since the dark ages, long before silicone baking mats and stand mixers. You can still make a good pastry dough with a bowl, two butter knives and a rolling pin (or a wine bottle in a pinch).

Once you delve into baking, you'll discover all sorts of quirky specialized tools—everything from rings that attach to your rolling pin and gauge a dough's thickness, to rolling pin stockings that prevent dough from sticking. There are even contraptions that cut your pie into even slices. I don't bother with these gadgets, but some bakers swear by them. Baking is as individual as your tastes—find the tools that work best for you.

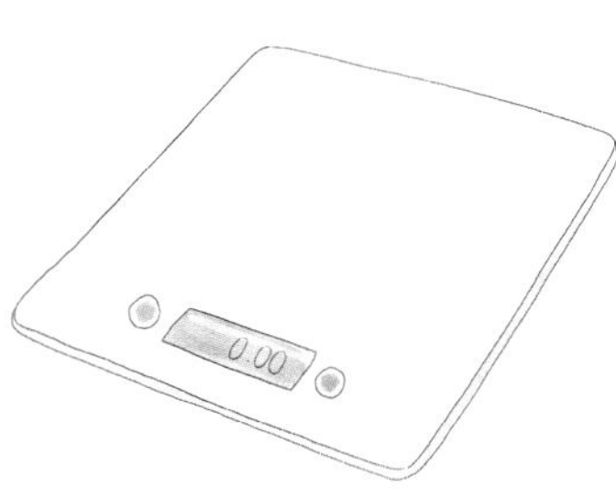

KITCHEN SCALE

If you enjoy baking, you'll appreciate the precision and convenience of a digital kitchen scale. The pastry dough recipes in this book include weight measurements, which makes baking a lot more convenient. Once you're accustomed to measuring by weight—especially sticky ingredients like butter—you'll wish all ingredients were measured using a scale. To read more about the importance of a kitchen scale, see A Weighty Note on page 30.

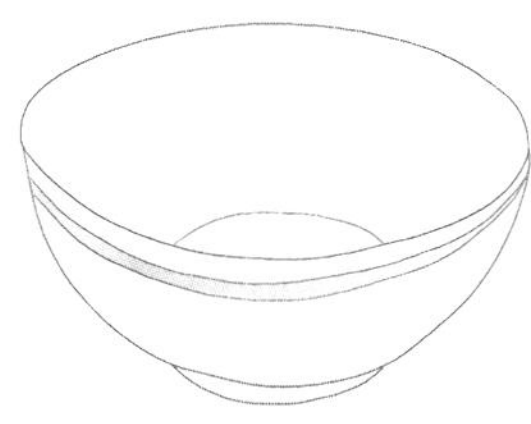

LARGE BOWL

You'll need a set of bowls for mixing—ceramic, glass, stainless steel or plastic are all fine. I mix my pastry in a large 4-quart (3.8 L) bowl. Always default to a larger bowl when mixing dry ingredients.

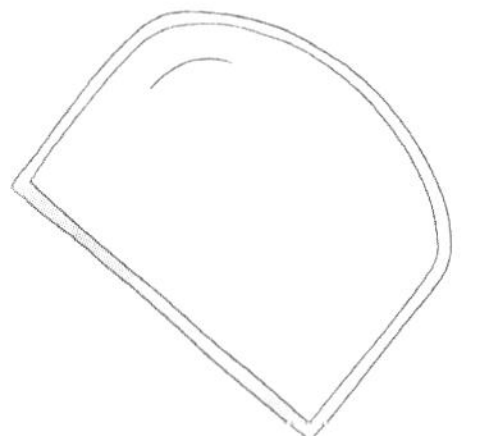

FLEXIBLE SCRAPER

Inexpensive plastic scrapers are very handy for scraping dough, custards and sticky ingredients from bowls. I always keep one near my baking bowls.

DOUGH SCRAPER

These sturdy scrapers, usually made of stainless steel (with a wooden or rubber handle), are great for scraping dough and flour and all sorts of other sticky things from your countertop. They're also handy for dividing pastry dough (and essential for bread makers).

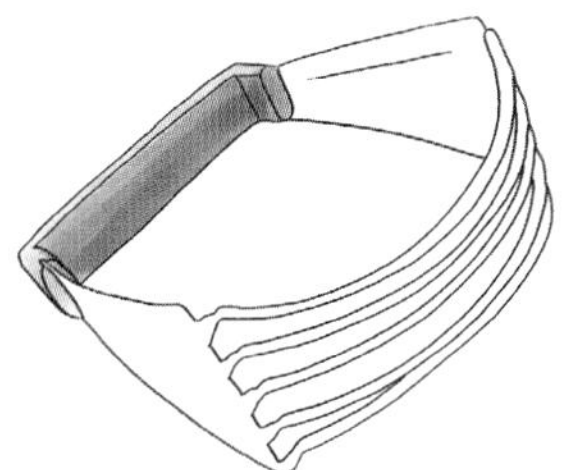

PASTRY BLENDER

This is my preferred tool for cutting butter (or lard) into flour. The metal blades cut through the fat easily, and my blender has lasted for ages. Two knives will achieve the same results, but I find the blender easier to use and more efficient.

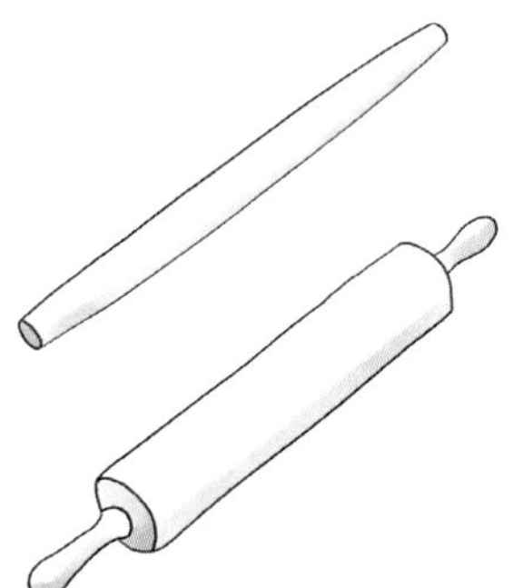

ROLLING PINS

There's no right or wrong when it comes to rolling pins, it's a matter of comfort.

I use a wooden French tapered rolling pin because it's light and offers more control, but some bakers prefer a classic North American rolling pin with handles and a rotating barrel. Rolling pins come in various sizes and materials—marble, stainless steel and non-stick silicone—but the key is to use what's most comfortable in your hands.

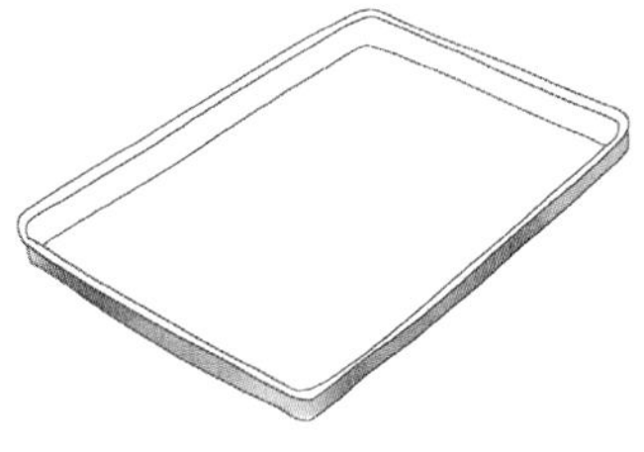

BAKING TRAYS

A heavy baking tray conducts heat more evenly than a lighter tray, and doesn't buckle in the oven. Alternatively, double up or stack lighter baking trays. Rimmed trays are a must for juicy pies in order to contain spilled juices and keep your oven clean. Don't toss out those weathered dark and dull trays—they conduct heat better than new shiny trays, which reflect heat away from the dough. Both work, but the latter requires a bit more time for your pastries to brown.

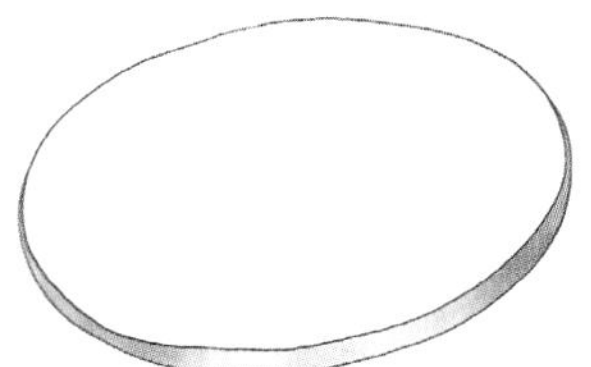

PIZZA STONES

Bake a pie on a preheated pizza stone and your bottom crust will brown beautifully. However, if your pie has the potential to overflow (e.g., a berry pie), use a rimmed baking tray instead.

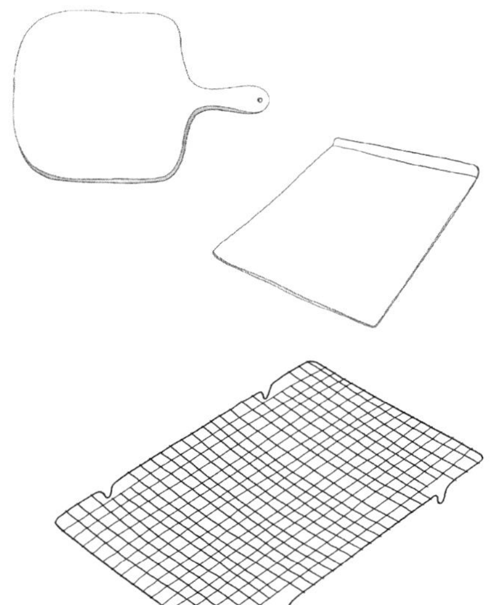

PIZZA PEEL OR FLAT-EDGED BAKING TRAY

There's no better way to transfer free-form tarts and galettes, or any pastry without a container, to a preheated baking tray than with a pizza peel (sometimes called a paddle) or a flat-edged baking tray.

WIRE BAKING RACKS

Wire racks lift pies and pastries off counters for better airflow (preventing a soggy pastry) and faster cooling times. If you don't have one, use a toaster oven rack, a trivet or a grate from a gas oven. Anything that allows air circulation beneath the pastry works.

PARCHMENT PAPER

Parchment paper is my go-to paper. I roll my dough on it (to prevent it from sticking to the counter or my rolling pin) and use it to line tart pans, big and small, as well as cake pans (for quiche and apple pie). I use parchment to separate and stack dough—and, because it withstands heat up to 425°F (220°C), it can also be used to line baking trays. Depending on the situation, it can even be reused.

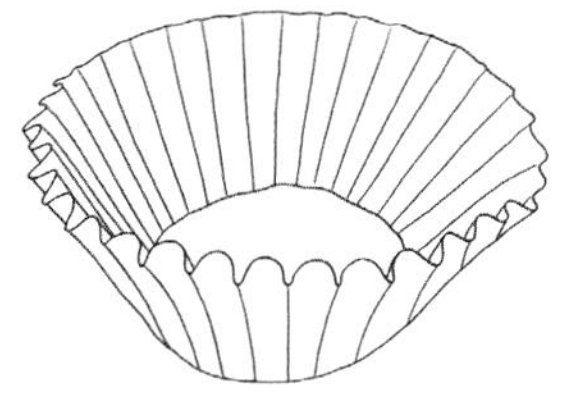

PARCHMENT BAKING CUPS

If you plan to make small tarts, parchment baking cups are ideal for lining the tart molds. Pastry dough tends to stick to the molds, and baking cups (or parchment) allow your tarts to release easily, without breaking.

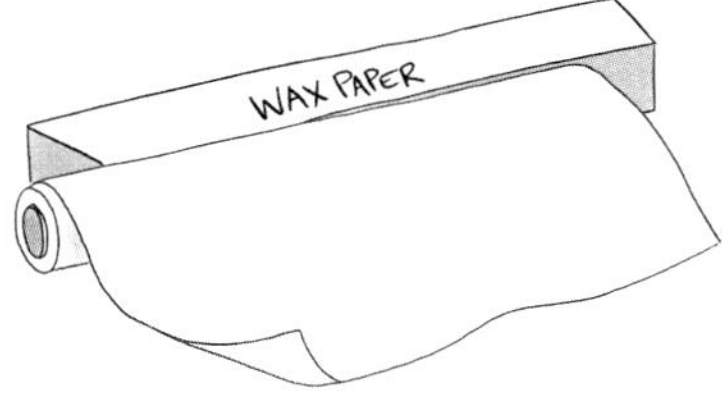

WAXED PAPER

You can't use wax paper in the oven, but you can roll your dough on it (to prevent it from sticking to the counter) and use it to separate and stack dough destined for the fridge or freezer.

PLASTIC WRAP

Plastic wrap has a lot of uses in a pastry kitchen. It's used to cover dough before it goes into the fridge, preventing the dough from drying out and cracking, which affects its ability to rise. I can still hear my chef instructors yelling "air is death to dough!" every time I wrap my pastry in plastic wrap.

Doughs are rolled between parchment and plastic wrap to prevent them from sticking to the counter or your rolling pin. Alternatively, large plastic freezer bags can be cut open and used to cover pastry when rolling out the dough, then washed and reused. Sturdy reusable freezer bags are a good option for refrigerating and freezing pastry.

ALUMINUM FOIL

Foil is handy for tenting pies to prevent them from burning. It's also useful for lining baking trays (for a quick cleanup) and can hold pie weights in place when blind baking (prebaking) pastry.

SILICONE BAKING MATS

I use reusable baking mats for lining baking trays. They're great for pie spills and anything that sticks.

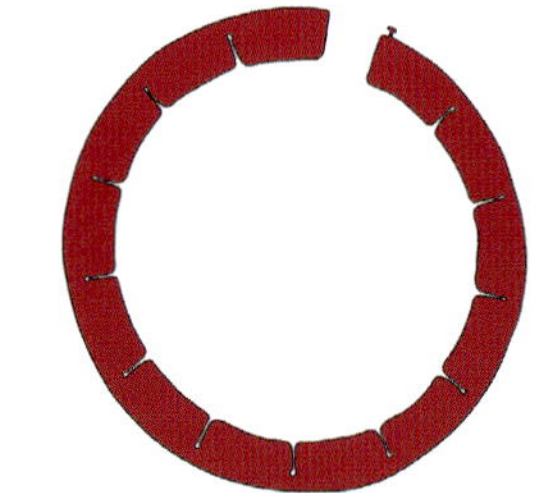

SILICONE PASTRY SHIELDS

Pastry shields are round or adjustable strips that fit on the rim of your pie to protect the pastry's edges from becoming too brown. They're great for *some* pies, but if your crimping is too pronounced, they tend to fall off. If you enjoy baking, they're nice to have, but not essential.

PIE PLATES AND CONTAINERS

I've baked pies in just about every cooking vessel imaginable, from cake pans and cast iron skillets to muffin tins and ceramic casserole dishes. A no-frills, 9-inch (23 cm) glass plate is my go-to for traditional pies; it conducts the heat well, and I can see the colour of the crust to ensure that the pastry's properly baked. Metal is also a good choice both for tarts and pies; it browns the pastry a bit faster than glass. Tart pans have removable bottoms and make for beautiful pastries. Pie plates with perforated bases are a fine option, and are said to create a crisper bottom due to air circulation, but I still lean toward glass.

It's fun to play around with different containers but if they're not the size specified you'll end up with too little or too much filling.

PIE WEIGHTS

Pie weights are used when pastries are blind baked (i.e., baked without a filling). This technique is used when fillings require no baking, such as custard, or when a filling is especially moist or requires only a brief period of baking.

Before the pastry goes into the oven it's covered with parchment or foil, then filled with pie weights to prevent the pastry from buckling in the oven. Once the pastry is sufficiently cooked, the pie weights (and parchment and foil) are removed and the pie is returned to the oven to brown. Pie weights are often ceramic or metal, but beans and rice work just as well. (When I found myself short on pie weights one day, I added beans and rice to the weights and have kept them mixed together ever since.) If you opt to use beans and rice, set them aside in a canister or separate container, so you don't end up cooking with them.

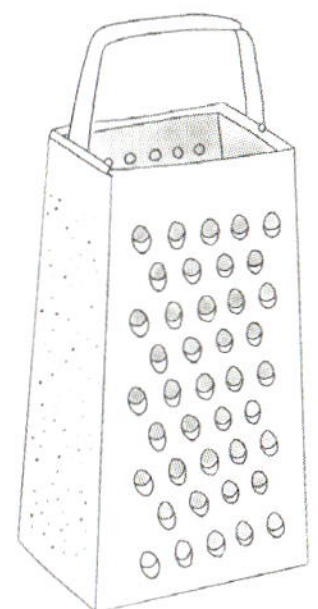

CHEESE GRATER

In addition to grating cheese—and chocolate—a grater is ideal for quickly softening chilled butter.

SPICE GRINDER AND/OR MORTAR AND PESTLE

If you enjoy fruit pies made with tapioca, you'll love having a spice grinder and/or mortar and pestle on hand to grind quick-cooking tapioca. Crushing the tapioca ensures your fruit fillings are free of gelatinous lumps. They can also be used to crush whole spices, which are always more flavourful than preground. A spice grinder is used to make the homemade garam masala featured in the Indian-spiced pastries.

SMALL WHISK

A small compact whisk (not a balloon whisk) is my go-to kitchen tool for everything from mixing eggs to custards and savoury sauces. About 9 inches (23 cm) in length, it sits in a canister near the stove, as it's just the right size for mixing many ingredients.

SIFTERS/STRAINERS

Gone are the days of sifting flour before using, but fine-mesh strainers of all sizes still come in handy for everything from dusting pastries with powdered sugar to straining juices and custards. I can't imagine a kitchen without a few of varying sizes on hand.

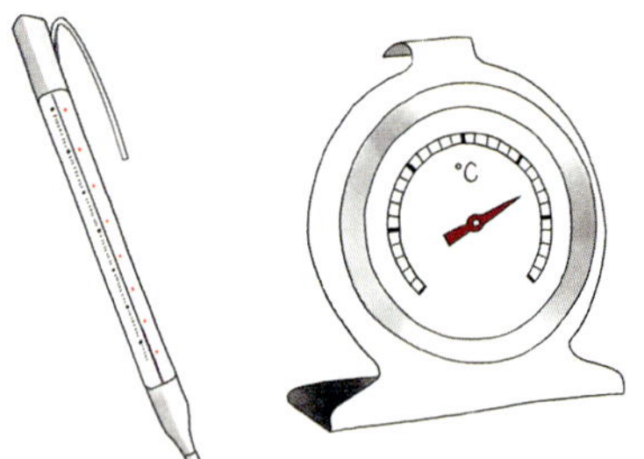

OVEN AND CANDY THERMOMETERS

I've had my share of wonky ovens, but an oven thermometer always keeps me on track. They're not expensive, and once you know if your oven runs hot or cold you can adjust accordingly.

Candy thermometers are essential for recipes that involve cooked sugar, such as Italian meringue or candied hazelnuts.

PASTRY BRUSH

You'll need a good pastry brush with a silicone or natural bristle for coating your pastries with egg or cream before they go in the oven. Silicone brushes are ideal when cooking sugar, allowing you to brush down the sides of the pan and prevent crystals from forming (which can seize the sugar). If you're an ambitious baker, a wide, natural bristle pastry brush is a cherished tool for dusting off excess flour from handcrafted or rough puff pastry.

OFFSET PALETTE KNIFE

A handy tool for smoothing the tops of creamy pies and levelling fillings. It's one of those tools you might not consider handy until you start using it.

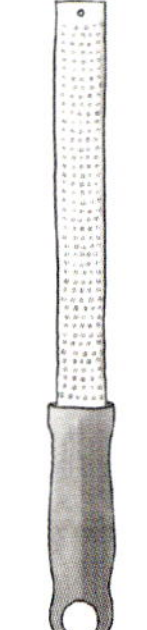

MICROPLANE ZESTER

An exceptional tool for zesting lemons and finely mincing garlic and ginger.

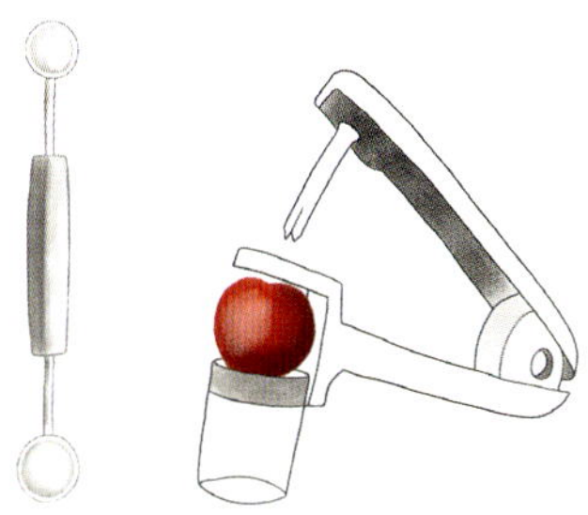

FRUITY TOOLS

I usually dismiss single-use tools as unnecessary, but if you're making cherry pie, a cherry pitter is the way to go. A melon baller is handy for coring pears and apples.

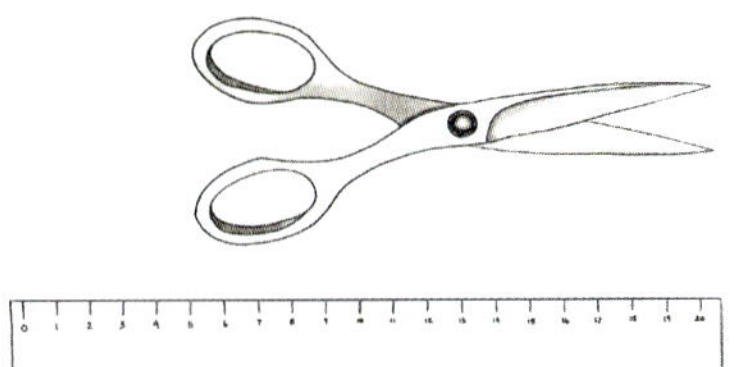

RULER AND SCISSORS

If you're making a lattice topping or cutting squares or rectangles of pastry, and are a stickler for uniformity, a ruler is essential. I use scissors for cutting off excess pastry from trims. Great tools for the baking drawer.

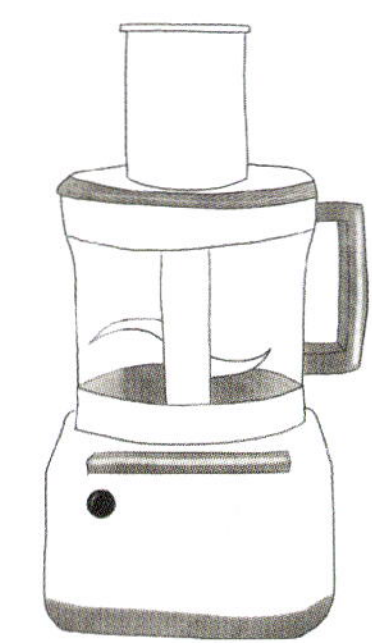

FOOD PROCESSORS

A food processor can bring together a shortcrust buttermilk dough or rough puff pastry in minutes. The key to using a food processor is to pulse the dough briefly in short bursts until just blended. If not careful, the dough can turn to a paste.

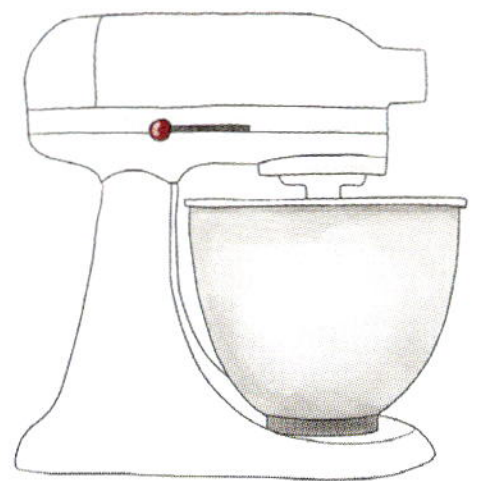

STAND MIXERS

I use a stand mixer for mixing together quick sweet doughs. Whipping cream and meringue-based fillings are easily made in a stand or hand-held mixer, but with a strong arm, and steely determination, everything can be made by hand.

BAKING STAPLES

FLOUR

All-purpose unbleached flour is my go-to flour. Reliable, inexpensive and readily available, it is used in most of the pastry recipes in this book. It's a well-balanced blend of hard and soft wheat flours that is suitable for most baked goods. After milling, flours are naturally bleached with age, or chemically bleached, a process that produces a whiter, finer-grained flour. Bleached and unbleached can be used interchangeably.

Whole wheat flour has the nutritious bran and germ still intact. It is sometimes mixed with all-purpose flour in pastries to lend a subtle nutty nuance. It's a bit heavier than all-purpose, so it's used with a light hand.

Pastry flour is a finely milled, low-protein specialty flour. Protein (in the form of gluten) is great for breads but not for delicate pastries. Pastry flour is used in the Buttermilk Shortcrust Dough (page 36) and mixed with all-purpose flour in the Rough Puff Pastry (page 54).

Refined flours (all-purpose and pastry) have a shelf life of one to two years and should be stored in an airtight container in a cool dark place. Whole wheat flour is more susceptible to spoilage (owing to the oil-rich bran and germ) and should be used within a few months and stored in the freezer. If you don't have the space, refrigeration is the next best option.

FATS

These are key to pastry dough, and you have loads of options.

Lard made from pork provides the flakiest pastry crusts imaginable, and because it has a higher melting point than butter, it's easy to work with. It is a time-honoured option.

Butter doesn't offer the flakiness of lard, but it does provide the most flavour. I prefer European-style unsalted butter for its higher fat content (it contains less water, which is preferable when making pastry). Unsalted is preferred in baking (I use it for all my cooking) because the salt content varies by brand. More importantly, salt acts as a preservative, so unsalted butter is often fresher, as salted butter can sit on the shelf a lot longer.

Vegetable shortening is a flavourless fat made from soybean, cottonseed or palm oil, and is a great option for vegans. It is more forgiving than butter, as it remains solid in warm temperatures. Select brands that are free of trans fats.

COCONUT OIL

In its solid state, coconut oil can be used in place of the abovementioned fats when at room temperature. Unrefined coconut oil has a more pronounced coconut flavour than refined, so choose accordingly.

THICKENERS

Quick-cooking tapioca (also called instant) is my go-to starch for juicy fruit pies. Made from cassava, a starchy root vegetable, it thickens without clouding the filling. Tapioca needs to sit with a fruit filling for at least 15 minutes before baking so that the tapioca can absorb the fruit juices. If you're like me and don't care for gelatinous bits of tapioca in your pies, grind the tapioca in a spice grinder *before* using—this is a fabulous tip I learned from a pastry chef friend. I grind a box in one go so I have finely ground tapioca whenever I need it.

Cornstarch is a smooth and fast-acting thickener that's easy to use but can break down (and hinder the thickening process) when combined with acidic ingredients like rhubarb and lemon. Used in small quantities, it doesn't affect the flavour of the filling.

GELATIN

Gelatin firms mousse-type fillings and makes sparkling jellies for topping custards such as the Ruby Red Grapefruit Tart (page 278).

Although recipes call for powdered gelatin (as it's readily available), gelatin sheets are starting to show up in baking aisles. These are easy to work with and you never have to worry about undissolved granules. Gelatin sheets are first softened in cold water, squeezed dry, then added to warm ingredients such as warm juice or custard. Gelatin sheets vary in size and strength, so read the package carefully to determine the firming/setting strength. Replace 1 Tbsp (15 mL) unflavoured gelatin powder with enough sheet gelatin to firm 2 cups (500 mL) liquid.

Gelatin is made from animal by-products. Vegetarians have a number of gelling options, including agar powder and carrageen, but these products behave differently than gelatin so follow the directions on the package.

EGGS

Large eggs are used in these recipes, and local farm fresh or organic are always your best bet.

If using a kitchen scale, it's helpful to know large eggs weigh about 50 g (20 g per yolk, 30 g per white).

SUGAR

White granulated cane sugar is used in these recipes unless otherwise specified. I dust my sweet pies with coarse raw sugar (large crystal turbinado or demerara are good choices) just before they're baked.

FRUIT

Fruit pies are only as good as the fruit they contain, so select local, seasonal fruit with care. Taste fruit before you use it to ensure it's at its peak. Citrus peel should be from lemons free of pesticides or a wax coating.

NUTS

Purchase nuts in quantities you can use in a reasonable time period, as they go rancid. Store nuts in an airtight container in the fridge or freezer.

CHOCOLATE

Purchase the best you can afford. I prefer to bake with bittersweet chocolate containing 65%–70% cacao. Even if you love dark chocolate, don't be tempted to use a higher percentage of cocoa than that—the more cocoa, the less cocoa butter (the ingredient that gives chocolate its luxurious mouthfeel). Some manufacturers classify bittersweet as chocolate containing more than 50% cocoa solids, whereas semisweet contains 35%–50% percent cocoa solids.

SALT

Table salt is used in the pastry dough recipes and kosher salt is used in the savoury fillings. Refer to A Salty Note on page 130 for more detailed information.

PASTRY DOUGH

Flaky
Flaky Whole Wheat
Chocolate Walnut
Lemon Almond
Whole Wheat Flax
Cream Cheese

Sweet Tart
Chocolate Tart
Roasted Almond
Chocolate Linzer
Hazelnut
Cookie Crumb
Gateau

The following recipes represent a small slice of the world's pastry, but have seen me through a lifetime of pie projects.

The pastry doughs featured in this book have been divided into four categories:

Pie Dough, for sweet and savoury pies, with textures ranging from flaky to tender. Suitable for single- and double-crust pies, galettes, tarts and turnovers, these pastry recipes include the Flaky Pastry Dough (page 32) and Buttermilk Shortcrust Dough (page 36), and can be used interchangeably.

Tart Dough, for sweet tarts and single-crust pies. Similar to a sugar-cookie or shortbread dough, these doughs can be rolled out and in some cases pressed directly into a pan. Doughs in this category include the Sweet Tart Dough (page 38), Chocolate Walnut Dough (page 42), Roasted Almond Dough (page 43), Chocolate Linzer Dough (page 44), Hazelnut Tart Crust (page 45), Cookie Crumb Crust (page 46) and Lemon Almond Dough (page 47).

Speciality Doughs have unique pastry applications and straddle the texture of pie and tart, such as the Cream Cheese Dough (page 48) and Gâteau Pastry Dough (page 49).

Laminated Dough, or puff pastry, is a butter-rich speciality pastry that puffs as it bakes. It is made by laminating, or sandwiching, butter between dough, then folding the dough to create multiple layers that puff in the oven. It can be used for sweet and savoury pies, tarts and specialty cookies. Doughs include the Handcrafted Puff Pastry (page 50) and Rough Puff Pastry (page 54).

A WEIGHTY NOTE

Dry ingredients in this section are listed by volume *and* weight. This is because measuring by weight is more accurate—a cup of flour or brown sugar can be loosely or firmly packed but the scale is always correct. At culinary school, we didn't even have measuring cups in our pastry kitchen!

It's a challenge convincing new bakers to buy a kitchen scale, but once they own one, they wonder how they'd managed before. In addition to consistent results, a digital scale means less cleanup. Your mixing bowl is placed on the scale and reset to zero (with the press of a button), then each subsequent ingredient is added to the *same* bowl and reset to zero again after each addition. Forget how many egg yolks you added? A scale will keep you on track: yolks weigh ⅔ oz (20 g), whites 1 oz (30 g). It doesn't sound like a big deal, but if you enjoy baking, a scale is a game changer.

PIE CHART

DOUGH
PIE
FLAKY
BUTTERMILK
SPECIALTY
CREAM CHEESE
GATEAU
LAMINATED
HAND PUFF
ROUGH PUFF
SWEET TART
CHOCOLATE WALNUT
ROASTED ALMOND
CHOCOLATE LINZER
HAZELNUT
COOKIE CRUMB
LEMON ALMOND

FLAKY PASTRY DOUGH

YIELD

Makes about 2 lb (910 g)

INGREDIENTS

2¾ cups (685 mL) all-purpose flour (440 g)

1 tsp (5 mL) table salt (6 g)

1 cup (250 mL) lard, vegetable shortening or unsalted butter (227 g), chilled and cut into 1- to 2-inch (2.5–5 cm) pieces

1 large egg, lightly beaten

1 Tbsp (15 mL) white or cider vinegar

Ice cold water

FLAKY PASTRY DOUGH is featured in the majority of the pies in this book, both savoury and sweet. If you use only one pastry recipe in this book, let it be this one. It is the workhorse of pastry dough and offers loads of flexibility: it can be made with lard, vegetable shortening or unsalted butter.

Lard produces the flakiest pastry, but butter provides the most flavour. Some bakers use half butter, half lard (or shortening). Try a few options and you'll find the fat that works best for you.

The key to a flaky pastry is keeping the fat cold and distinctive; you should see traces of fat in the dough once it's rolled out. In the oven, the moisture in the fat creates steam, causing the pastry to puff and pull apart and producing a flaky pastry.

The exact amount of liquid isn't specified because it varies depending on the age of your flour, the harvest, the humidity and other factors. Go easy with liquid and keep in mind that you can always add more, but you can't take it away.

Place the flour and salt in a large bowl and mix to combine. Add the lard, shortening or butter and cut into the flour with a pastry blender or 2 knives until the mixture is crumbly with some larger, irregular (bean-sized) pieces along with the mostly finer crumbs.

. . . recipe continued

Images depict the combination of the flour and fat, the "shaggy mass" stage, the rolled dough (note the visible traces of fat), transferring the dough to a pie plate (with plastic wrap intact) and trimming the edges.

WHOLE WHEAT VARIATION: Replace 1 cup (250 mL/160 g) all-purpose flour with 1 cup (250 mL/160 g) whole wheat flour. Featured in the Nectarine Slab Crumble (page 222).

WHOLE WHEAT FLAX VARIATION: Replace 1¼ cups (310 mL/200 g) all-purpose flour with 1 cup (250 mL/160 g) whole wheat flour and ¼ cup (60 mL/32 g) flax meal. Featured in the Pan-Seared Brussels Sprout Tart (page 110).

. . . Flaky Pastry Dough (cont.)

In a spouted measuring jug, combine the egg, vinegar and enough ice cold water to equal 1 cup (250 mL); mix with a fork. Gradually pour about half the liquid into the flour and mix with a fork, adding only enough additional liquid so that the dough clings together. You'll know you've added enough liquid when you can grab a portion of dough with your hands and it sticks together, and when there are few (if any) crumbs at the bottom of your bowl.

Portion the dough (a shaggy mass at this stage) into 2 squat discs, each about 1 inch (2.5 cm) thick. Wrap in plastic wrap and refrigerate for at least an hour before using, or up to 3 days.

Refrigerated dough needs to rest at room temperature for a while before it's rolled out. Lard and shortening-based doughs need little rest, but doughs made with butter take time. You'll know it's ready to roll when you press the dough with your finger and it leaves a slight imprint.

BUTTERMILK SHORTCRUST DOUGH

YIELD

Makes about 2 lb (910 g)

INGREDIENTS

3½ cups (875 mL) pastry flour (455 g)

1 tsp (5 mL) table salt (6 g)

1⅓ cups (330 mL) unsalted butter (305 g), chilled and cut into 1-inch (2.5 cm) cubes

¼ cup + 2 Tbsp (90 mL) buttermilk*

¼ cup + 1 Tbsp (75 mL) whole milk

*If you don't have buttermilk you can make a substitute by placing 1 Tbsp (15) lemon juice or vinegar in a measuring cup and adding just enough whole milk to equal 1 cup (250 mL). Be sure to use only the amount needed for this recipe.

I ONCE DISMISSED PASTRY made with a food processor, but my dear friend Karri Smith, pie aficionado and Cordon Bleu graduate, encouraged me to try her standout buttermilk shortcrust dough. This recipe, generously shared by Karri, comes together quickly, is easy to work with and can be used interchangeably with the Flaky Pastry Dough (page 32). Made of finely milled pastry flour, the dough has a lovely texture and yields a tender crust.

If you don't have a food processor, you can still make this dough with a pastry blender or two knives, as directed in the Flaky Pastry Dough recipe.

Place the flour and salt in the bowl of a food processor and pulse to mix. Add the cubes of butter and pulse until you achieve pea-sized pebbles of butter, removing the lid now and then to check the size.

Add the buttermilk and whole milk all at once and pulse just until the dough comes together. The mixture will look crumbly, but if you grab a handful, it should hold together. If it doesn't, add a bit of milk, by the teaspoon, until the mixture holds together.

Transfer the dough, still crumbly but holding together, to a sheet of parchment. Shape the dough into 2 squat disks, each about 1 inch (2.5 cm) thick. Wrap in plastic wrap and refrigerate for about an hour before using, or up to 3 days.

Refrigerated dough needs to rest at room temperature for a while before it's rolled out. You'll know it's ready to roll when you press the dough with your finger and it leaves a slight imprint.

Images depict the combination of the flour and butter, the crumbly (but still holding together) mixture and rolling the dough between parchment and plastic wrap.

SWEET TART DOUGH

YIELD

Makes about 1½ lb (680 g)

INGREDIENTS

1 cup (250 mL) unsalted butter (227 g), room temperature

⅔ cup (160 mL) powdered (icing) sugar (90 g)

4 large egg yolks (about 3 oz/80 g), room temperature*

2½ cups (625 mL) all-purpose flour (400 g)

¼ tsp (1 mL) table salt (2 g)

*Meringue is a great way to use up leftover egg whites; see Pavlova recipe, page 66.

THIS BUTTERY DOUGH forms the base for many of the sweet tarts featured in this book. The pastry, a shortcrust dough, comes together as easily as cookie dough, and your biggest challenge will be to resist the temptation to nibble it all before it's baked.

The dough is rolled and either draped over a rolling pin and transferred to a tart pan, or gently pressed, piecemeal, into the pan. The dough has a similar texture to a rolled sugar cookie dough, and if it's not rolled at the optimum temperature (chilled but not too cold) it tends to break.

The dough is usually prebaked (blind baked) before the filling is added. Leftover dough, like all of the tart doughs featured in this book, can be fashioned into cookies or tart shells (see page 65 for info).

In either the bowl of a stand mixer (fitted with the paddle attachment) or a medium bowl, cream together the butter and powdered sugar. Add the yolks and mix until combined. Add the flour and salt and combine just until the mixture comes together and forms a soft dough.

Shape the dough into a squat disc about 1 inch (2.5 cm) thick. Wrap in plastic and refrigerate for about an hour before using, or up to 3 days. The buttery dough becomes very firm in the fridge and needs to rest at room temperature for at *least* 30 minutes before rolling out. You'll know it's ready when you press the dough with your finger and it leaves a slight imprint.

. . . recipe continued

Images depict the mixed dough, rolling of the dough between parchment and plastic, draping the dough over a rolling pin (to transfer to a tart pan) and pressing the dough into a pan with the plastic wrap intact.

. . . Sweet Tart Dough (cont.)

CHOCOLATE VARIATION: Omit the lemon zest and replace 3 Tbsp (45 mL/30 g) flour with 3 Tbsp (45 mL/30 g) cocoa powder. Featured in the Chocolate Soufflé Tart (page 242).

LEMON VARIATION: Add the zest of 2–3 lemons into the butter/powdered sugar mixture when preparing the dough. Featured in the Lemon Cream Tart (page 282) and the Lemon Mousse Tart (page 290).

Images depict cutting the dough with a rolling pin and levelling the dough with the bottom of a measuring cup, with the plastic wrap intact.

CHOCOLATE WALNUT DOUGH

YIELD

Makes about 1 lb (450 g)

INGREDIENTS

¾ cup (185 mL) chopped walnuts (98 g)

½ cup (125 mL) unsalted butter (114 g), room temperature

¼ cup (60 mL) firmly packed dark brown sugar (45 g)

3 Tbsp (45 mL) maple syrup

½ tsp (2.5 mL) vanilla extract

½ cup (125 mL) all-purpose flour (80 g)

½ cup (125 mL) whole wheat flour (80 g)

2 tsp (10 mL) cocoa powder (6 g)

½ tsp (2.5 mL) baking powder (2 g)

¼ tsp (1 mL) baking soda (1 g)

¼ tsp (1 mL) table salt (2 g)

THIS DELICIOUS BUTTERY tart dough, made with all-purpose and whole wheat flours, smacks of chocolate shortbread with a nutty crunch. It is featured in the Triple-Chocolate Tart (page 232).

Pulse the walnuts in a food processor until the nuts are mostly fine-textured with some irregular coarse pieces.

In either the bowl of a stand mixer (fitted with the paddle attachment) or a medium bowl, cream together the butter and brown sugar. Add the maple syrup, vanilla and chopped walnuts, stirring to combine. Add the remaining ingredients just until the mixture comes together and forms a soft dough.

Shape the dough into a squat disc about 1 inch (2.5 cm) thick. Wrap in plastic and refrigerate for about an hour before using, or up to 3 days.

Refrigerated dough needs to rest at room temperature for a while before it's rolled out. You'll know it's ready to roll when you press the dough with your finger and it leaves a slight imprint.

ROASTED ALMOND DOUGH

THIS ROASTED NUT crust makes a cookie-like base that's perfect for tarts. The longer the almonds are roasted, the more pronounced the nutty flavour. Featured in the Labneh Tart recipe (page 260).

Spread the almonds on a baking tray in a single layer and bake at 375°F (190 °C) until lightly browned, about 8–10 minutes. When the nuts have cooled, tip them into a food processor with the granulated sugar and process until finely ground.

In a separate bowl, mix together the flour, cinnamon, baking powder and salt.

In either the bowl of a stand mixer (fitted with the paddle attachment) or a medium bowl, beat the butter with the brown sugar until the mixture is light and fluffy. Beat in the egg, ground almonds and flour mixture until well incorporated. The mixture will resemble cookie dough.

Line the base of a 10½-inch (26 cm) tart pan (with a removable base) with parchment paper. Scrape the dough into the parchment-lined tart pan, cover with plastic wrap and, using your hands or the bottom of a flat measuring cup, smooth the dough into place over the plastic, assuring the dough is evenly distributed along the bottom and sides of the pan. Refrigerate for at least 40 minutes.

YIELD

Makes about 1½ lb (680 g)

INGREDIENTS

¾ cup (185 mL) whole almonds (128 g), outer skin intact

3 Tbsp (45 mL) granulated sugar (38 g)

1¾ cup (435 mL) all-purpose flour (280 g)

½ tsp (2.5 mL) ground cinnamon (2 g)

½ tsp (2.5 mL) baking powder (2 g)

½ tsp (2.5 mL) salt (3 g)

¾ cup (185 mL) unsalted butter (168 g), room temperature

⅓ cup (80 mL) firmly packed golden (light) brown sugar (60 g)

1 large egg

CHOCOLATE LINZER DOUGH

YIELD

Makes about 2½ lb (1.13 kg)

INGREDIENTS

1 cup (250 mL) whole almonds (170 g), outer skin intact

¼ cup (60 mL) granulated sugar (50 g)

2 cups (500 mL) all-purpose flour (320 g)

½ tsp (2.5 mL) ground cinnamon (2 g)

¼ tsp (1 mL) allspice (1 g)

½ tsp (2.5 mL) baking powder (2 g)

½ tsp (2.5 mL) salt (3 g)

1 cup (250 mL) unsalted butter (227 g), room temperature

½ cup (125 mL) firmly packed golden (light) brown sugar (90 g)

4 large egg yolks

3½ oz (100 g) good-quality dark chocolate (about 65%–70% cocoa), finely grated using the smallest holes on a box grater

THIS RICH, ALMOND-spiced pastry is flecked with grated dark chocolate and rolled a bit thicker than most pastries for a more substantial crust. Featured in the Chocolate Linzer Tartlets (page 246).

Spread the almonds on a baking tray in a single layer and bake in a 375°F (190°C) oven until lightly browned, about 8–10 minutes. When the nuts have cooled, tip them into a food processor with the granulated sugar and process until finely ground.

In a separate bowl, mix together the flour, cinnamon, allspice, baking powder and salt.

In either the bowl of a stand mixer (fitted with the paddle attachment) or a medium bowl, beat the butter with the brown sugar until the mixture is light and fluffy. Beat in the egg yolks and mix well. Add the ground almonds, flour mixture and grated chocolate. Mix until well incorporated.

Scrape the dough from the bowl and shape into 2 squat discs, each about 1 inch (2.5 cm) thick. Wrap in plastic and refrigerate for about an hour before using, or up to 3 days.

Refrigerated dough needs to rest at room temperature for a while before it's rolled out. You'll know it's ready to roll when you press the dough with your finger and it leaves a slight imprint.

HAZELNUT TART CRUST

THIS NUTTY HONEY dough with a hint of cinnamon is pressed directly into the tart pan, rather than rolled out. Featured in the Cheesecake Tart (page 258).

YIELD

Makes about 1 lb (450 g)

INGREDIENTS

½ cup (125 mL) chopped hazelnuts (65 g)

½ cup (125 mL) unsalted butter (114 g), room temperature + extra for brushing the pan

¼ cup (60 mL) firmly packed golden (light) brown sugar (45 g)

3 Tbsp (45 mL) liquid honey

½ cup (125 mL) all-purpose flour (80 g)

½ cup (125 mL) whole wheat flour (80 g)

½ tsp (2.5 mL) baking powder (2 g)

¼ tsp (1 mL) baking soda (1 g)

¼ tsp (1 mL) table salt (2 g)

½ tsp (2.5 mL) cinnamon (2 g)

Pulse the nuts in a food processor until mostly fine-textured with some irregular coarse pieces.

In the bowl of a stand mixer (fitted with the paddle attachment) or a medium bowl, blend the butter with the brown sugar and honey. Add the ground nuts and remaining ingredients and mix until combined. The mixture will resemble a cookie dough.

Using either a 13¾- × 4¾-inch (35 × 12 cm) or an 11- × 7-inch (28 × 18 cm) fluted tart pan with a removable base, lightly brush the base and sides with butter. Line the base and sides with parchment paper cut to size (the butter helps the parchment stay in place). Scrape the dough into the parchment-lined tart pan, cover with plastic wrap and, using your hands or the bottom of a flat measuring cup, smooth the dough into place over the plastic, assuring the dough is evenly distributed along the bottom and sides of the pan. Refrigerate for at least 30 minutes.

COOKIE CRUMB CRUST

YIELD

Makes nearly 1 lb (450 g)

INGREDIENTS

2½ cups (625 mL) firm cookie crumbs (360 g), such as gluten-free ginger snaps

¼ cup + 2 Tbsp (90 mL) unsalted butter (84 g), room temperature, plus more as needed

THIS NOSTALGIC, two-ingredient crumb crust features gluten-free cookies, but any firm cookie works well. You can make cookie crumbs in a food processor, but if you don't have one, place cookies in a freezer bag and rap them with your rolling pin until you achieve fine crumbs. Although it's not necessary to bake this crust (the cookies are already baked), I prefer the firmer texture of a briefly baked crust. Featured in the Peanut Butter Chocolate Pie (page 240).

In a medium bowl, combine the cookie crumbs and butter and mix until the crumbs are evenly coated. The mixture should hold together when you grab a portion with you hands. If not, add additional butter by the teaspoon just until the crumbs hold together.

Line the base of a 9½- to 10-inch (24–25 cm) tart pan (with a removable base) with parchment paper. Tip the crumbs into the parchment-lined tart pan, cover with plastic wrap and press the mixture into the tart pan using your fingers or a flat-bottomed cup. Wrap in plastic and refrigerate for 20 minutes to firm.

LEMON ALMOND DOUGH

MADE OF ALMONDS, egg yolks and lemon zest, this is a rich tender dough. If you have a food processor, grind the almonds rather than purchasing pre-ground—they're much more flavourful. Featured in the Lemon Meringue Tartlets (page 274).

Place the almonds in a food processor with the granulated sugar and process until finely ground.

In either the bowl of a stand mixer (fitted with the paddle attachment) or a medium bowl, cream together the butter, powdered sugar and lemon zest until light and fluffy, about 2–3 minutes. Add the yolks and mix until well combined. Add the flour, salt and ground almond mixture. The mixture should resemble a sticky cookie dough.

Scrape the dough from the bowl and shape into a squat disc about 1 inch (2.5 cm) thick. Wrap in plastic and refrigerate for about an hour before using, or up to 3 days.

Refrigerated dough needs to rest at room temperature for a while before it's rolled out. You'll know it's ready to roll when you press the dough with your finger and it leaves a slight imprint.

YIELD

Makes about 1¾ lb (795 g)

INGREDIENTS

1¼ cups (310 mL) whole almonds (212 g), outer skin intact

¼ cup (60 mL) granulated sugar (50 g)

1 cup (250 mL) unsalted butter (227 g), room temperature

¼ cup (60 mL) powdered (icing) sugar (30 g)

Zest from 2 organic lemons

4 large yolks, room temperature

1½ cups (375 mL) all-purpose flour (240 g)

¼ tsp (60 mL) table salt (2 g)

CREAM CHEESE DOUGH

YIELD

Makes about 2 lb (910 g)

INGREDIENTS

- 1 cup (250 mL) unsalted butter (227 g), room temperature
- One 8½ oz (250 g) brick Philadelphia-style cream cheese, room temperature
- Zest from 1 lemon
- 2 Tbsp (30 mL) granulated sugar (25 g)
- ½ tsp (2.5 mL) table salt (3 g)
- 2 large egg yolks, room temperature
- 2¼ cups (530 mL) all-purpose flour (360 g)

THIS TENDER DOUGH, enriched with egg yolks and cream cheese, is featured in the Apple Rugelach (page 194) and Blueberry Cream Cheese Turnovers (page 88), with the latter using the Whole Wheat Flour Variation below.

In either the bowl of a stand mixer (fitted with the paddle attachment) or a medium bowl, beat the butter, cream cheese and lemon zest until fluffy, about 2 minutes. Add the sugar, salt and egg yolks until well combined. Gradually add the flour and mix until combined. Scrape the dough from the bowl. Divide the dough into 3 portions.

Shape each portion into a disc about 1 inch (2.5 cm) thick. Wrap in plastic and refrigerate for about an hour before using, or up to 3 days.

Refrigerated dough needs to rest at room temperature for a while before it's rolled out. You'll know it's ready to roll when you press the dough with your finger and it leaves a slight imprint.

WHOLE WHEAT FLOUR VARIATION: Replace 1 cup (250 mL/160 g) all-purpose flour with whole wheat flour. Divide into 2 portions (instead of 3 portions).

GÂTEAU PASTRY DOUGH

GÂTEAU PASTRY, OR cake pastry, is a soft, sweet, eggy dough unlike any other. It features just enough baking powder to lend a cake-like quality to pastry. Featured in the Gâteau Basque recipe (page 268), it also makes delicious turnovers, although this is one of the few doughs that doesn't translate well to other pie recipes.

YIELD

Makes about 1½ lb (680 g)

INGREDIENTS

2 cups (500 mL) all-purpose flour (320 g)

2 tsp (10 mL) baking powder (8 g)

½ tsp (2.5 mL) table salt (3 g)

½ cup (125 mL) unsalted butter (114 g), room temperature

½ cup (2.5 mL) granulated sugar (110 g)

Zest from 1 organic lemon

3 large eggs, room temperature

In a medium bowl, mix together the flour, baking powder and salt.

In the bowl of a stand mixer (fitted with the paddle attachment) or a medium bowl, mix together the butter, sugar and lemon zest. Add the eggs one at a time, mixing after each addition. Add the flour mixture and combine until the mixture resembles a soft cookie dough.

Scrape the dough from the bowl and shape into 2 squat discs, each about 1 inch (2.5 cm) thick. Wrap in plastic and refrigerate for about an hour before using, or up to 3 days.

Refrigerated dough needs to rest at room temperature for a while before it's rolled out. You'll know it's ready to roll when you press the dough with your finger and it leaves a slight imprint.

HANDCRAFTED PUFF PASTRY

YIELD

Makes about 3½ lb (1.6 kg)

BUTTER

2 cups (500 mL) unsalted butter (454 g), room temperature

¼ cup (60 mL) all-purpose flour (40 g)

DOUGH

4 cups (1 L) all-purpose flour (640 g) + more as needed

¼ cup (60 mL) unsalted butter (56 g), room temperature

2½ tsp (12.5 mL) table salt (15 g)

1½ cups (375 mL) cool water + more as needed

PUFF PASTRY IS the prima donna of all pastries. With light flaky layers that shatter with every bite, it's a diva of a pastry, a little temperamental at times but a worthy endeavour for ambitious home bakers up for a challenge.

Puff pastry takes time, but it's not difficult once you understand the ingenuity of laminated dough. Simply put, one slab of butter is sandwiched, or laminated, between two layers of dough. The "sandwich" is then rolled into a rectangle and folded in three, as you might fold a letter. This process is repeated a total of six times, with a resting period between folds.

This technique creates a multi-layered pastry separated by butter. In a hot oven, the butter creates steam that pushes up the individual layers to create the pastry's magical puff.

The secret to working with the dough is managing the butter's temperature—too warm and it will squish out the sides when you roll it; too cold and the pastry will tear. If you think of your fridge as the tool for firming butter and your countertop as the butter softener, you can move the dough between the two to manage it at its most pliable. It takes a bit of practice, but you'll get comfortable after the first fold.

I've offered instructions for mixing the dough with a stand mixer, but it can be made just as easily by hand. Plan to make puff pastry over a day or two.

BUTTER

Blend together 2 cups (500 mL) butter and ¼ cup (60 mL) flour in the bowl of a stand mixer fitted with the paddle attachment.

Scrape the butter onto a sheet of parchment paper, cover with plastic wrap and smooth into a rectangle using your hands or a pastry blender. Form into a neat packet measuring about 6 × 8 inches (15 × 20 cm). The parchment helps to shape the butter and the rolling pin smooths it evenly. Wrap and refrigerate.

DOUGH

Using the same bowl in which the butter was mixed, combine 4 cups (1 L) flour, ¼ cup (60 mL) butter and the salt until the butter forms small nuggets in the flour.

Replace the stand mixer paddle with the dough hook and add about 1½ cups (375 mL) water, mixing on low speed for about 3 minutes. If the dough is not holding together, add additional water by the spoonful. If the dough sticks to the hook or the sides of the bowl, add additional flour by the tablespoonful until the dough comes off the sides of the bowl easily.

. . . recipe continued

Transfer the dough (still rough at this stage) to a sheet of parchment dusted with flour. Roll the dough into a 12 × 16 inch (30 × 40 cm) rectangle, or to fit the size of your baking tray.

Transfer the dough and the parchment beneath it to a baking tray, cover completely with plastic wrap and refrigerate for at least 40 minutes.

Retrieve the butter mixture from the refrigerator and allow it to rest at room temperature, covered, until it becomes more manageable.

After the dough has rested, transfer it to your work surface, keeping the rectangle's edges straight and the corners square. Place the butter mixture on half of the dough; fold the remaining dough over the butter, like a butter sandwich.

Seal the edges by pinching them together and roll the dough into a rectangle measuring approximately 12 × 16 inches (30 × 40 cm), or the size of your baking tray, dusting with flour as necessary and aiming for straight edges and square corners. Brush off any excess flour.

After you've rolled the dough into a rectangle, place on a baking tray, cover with plastic and refrigerate for at least 40 minutes.

Once the dough has rested, transfer it to a lightly floured sheet of parchment. Brush off any excess flour from the dough and fold the dough into thirds, as you would a letter; cover with plastic and refrigerate. This is your first of 6 folds (or "turns" in pastry speak).

Note the seam along one side of your pastry. Each time the dough is rolled out, keep the folded seam on the same side. (Some bakers leave the seam on the right side, like a book, to remember the direction.) This technique helps your pastry rise evenly by stretching the gluten in the flour in equal directions.

If you're still with me, the rest is rote: Roll out the folded dough and shape into a rectangle about 12 × 16 inches (30 × 40 cm), fold in thirds again, refrigerate for at least 40 minutes and repeat the entire process—for a total of 6 "folds."

To help remember which "fold" you're on, make an indentation in the dough with your finger before resting the dough in the fridge—one fingerprint for each turn. The fingerprints will disappear when the pastry is re-rolled.

Ensure the dough is well covered with plastic wrap before it's refrigerated, otherwise it will dry and crack and not rise properly. The dough can be refrigerated between intervals up to 24 hours, so don't worry about finishing the dough in a single day.

When you've completed 6 "turns," wrap the pastry in plastic and refrigerate up to 3 days, or freeze up to 3 months.

ROUGH PUFF PASTRY

YIELD

Makes 3 lb (1.5 kg)

INGREDIENTS

2 cups (500 mL) all-purpose flour (320 g)

2 cups (500 mL) pastry flour (260 g)

½ Tbsp (7.5 mL) table salt (9 g)

2 cups (500 mL) unsalted butter (454 g), chilled and cut into cubes

1 cup (250 mL) ice cold water

ROUGH PUFF PASTRY is the next best thing to handcrafted puff pastry. It's a beautifully light, buttery, flaky pastry that doesn't rise quite as high as standard puff pastry, but it's not as temperamental or labour-intensive. Rough puff pastry can be mixed by hand, in a food processor or with a stand mixer—all three methods are listed below. Use the one you find most convenient, then continue on to "Preparing the Pastry."

FOOD PROCESSOR METHOD

Place the flours and salt in the bowl of a food processor and pulse to mix. Add the cubes of butter and pulse until you achieve pea-sized pebbles of butter, removing the lid now and again to check the size of the butter pieces.

Add the water all at once and pulse just until the dough comes together. The mixture will look crumbly, but if you grab a handful it should hold together. If not, add a bit of ice water by the spoonful until the mixture holds together.

STAND MIXER METHOD

Combine the flours and salt in the bowl of a stand mixer fitted with the paddle attachment. Add the cubes of butter and toss with your hands or a spoon to ensure they are coated with flour (rather than clumped together). Mix on medium-low speed until the flour mixture appears crumbly, about 3–4 minutes.

Replace the paddle attachment with the dough hook and mix on medium-low speed while adding the water all at once. Continue mixing until the dough comes together and there are no crumbs at the bottom of the bowl. If the mixture is not holding together, add a bit of ice water, by the spoonful, until the mixture comes together in a shaggy mass.

HAND METHOD

Combine the flours and salt in a large bowl. Add the cubes of butter and work the flour and butter together with your fingertips, squishing the butter until the mixture resembles grainy crumbs. This takes about 10 minutes, but the process—scooping both hands through the flour and letting it fall through your fingers while you knead the butter between your fingers—is a pleasant, contemplative task.

Add the water all at once and mix with your hands or a spoon until the mixture clings together. Transfer to a floured work surface and knead the dough with the palm of your hand about 8 times, until the mixture is fairly smooth. You should see traces of butter throughout the dough.

. . . recipe continued

. . . Rough Puff Pastry (cont.)

PREPARING THE PASTRY

Regardless how you mix the ingredients, transfer the dough (which should still be crumbly at this stage, but should hold together when you grab a portion in your hands) to a sheet of parchment lightly dusted with flour.

Shape the dough with your hands (or a rolling pin) into a squat rectangle about 6 × 9 inches (15 × 22 cm). Wrap in plastic and refrigerate for 1 hour.

Place the dough on a sheet of parchment dusted with flour. Cover with plastic wrap and roll the dough, over the plastic wrap, forming a 9- × 14-inch (23 × 36 cm) rectangle.

Fold the rectangle into thirds, as if folding a letter for an envelope. This is considered your first "turn." (Some bakers note each turn with a finger depression in the dough, see previous recipe.) You will need a total of 4 "turns" with at least 40 minutes refrigeration (with the pastry tightly wrapped in plastic) between each turn.

Be sure to roll the dough with the seam facing the same direction every time. This will stretch your dough in all directions, helping to ensure your pastry rises evenly.

Use as directed in recipes calling for puff pastry.

FRENCH PALMIERS

YIELD

Makes about 48 palmiers

INGREDIENTS

1 lb (450 g) puff pastry, either handcrafted (page 50), rough (page 54) or commercial (frozen)

About ½ cup (125 mL) granulated sugar, divided

1 large egg, lightly beaten

THIS RECIPE IS a bit of an outlier, but it showcases the versatility of puff pastry. Palmiers (French for palm tree leaf, pronounced pahlm-yays) are crisp, caramelized, sugar-dusted cookies that are so good that I make a batch whenever I prepare puff pastry.

This is the sort of pastry that makes guests ask mid-bite "What is this and where can I buy some?"

Scatter a large sheet of parchment with about 3 Tbsp (45 mL) sugar. Roll the dough onto the sugar-dusted parchment until approximately 14 × 16 inches (35 × 40 cm). Cover the dough with an additional 3 Tbsp (45 mL) sugar and gently press on the pastry with your hands to embed the sugar.

Fold in one edge of the longer side of the pastry about 2⅓ inches (5.5 cm), then do the same with the opposite edge. Repeat each fold again until the two edges meet in the middle.

Brush the beaten egg along both sides of the seam. Fold the dough in half, along the seam, to create a cylinder.

. . . recipe continued

THÉ
EARL GREY
TEA

. . . French Palmiers (cont.)

Cut the 16-inch (40 cm) cylinder in half to create two 8-inch (20 cm) cylinders. Dust with additional sugar, cover tightly with plastic wrap and refrigerate for at least 40 minutes. The dough can be frozen at this stage, if desired.

Cut the chilled dough into ⅓-inch (8 mm) thick slices and transfer to parchment paper. Dust with more sugar, cover with another sheet of parchment (or plastic wrap) and gently flatten with a rolling pin.

Arrange the slices on a parchment-lined baking tray, leaving 1 inch (2.5 cm) between each slice. Cover and refrigerate for at least 30 minutes before baking.

Preheat oven to 425°F (220°C).

To promote caramelization, lightly spritz the cookies with a bit of water just before baking. Fill a spray bottle with cold water or place a hand under a water faucet and flick the excess water from your fingertips directly over the pastries.

Bake in the preheated oven for 6–7 minutes, or until edges are golden. Remove the baking tray, turn the cookies over with a spatula and return to the oven for 4–5 additional minutes, or until golden.

Cool on a wire rack.

PRECIOUS SCRAPS

Bakers love a challenge, and nothing sparks our creativity like a few scraps of dough, leftover egg whites or a bit of filling. Here are but a few ideas for rounding up those odds and ends.

MINI SWEET AND SAVOURY PASTRIES

A cookie cutter is all that's needed to stamp out these sweet and savoury pastries.

You don't need a recipe (or a tart mold) to create delicious pastries. In this case, a circle of Flaky Pastry Dough (page 32) or Buttermilk Shortcrust Dough (page 36) is dusted with sugar, topped with half a plum and sealed with another circle of pastry. Vents are cut into the centre of each pastry, then the dough is brushed with lightly beaten egg or cream and sprinkled with sugar. The pastries are refrigerated until firm, then baked in a 425°F (220°C) preheated oven for about 15 minutes.

Tinker with your choice of sweet fillings, including soft or cooked fruit or jam (a raw apple doesn't work, but cooked caramelized apples and soft plums are delightful). Or, create a savoury pastry using seasoned (precooked) leftovers—think curried chicken, chopped beef and potatoes, ham and cheese, tofu and mushrooms . . . anything your fridge has to offer. Simply swap the sugar topping for Parmesan cheese.

SWEET PASTRY STRAWS

Especially delicious using Handcrafted Puff Pastry (page 50) or Rough Puff Pastry (page 54), these pastry straws also make good use of the Flaky Pastry or Buttermilk Shortcrust doughs. You'll need at least 1 oz (30 g) leftover pastry per straw. They're so good, you may not want to wait for leftovers to make a batch.

Roll the leftover dough onto a sheet of parchment paper generously dusted with sugar. Shape into a rectangle about 12 inches (30 cm) long × ⅛ inch (3 mm) thick, and as wide as your pastry allows.

Top with more granulated sugar, brown sugar or cinnamon sugar. Using a sharp knife, cut the pastry into long, ½-inch (1 cm) wide strips.

Grasping a strip of pastry from opposing ends, gently twist the strip of dough in opposite directions to fashion a spiral, then transfer to a parchment-lined baking tray. Continue with the remaining strips, leaving about ¾ inch (2 cm) between each straw. Cover the straws with plastic wrap and firm in the fridge until ready to bake.

Bake the chilled dough in a preheated 425°F (220°C) oven for 10–15 minutes, or until golden, turning the straws over once during baking.

SAVOURY PASTRY STRAWS

Follow the directions above, replacing the sugar with freshly grated Parmesan cheese. For a flavourful savoury straw that yields an addictive chewy texture, layer the pastry with a thin smear of Rustic Tapenade (page 303) or Sun-Dried Tomato & Roasted Garlic Pesto (page 303).

CLOCKWISE, FROM TOP LEFT: Mini Sweet and Savoury Pastries, Pastry Straws, Pastry Puffs, Sweet Pastry Rings.

CLOCKWISE, FROM TOP LEFT: Lemon Mousse, Sweet and Savoury Tart Shells, Pastry Crisps, Cookies.

SWEET PASTRY RINGS

Prepare unbaked Sweet Pastry Straws (page 62) and fashion into circles, dusting with cinnamon sugar. Cover with plastic wrap and firm in the fridge, then bake the chilled dough in a preheated 425°F (220°C) oven for 10–15 minutes or until golden, rotating the baking tray once during baking.

PASTRY PUFFS

These light, crisp pastries are created by deep-frying scraps of the Flaky Pastry or Buttermilk Shortcrust dough until they puff and turn golden.

Pour about 2 inches (5 cm) of oil into a heavy skillet. Bring the oil slowly to temperature, until an instant-read thermometer reaches 350–360°F (175–180°C), or a cube of bread dropped in the oil turns golden after about 30–40 seconds. Carefully lower chilled scraps of pastry into the oil, being mindful not to overcrowd the pan, which will render your pastry soggy rather than crisp. Rotate the pastry with tongs or a fork to brown evenly. Transfer to a paper towel to drain and sprinkle lightly with powdered sugar. Serve immediately.

SWEET CREAMY FILLINGS

Although it's tempting to lick the bowl, consider spooning sweet leftover fillings (such as the mousse in the Lemon Mousse Tart, page 290) into dessert glasses.

SWEET AND SAVOURY TART SHELLS

With miniature tart molds on hand, any scrap of dough can be fashioned into a base for a sweet or savoury tart. Unbaked or prebaked blind (without filling), tart shells freeze beautifully. Follow the directions for the Lemon Meringue Tartlets (page 274) and keep tart shells on hand for whenever you have extra filling.

COOKIES!

All the sweet tart doughs featured in this book make excellent cookies. Left plain or doubled and sandwiched with jam or chocolate ganache (page 232), these cookies freeze beautifully. If you opt to use a filling, do so just before serving, unless you prefer a softer, more yielding cookie (as I do).

PASTRY CRISPS

Granulated sugar is sprinkled over squares of the Flaky Pastry or Buttermilk Shortcrust doughs to create these playful, sweet, crispy snacks. Cinnamon sugar and brown sugar make excellent choices too.

For savoury crisps, dust the pastry squares with lightly beaten egg, then with Parmesan cheese and finely chopped rosemary or cumin and coriander.

The dough is refrigerated until firm, then baked in a 425°F (220°C) preheated oven for about 10 minutes.

PAVLOVA

YIELD

Makes 6 large meringues

MERINGUE

4 large egg whites, room temperature

1 cup (250 mL) granulated or fine (berry) sugar (about 200 g)

½ Tbsp (7.5 mL) cornstarch (about 3 g)

½ tsp (2.5 mL) white vinegar

TOPPINGS

1½ cups (375 mL) whipping cream, chilled

1½ Tbsp (22 mL) granulated sugar (about 18 g)

1 lb (450 g) fresh strawberries, cleaned and hulled (green leafy tops removed, if desired)

Blackberry Coulis (page 298), made with strawberries or raspberries

¼ cup (60 mL) dried or fresh blueberries (optional)

Fresh mint (optional)

Icing (powdered) sugar (optional)

As many of the pastry doughs call for yolks only, it's only fitting to include a recipe that makes use of the whites. Enter meringue: light and airy with a crisp shattering exterior and a marshmallow-y centre.

In this recipe, billows of meringue are dropped from a large spoon to fashion a freestyle Pavlova. Tossed with just-picked strawberries, a dollop of whipped cream and a splash of fruit coulis, this breezy dessert smacks of summer entertaining.

For individual servings, refer to the Eton Mess Variation following the recipe.

Line a baking tray with parchment paper or a non-stick baking mat. Preheat oven to 200°F (95°C).

Before you start, ensure your metal, glass or ceramic mixing bowl and whisk are scrupulously clean—the egg whites will not increase in volume if inadvertently mixed with traces of fat such as egg yolk.

Using a stand or hand-held mixer, whisk the egg whites at medium-high speed until a dense network of foam appears. Slowly add 1 cup (250 mL) granulated or fine sugar in a thin stream, continuing to whisk as you do so. Increase the speed to high and whip until glossy, stiff peaks appear. Reduce speed to low, add the cornstarch and vinegar and whisk until just incorporated.

Spoon the meringue in large mounds onto the prepared baking tray and flatten them slightly with the back of a spoon.

Bake the meringues for about an hour or longer, until completely dry (the smaller the meringue, the faster it will dry). Turn the oven off and leave the meringues inside until they have cooled completely. The meringues will crack slightly, and the colour will change from bright white to ivory. If not using immediately, store meringues in a cool dry place in an airtight container, with parchment layered between each meringue, for up to 2 weeks.

PUTTING IT ALL TOGETHER

When ready to serve, whip the cream with 1½ Tbsp (22 mL) granulated sugar until soft peaks appear. Place the baked meringue on a plate or tray, add as much whipped cream as desired, scatter with strawberries and drizzle with a bit of fruit coulis. Garnish with dried or fresh blueberries, fresh mint and icing sugar, if desired. Serve additional whipped cream and fruit coulis on the side.

. . . recipe continued

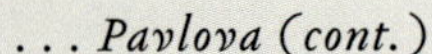
. . . Pavlova (cont.)

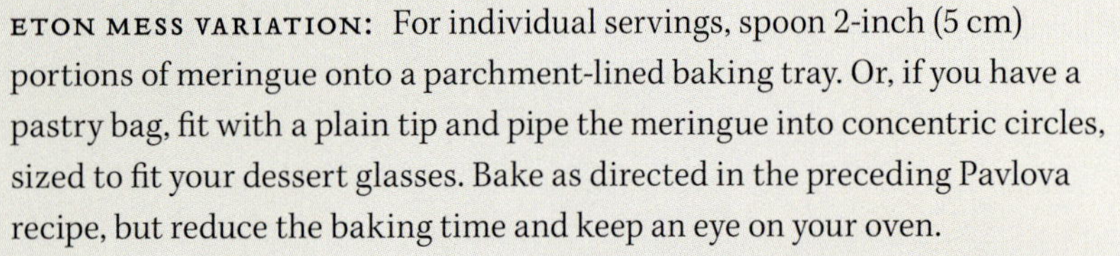
ETON MESS VARIATION: For individual servings, spoon 2-inch (5 cm) portions of meringue onto a parchment-lined baking tray. Or, if you have a pastry bag, fit with a plain tip and pipe the meringue into concentric circles, sized to fit your dessert glasses. Bake as directed in the preceding Pavlova recipe, but reduce the baking time and keep an eye on your oven.

To serve, layer glasses with fruit, cream, coulis and meringue (whole or broken into pieces). Garnish with pistachio nuts, if desired.

CHERRY & BERRY

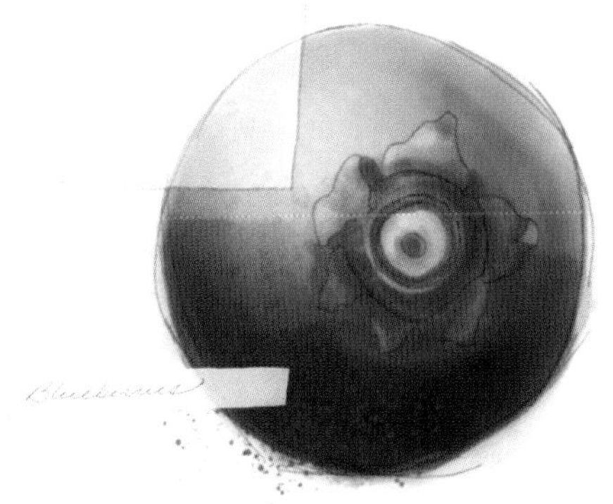

SWEET BING PIE

YIELD

Makes one 9-inch (23 cm) pie

PASTRY

1 recipe Flaky Pastry Dough (page 32), divided into 2 portions

1 large egg, lightly beaten, for brushing the pastry + more as needed

1–2 Tbsp (15–30 mL) coarse raw or granulated sugar

FILLING

½ cup (125 mL) granulated sugar

3 Tbsp (45 mL) quick-cooking tapioca, ideally ground in a spice grinder (see page 19 for info)

8 cups (2 L) Bing or other sweet cherries (about 1.25 kg), pitted (see note)

2 tsp (10 mL) balsamic vinegar

¼ cup (60 mL) chopped hazelnuts or almonds

2 Tbsp (30 mL) unsalted butter (about 30 g), chilled and cut into small pieces

SPECIAL EQUIPMENT

Shallow 9-inch (23 cm) pie plate (0.75 quart)

CHERRIES

I usually dismiss "single-use" kitchen tools—the cherry pitter not so. It's the only way to go when pitting a couple pounds of cherries. And it's a perfect job to delegate.

Cherries vary in sweetness, depending on the variety and season. I note the date and variety so I can adjust the sweetness, if necessary, for my next pie.

THIS QUINTESSENTIAL SUMMER pie includes a couple of unlikely ingredients—a touch of balsamic vinegar to brighten the sweet cherry filling, and ground hazelnuts to lend a nutty note. The hazelnuts also prevent the crust from getting soggy.

If you've never made a lattice pie, refer to the step-by-step photos on page 183. I've added a little variation by replacing a few strips of lattice with twists of pastry. It's easier than it looks.

If you plan to serve the pie for tonight's dessert, you'll want to make it early in the day. A fruit pie takes a few hours to firm.

Cherry pie is especially delicious with Handcrafted Vanilla Ice Cream (page 300).

PASTRY

Prepare the pastry and place one portion of dough onto a sheet of parchment paper dusted with flour. Layer a sheet of plastic wrap over the dough and roll (over the plastic) from the centre toward the pastry's edge in all directions until approximately 11 inches (28 cm) in diameter and about ⅛ inch (3 mm) thick.

Drape the dough onto your rolling pin and transfer to the pie plate, being mindful not to pull or stretch the dough. Gently press the dough into the sides of the pie plate and trim the edges. Cover with plastic wrap and refrigerate for at least 45 minutes.

LATTICE

Place the second portion of dough onto a sheet of parchment paper generously dusted with flour. Place a sheet of plastic wrap on top of the dough and roll (over the plastic) from the centre toward the pastry's edge in all directions until approximately 10 inches (25 cm) in diameter and ⅛ inch (3 mm) thick. Remove the plastic and cut the pastry into 8 strips, each 1½ inches (4 cm) wide.

Gather and re-roll the remaining dough, then cut the pastry into 8 more strips, each ¼ inch (6 mm) wide. Twist two ¼-inch (6 mm) strips together to create 4 twisted strips. You should have eight 1½-inch (4 cm) strips and 4 twisted strips. Cover with plastic wrap and refrigerate.

FILLING

In a large bowl, combine ½ cup (125 mL) sugar with the tapioca, cherries and balsamic vinegar; stir to coat the fruit. Allow to rest for 30 minutes to soften the tapioca.

. . . recipe continued

. . . Sweet Bing Pie (cont.)

PUTTING IT ALL TOGETHER

Retrieve the chilled pastry base from the fridge and sprinkle it with the chopped nuts. Stir the cherry/sugar mixture and spoon it into the pastry, mounding the fruit in the middle. Gently tap the pie plate on your work surface to distribute the fruit and sugar. (If using a glass pie plate, place a tea towel beneath your plate to protect the glass.) Dot with butter.

If you've never made a lattice before, refer to the step-by-step images for the Pure & Simple Apple Pie (page 180). Place five 1½-inch (4 cm) strips of pastry loosely across the pie in one direction, leaving about a ½-inch (1 cm) gap between each strip. Do not press the dough in place.

To weave in the first ½-inch (1 cm) pastry strip, gently fold back every other pastry strip to the pastry's edge and lay a perpendicular strip of pastry over the remaining strips. Fold the strips back in place and you'll see you've created your first weave. Repeat the process with each new strip, alternating the pastry twists with the plain strips.

When the weaving is complete, trim the edges and carefully press the lattice into the pastry base with your fingers. Brush the lattice with beaten egg and dust with 1–2 Tbsp (15–30 mL) coarse raw or granulated sugar. Refrigerate or freeze for about 20 minutes to firm the lattice.

Preheat a foil or parchment-lined, rimmed baking tray in a 425°F (220°C) oven. Place the chilled pie on the preheated tray and bake for 20 minutes, then reduce the temperature to 375°F (190°C) and continue to bake for another 30–40 minutes until the pastry is cooked through and the cherries are soft. Rotate the baking tray once during baking and cover with foil as necessary to prevent burning.

Cool on a wire rack. Allow to cool for a few hours before serving. Serve at room temperature or rewarm and serve with ice cream.

CLASSIC BERRY TARTS

YIELD

Makes ten to twelve 3½-inch (9 cm) tarts

PASTRY

1 recipe Sweet Tart Dough (page 38), only half the dough needed

FILLING

1½ cups (375 mL) preserves or jam

1 recipe Pastry Cream (page 296)

5 cups (1.25 L) fresh berries (blueberries, raspberries, strawberries and/or blackberries; about 2 lb/910 g)

Mint sprigs, for garnish (optional)

SPECIAL EQUIPMENT

Twelve 4-inch (10 cm) tart molds

24 baking cups or parchment paper, cut to fit the molds

Pie weights (or beans or rice)

WHAT BETTER WAY to show off fresh berries and cherries than perched on a tart? Filled with a dollop of jam and a light custard laced with rum, these time-honoured tarts are always well received.

The pastry, similar to a buttery shortbread, comes together as easily as cookie dough and can be baked days in advance (and frozen even longer). The custard, too, can be made in advance, and because it's stabilized with gelatin, it won't become weepy or runny like some creamy fillings. You'll want to assemble these tarts just before serving.

PASTRY

Line the tart molds with half the paper baking cups or parchment paper cut to size (the balance of the baking cups/parchment will be used later). The molds need to be *completely* covered with paper, otherwise you won't be able to release the tarts without breaking them (it's fine if your paper overlaps the molds).

Prepare the pastry and place the dough onto a sheet of parchment paper dusted with flour. Layer a sheet of plastic wrap over the dough and roll (over the plastic) until approximately ⅛ inch (3 mm) thick. Remove the plastic and cut the dough into circles slightly larger than your tart molds using a cup or small bowl as a guide.

Carefully transfer the circles of dough with a spatula, or your hands, to the paper-lined molds. Use a scrap of plastic wrap to gently press the dough (through the plastic) against the base and edges of each mold, aiming for a uniform thickness.

The parchment-lined tart molds can be stacked in bundles and wrapped in plastic, so as not to take up too much room in the fridge. Or, if you have the space, place them on a baking tray and cover with plastic wrap.

Preheat oven to 375°F (190°C).

Pierce the base and sides of each pastry with the tines of a fork. Cover each pastry with the remaining 12 baking cups or squares of parchment and fill with pie weights to the top of the mold. Place the tarts on a baking tray, leaving plenty of room between each.

Bake 20 minutes in the preheated oven, rotating the baking tray once during baking to ensure the tarts bake evenly. Remove the tarts from the oven and carefully remove the pie weights and baking cups (or parchment). Return the tarts to the oven and continue to bake, uncovered, for another 5–7 minutes, or until the pastries are browned and cooked through.

Cool on a baking rack. Do not remove the molds until the tarts have cooled completely.

. . . recipe continued

. . . Classic Berry Tarts (cont.)

FILLING

Up to an hour before serving, spread the base of each tart with a dollop of preserves. Top with about 2 Tbsp (30 mL) chilled Pastry Cream (mix before using) and smooth the tops with a knife. Garnish with your choice of fresh berries and mint, if desired.

MINI TARTS VARIATION: To make a smaller version of the Classic Berry Tarts, use twenty-four 2½-inch (6 cm) tart molds, with 48 miniature baking cups. You'll only need half the Pastry Cream. Yields 24 tarts.

BLUEBERRY BLACKBERRY GALETTE

YIELD

Makes 6–8 servings

PASTRY

1 recipe Flaky Pastry Dough (page 32)

1 large egg, lightly beaten, for brushing the pastry + more as needed

1–2 Tbsp (15–30 mL) coarse raw or granulated sugar

ALMOND CREAM

2 Tbsp (30 mL) unsalted butter (about 30 g), room temperature

2 Tbsp (30 mL) powdered (icing) sugar

¼ cup + 1 Tbsp (75 mL) ground almonds

1 large egg yolk, lightly beaten

1 Tbsp (15 mL) rum, cognac or Grand Marnier (optional)

BERRY FILLING

¼ cup + 3 Tbsp (105 mL) granulated sugar

3 Tbsp (45 mL) cornstarch

2 cups (500 mL) fresh blueberries + 1 cup (250 mL) for the topping

2 cups (500 mL) fresh blackberries + 1 cup (250 mL) for the topping

2 tsp (10 mL) unsalted butter (about 15 g), chilled and cut into small pieces

---

BLUEBERRY BLOOM

A dusty finish on blueberries (the "bloom') is a sure sign of freshness. It serves as a protective barrier and seals in moisture. Rinse blueberries just before using.

IF YOU FAVOUR simplicity over form, this freestyle galette is the way to go. A rectangle of pastry is smeared with almond cream then scattered with plump berries. You needn't be fussy about the way you fold the edges to encase the fruit, galettes are meant to be rustic. Once baked, the galette is topped with even more berries.

Served with a scoop of Handcrafted Vanilla Ice Cream (page 300), this galette sums up the best of summer.

PASTRY

Prepare the pastry and place all of the dough onto a sheet of parchment paper dusted with flour. Layer a sheet of plastic wrap over the dough and roll (over the plastic) into a rectangle approximately 10 × 15 inches (25 × 38 cm) and about ⅛ inch (3 mm) thick.

To prevent the pastry from bunching at the corners, snip off the four corners to prevent excess pastry when folded (think gift wrapping a box). Transfer the dough with the parchment underneath to a tray or platter; cover with plastic and refrigerate until needed.

ALMOND CREAM

In a small bowl, combine 2 Tbsp (30 mL) butter with the powdered sugar, ground almonds, egg yolk and liquor, if using. Mix well to combine.

BERRY FILLING

In a large bowl, combine ¼ cup + 3 Tbsp (105 mL) granulated sugar and the cornstarch. Add 2 cups (500 mL) each of the fresh berries and toss to combine.

Preheat a foil- or parchment-lined baking tray in a 425°F (220°C) oven.

PUTTING IT ALL TOGETHER

Place the chilled pastry, with the parchment beneath it, onto your work surface. Spread the almond cream over the pastry, leaving a 2-inch (5 cm) border on each side. Tip the blueberry mixture onto the almond cream, being mindful to retain the border.

. . . recipe continued

. . . Blueberry Blackberry Galette (cont.)

Fold the pastry borders over the filling toward the centre, to create a neat rectangular package. Brush the corners with beaten egg to help seal the edges. Dot the exposed fruit with 2 tsp (10 mL) butter.

Brush the exposed pastry with additional beaten egg and sprinkle generously with coarse raw or granulated sugar.

Transfer the galette, and the parchment beneath it, to the preheated tray in the oven using a rimless baking tray or a pizza peel. Alternatively, carefully remove the preheated baking tray and place the galette on it. Bake for 15 minutes, reduce heat to 375°F (190°C) and continue to bake for another 20–30 minutes until the pastry is golden and cooked through. Rotate the tray halfway during baking and tent with foil as necessary to prevent burning.

Cool on a wire rack. Top with 2 cups (500 mL) mixed berries. Serve at room temperature or rewarmed.

QUILT BERRY PIE

YIELD

Makes one 9-inch (23 cm) square pie

PASTRY

1 recipe Flaky Pastry Dough (page 32), divided into 2 portions

1 large egg, lightly beaten, for brushing the pastry

1–2 Tbsp (15–30 mL) coarse raw or granulated sugar

BERRY FILLING

¼ cup + 3 Tbsp (105 mL) granulated sugar

3 Tbsp (45 mL) cornstarch

5 cups (1.25 L) fresh assorted berries (blueberries, raspberries and blackberries)

2 tsp (10 mL) unsalted butter (about 15 g), chilled and cut into ½-inch (1 cm) pieces

SPECIAL EQUIPMENT

9-inch (23 cm) square tart pan with a removable base, or a shallow 8¾-inch (22 cm) pie plate

A SQUARE-PEG IN a world of round pies, this triple-berry pastry is distinctive. Reminiscent of a quilted square, it's a folksy pie that's bursting with fresh-picked raspberries, blackberries and blueberries.

Berries range from sweet to tart depending on the variety and season. Taste your berries before you bake them; if they're especially tart, tame them with an extra spoonful of sugar. Conversely, if they're at their sweetest peak, dial back the sugar.

Fruit pies take a few hours to firm, so plan accordingly. Delicious with Handcrafted Vanilla Ice Cream (page 300).

PASTRY BASE

Prepare the pastry and place one portion of dough onto a sheet of parchment paper dusted with flour. Layer a sheet of plastic wrap over the dough and roll (over the plastic) from the centre toward the pastry's edge in all directions until approximately 11 inches (28 cm) in diameter and about ⅛ inch (3 mm) thick. Remove the plastic and cut the dough with a sharp knife into a square measuring 11 × 11 inches (28 × 28 cm).

Drape the dough onto your rolling pin and transfer to the tart pan, being mindful not to pull or stretch the dough. Gently press the dough into the sides of the pan and trim the edges. Cover with plastic wrap and refrigerate for at least 20 minutes.

PASTRY TOP

Place the remaining portion of dough onto a sheet of parchment paper dusted with flour. Place a sheet of plastic wrap over the dough and roll (over the plastic) from the centre toward the pastry's edge in all directions until approximately 12 inches (30 cm) in diameter and ⅛ inch (3 mm) thick. Remove the plastic and cut the dough with a sharp knife into a square measuring approximately 11 × 11 inches (28 × 28 cm). Transfer the dough with the parchment underneath to a tray or platter; cover with plastic and refrigerate for at least 20 minutes.

BERRY FILLING

In a large bowl, mix together ¼ cup + 3 Tbsp (105 mL) granulated sugar with the cornstarch. Add the berries and gently toss to combine.

... recipe continued

. . . Quilt Berry Pie (cont.)

PUTTING IT ALL TOGETHER

Tip the fruit/sugar mixture into the dough-lined tart pan and smooth the fruit evenly. Use a spatula to remove any sugar/cornstarch left in the bowl. Gently tap the tart pan on your work surface to distribute the fruit and sugar. Dot with butter.

Retrieve the remaining dough (the top) and cut either decorative or plain air vents into the pastry. Drape the dough onto a rolling pin and transfer to the tart pan, loosely covering the filling. Pinch the edges together and trim any excess dough. Cover with plastic wrap and firm in the fridge, or freezer, for 20 minutes.

Preheat a foil- or parchment-lined baking tray in a 425°F (220°C) oven.

Brush the pie liberally with beaten egg. Sprinkle generously with coarse raw or granulated sugar. Transfer to the preheated tray and bake for 15 minutes, then reduce the temperature to 375°F (190°C) and continue to bake another 30–40 minutes. Rotate the baking tray once during baking and tent with foil as necessary to prevent burning.

Cool on a wire rack. Cool for a few hours before serving. (The cooling helps the filling to set.) Serve at room temperature.

BLUEBERRY CREAM CHEESE TURNOVERS

YIELD

Makes fourteen 4½-inch (11 cm) tarts

PASTRY

1 recipe Cream Cheese Dough using the Whole Wheat Variation (page 48), divided into 2 portions

2–3 Tbsp (30–45 mL) whipping cream, for brushing the pastry

¼ cup (60 mL) coarse raw or granulated sugar

FILLING

1½ Tbsp (22 mL) cornstarch

¼ cup + 3 Tbsp (105 mL) granulated sugar, divided

One 8½ oz (250 g) brick Philadelphia-style cream cheese (original, not light)

2 Tbsp (30 mL) finely chopped candied ginger

Zest from 1 lemon + 2 tsp (10 mL) lemon juice

1 cup (250 mL) chopped walnuts

2 cups (500 mL) fresh or frozen blueberries (about 375 g), no need to thaw if using frozen

CANDIED GINGER AND walnuts team up with blueberries and cream cheese in these much-loved whole wheat pastries. Turnovers are great for snacks and picnics and they freeze beautifully. Made with fresh or frozen berries, they can be enjoyed anytime.

PASTRY

Prepare the pastry and place one portion of dough onto a sheet of parchment paper dusted with flour. Layer a sheet of plastic wrap over the dough and roll (over the plastic) into a circle about ⅛ inch (3 mm) thick. Using a small (4½ inch/11 cm) bowl or saucer as a guide, cut 7 circles into the dough, gathering and re-rolling the scraps as necessary. Place each circle between parchment or wax paper, wrap in plastic and refrigerate for at least 20 minutes.

Repeat the process with the remaining portion of dough for a total of 14 circles.

FILLING

In a small bowl, combine the cornstarch with ¼ cup + 2 Tbsp (90 mL) sugar.

In a medium bowl, mix the cream cheese with a wooden spoon or hand-held mixer until softened. Add the candied ginger, the remaining 1 Tbsp (15 mL) sugar and the lemon juice and zest. Mix to combine.

PUTTING IT ALL TOGETHER

Working with 7 circles of dough at a time, spread about 1 Tbsp (15 mL) of the cheese mixture evenly onto each circle of dough, ensuring the mixture reaches the edges. The cheese helps seal the pastry when it's folded in half.

Sprinkle about 1 Tbsp (15 mL) chopped walnuts onto one half of each circle. Cover the walnuts with a small heaping of blueberries (about 8–12 berries, depending on size). Sprinkle 1 tsp (5 mL) of the cornstarch/sugar mixture over the berries.

Carefully fold half the pastry over the filling to form a half-circle. Press the seams together and crimp the edges with the tines of a fork.

Place the pastries on a parchment-lined baking tray, cover with plastic wrap and refrigerate for at least 20 minutes. The pastries can be packed close together during refrigeration, but you'll need to divide the turnovers between 2 trays for baking to allow air to circulate and promote even browning.

. . . recipe continued

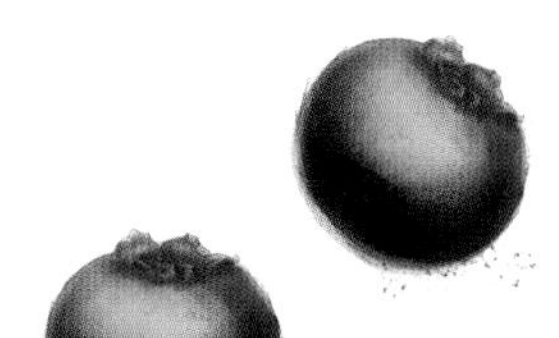

. . . Blueberry Cream Cheese Turnovers (cont.)

Preheat oven to 375°F (190°C).

Cut 3 small vents into each turnover. Brush with whipping cream and sprinkle with ¼ cup (60 mL) coarse raw or granulated sugar. Divide the hand pies between 2 baking trays or bake one tray at a time (7 pastries per tray). Bake in the preheated oven until golden brown, about 25–30 minutes, rotating the baking tray once during baking.

Cool on a wire rack. Serve warm or at room temperature.

FREEZING

Baked turnovers can be frozen up to 1 month. Store cooled pies in reusable freezer bags between layers of parchment or waxed paper. Note the date on the bags and remove as much air as possible before sealing. Thaw and serve at room temperature or reheat (thawed) pastries in a 250°F (120°C) oven until warm, about 15–20 minutes.

STRAWBERRY RASPBERRY GALETTE

YIELD

Makes one 9-inch (23 cm) galette

PASTRY

1 recipe Flaky Pastry Dough (page 32), only half the dough needed

2–3 Tbsp (30–45 mL) whipping cream, for brushing the pastry

1 Tbsp (15 mL) coarse raw or granulated sugar

FILLING

5 cups (1.25 L) hulled and quartered strawberries + 6–8 whole strawberries for the topping (about 1 kg in total)

¼ cup + 2 Tbsp (90 mL) granulated sugar

1¼ tsp (6 mL) balsamic vinegar

½ vanilla pod, split in two, seeds scraped out with a knife, or ½ Tbsp (7.5 mL) vanilla extract

Pinch salt (about ⅛ tsp/0.5 mL)

3 Tbsp (45 mL) quick-cooking tapioca, ideally ground in a spice grinder (see page 19 for info)

1½ cups (375 mL) fresh raspberries (about 250 g), divided

⅓ cup (80 mL) chopped walnuts, almonds or hazelnuts

I LOVE SERVING THIS French-style galette when strawberries and raspberries are at their peak. The berries are wrapped in pastry and baked until tender and juicy, then the galette is topped with plump fresh berries for a delicious textural contrast.

If you're lucky enough to have access to farm fresh strawberries, opt for those rather than the commercial berries sold in plastic clamshell containers. The two are not the same. Here on Vancouver Island, the summer strawberries are so fragrant that their scent alone draws you to the farm stands.

This galette is best enjoyed the day it's made. It's especially tempting with a dollop of Whipped Labneh (page 300) or Handcrafted Vanilla Ice Cream (page 300).

PASTRY

Prepare the pastry and place the dough onto a sheet of parchment paper dusted with flour. Layer a sheet of plastic wrap over the dough and roll (over the plastic) from the centre toward the pastry's edge in all directions, forming a circle about 12 inches (30 cm) in diameter and ⅛ inch (3 mm) thick.

Place the circle of dough onto a plate or tray lined with parchment and dusted with flour. Cover with plastic wrap and refrigerate for at least 20 minutes.

FILLING

In a large bowl, combine the sliced strawberries with ¼ cup + 2 Tbsp (90 mL) granulated sugar and the vinegar, vanilla, salt and tapioca; toss well. Leave for 30 minutes to macerate (soften). Add 1 cup (250 mL) raspberries and gently toss to evenly coat the fruit.

PUTTING IT ALL TOGETHER

Preheat a foil- or parchment-lined baking tray in a 425°F (220°C) oven.

Place the circle of dough onto your work surface (with the parchment beneath it). Sprinkle the dough with the nuts, leaving a generous border (see image, page 94).

Add the strawberry mixture, leaving the same trim. (This will seem like a lot of berries, but they shrink in the oven.) Fold the outer edges of the dough to partially cover the filling (see image, page 94), leaving the fruit exposed in the centre. The pastry's edges unfurl slightly in the oven, so you'll see more fruit after it's baked.

Brush the pastry's edge with whipping cream and dust with 1 Tbsp (15 mL) coarse raw or granulated sugar.

. . . recipe continued

. . . Strawberry Raspberry Galette (cont.)

Transfer the galette, and the parchment beneath it, to the preheated tray in the oven using a rimless baking tray or a pizza peel. Alternatively, carefully remove the preheated baking tray and place the galette on it. Bake for 15 minutes, reduce heat to 375°F (190°C) and continue to bake for another 20–30 minutes until the pastry is golden and cooked through. Rotate the tray halfway during baking and tent with foil as necessary to prevent burning.

Cool on a wire rack. Top with the whole strawberries and the remaining raspberries. Best served the same day.

VEGETABLE

RATATOUILLE TART

YIELD

Makes two 10½-inch (26 cm) tarts

PASTRY

1 recipe Flaky Pastry Dough (page 32), divided into 2 portions

¼ cup + 2 Tbsp (90 mL) grated Parmesan cheese (about 35 g)

VEGETABLE FILLING

2 Tbsp (30 mL) olive oil + more as needed

2 large onions (white, yellow or sweet), diced

½ cup (125 mL) blanched and peeled pearl onions (optional)

2 medium zucchini (about 140 g each), cut in half lengthwise, then into ¼-inch (6 mm) slices

2 large red peppers, diced

½ tsp (2.5 mL) kosher salt + more as needed

4 cloves garlic, minced

One 28 oz (794 g) can good-quality plum tomatoes

Two 6 oz (175 g) jars marinated artichoke hearts, drained and finely chopped, tough stems removed

36 Kalamata olives, pits removed and coarsely chopped

2 tsp (10 mL) hot sauce, such as Sriracha

¼ cup + 2 Tbsp (90 mL) freshly chopped parsley

2 Tbsp (30 mL) freshly chopped basil

. . . ingredients continued

TANGY FETA AND creamy ricotta cheese form the base for this sumptuous vegetable tart. Briny olives, marinated artichoke hearts and plenty of herbs brighten the rustic, Mediterranean-inspired topping. The tart is a simplified version of the double-crust Ratatouille Pie featured in my previous book, *British Columbia from Scratch*.

The pastry is prebaked and topped with a generous grating of Parmesan cheese to ensure the crust stays firm, never soggy. The filling and pastry can be made days in advance—always an attractive option when hosting guests.

Ricotta needs to be strained at least four hours, preferably overnight.

PASTRY

Prepare the pastry and place one portion of dough onto a sheet of parchment paper dusted with flour. Layer a sheet of plastic wrap over the dough and roll (over the plastic) from the centre toward the pastry's edge in all directions until about ⅛ inch (3 mm) thick.

Drape the dough over your rolling pin and transfer to one of the tart pans, being mindful not to pull or stretch the dough. Press the dough against the tart's edges with your fingers and trim the excess pastry. Cover in plastic and refrigerate for at least 40 minutes before baking.

Repeat the process with the remaining portion of dough to make the second tart.

Preheat oven to 375°F (190°C).

Pierce the base and sides of each pastry with the tines of a fork. Cover with parchment paper or foil and fill with pie weights. Transfer to a baking tray and bake for 20 minutes, rotating the tray once during baking.

Remove the tarts from the oven and carefully remove the pie weights and parchment (or foil). Sprinkle each tart with 3 Tbsp (45 mL) Parmesan cheese and return to the oven, uncovered, for another 10 minutes, or until the pastry is browned and cooked through. Cool completely on a baking rack.

VEGETABLE FILLING

Heat the oil in a large saucepan, add the large onions and cook over medium heat for about 5 minutes until translucent. Add the blanched pearl onions, if using, along with the zucchini, red peppers and salt. Cook until just tender, about 5 minutes. Add the garlic and stir for about half a minute until aromatic, then add the plum tomatoes, breaking them up with a wooden spoon. Add the artichokes, pitted olives and hot sauce. Simmer uncovered over medium heat until the liquid has completely evaporated and the mixture has thickened, about 15–20 minutes (a watery mixture will seep through the pastry). Taste and season with additional salt, if desired. Add the freshly chopped parsley and basil. Set aside to cool completely.

. . . recipe continued

. . . Ratatouille Tart (cont.)

CHEESE FILLING

Combine the strained ricotta, feta, ½ cup (125 mL) Parmesan and the egg in a medium bowl and mix well.

PUTTING IT ALL TOGETHER

Divide the cheese mixture in two and spread evenly along the base of each precooked tart. Divide the cooled vegetable filling and spread evenly over the cheese mixture.

Preheat oven to 350°F (175°C).

Scatter 6 or 7 small ripe tomatoes atop the filling and drizzle with a bit of olive oil. Alternatively, garnish the edge of the tart with thinly sliced zucchini rounds (slightly overlapping) drizzled with a bit of olive oil.

Bake the tarts on a baking tray in the preheated oven for 30–40 minutes, or until the cheese and filling have warmed through.

Cool on a wire rack. Serve at room temperature or slightly warm.

CHEESE FILLING

1¾ cups (435 mL) ricotta cheese (about 400 g), strained (see note, page 109)

1 cup (250 mL) crumbled feta cheese (about 120 g)

½ cup (125 mL) freshly grated Parmesan cheese (about 60 g)

1 large egg, slightly beaten

TOPPING

6–7 small ripe tomatoes on the vine, or 1 small, thinly sliced zucchini

SPECIAL EQUIPMENT

Two 10½-inch (26 cm) tart pans with removable bases

Pie weights (or beans or rice)

ASPARAGUS & LEEK TART

YIELD

Makes one 9-inch (23 cm) square tart

PASTRY

1 recipe Flaky Pastry Dough (page 32), only half the dough needed

3 Tbsp (45 mL) grated Parmesan (about 20 g)

FILLINGS

2 Tbsp (30 mL) unsalted butter (about 30 g)

6 cups (1.5 L) thinly sliced leeks (about 1.5 kg), white part only

¾ tsp (4 mL) kosher salt + more as needed

Zest from 1 lemon + 4 tsp (20 mL) freshly squeezed lemon juice, divided + more as needed

¼ cup + 2 Tbsp (90 mL) soft cheese (cream cheese or goat cheese; about 95 g)

½ cup (125 mL) shredded Gruyère cheese (about 60 g)

½ cup (125 mL) crumbled feta (about 70 g)

2 anchovies, rinsed and finely minced, or 1 tsp (5 mL) anchovy paste

1 tsp (5 mL) finely minced garlic (about 1 clove)

½ tsp (2.5 mL) dried chili flakes (reduce the amount if you prefer less heat)

2 lb (910 g) fresh asparagus

2 Tbsp (30 mL) vegetable oil

SPECIAL EQUIPMENT

9-inch (23 cm) square (or round) tart pan with removable base

Pie weights (or beans or rice)

LEMONY, SLOW-ROASTED leeks and a trio of cheeses form a rich savoury base for this outstanding asparagus tart. The star is grilled asparagus, so you'll want to make this in the appropriate season. The tart can be assembled and refrigerated up to 24 hours before baking (as if you need another excuse for making this).

PASTRY

Prepare the pastry and place the dough onto a sheet of parchment paper dusted with flour. Layer a sheet of plastic wrap over the dough and roll (over the plastic) from the centre toward the pastry's edge in all directions until about ⅛ inch (3 mm) thick. Remove the plastic and, using a sharp knife, cut the dough about 1½ inches (4 cm) wider than the tart pan. Drape the dough onto your rolling pin and transfer to the tart pan, pressing the dough against the sides. Trim the edges. Cover with plastic wrap and refrigerate for about 20 minutes.

Preheat oven to 375°F (190°C).

Using a fork, prick the dough in several places (this prevents the dough from buckling when heated). Transfer to a baking tray, cover with parchment or foil and add the pie weights.

Bake for 25 minutes in the preheated oven, rotating the baking tray once to promote even browning. Remove the tart from the oven, carefully remove the foil and pie weights and sprinkle the pastry evenly with the Parmesan cheese. Return to the oven, uncovered, and continue to bake until the Parmesan is golden, about 12 minutes.

Cool on a wire rack and turn off the oven.

LEEK FILLING

Melt the butter in a large saucepan; add the sliced leeks and salt. Cook, partially covered, over low heat, stirring occasionally until completely soft and tender, about 30 minutes. If the mixture becomes dry and threatens to burn, add a splash of water. Remove the lid for the last 5 minutes of cooking to allow any residual moisture to evaporate. Add 1 Tbsp (15 mL) lemon juice. Taste and adjust seasoning, if necessary, with additional salt or lemon juice. Cool completely.

CHEESE MIXTURE

In a small bowl, combine the soft cheese, Gruyère, feta, anchovies, garlic, chili flakes and lemon zest.

. . . recipe continued

. . . Asparagus & Leek Tart (cont.)

ASPARAGUS

Trim the asparagus: Hold a spear (one hand at each end) and bend the stalk until it snaps at its natural breaking point about 2–3 inches (5–8 cm) from the base. Preheat a barbecue or stovetop grill to medium-high. Lay the trimmed asparagus on the grill, brush with oil and cook, uncovered, for about 9–10 minutes or until slightly charred. Turn the asparagus over with tongs, cover and cook until tender, about 5 more minutes, depending on the thickness of the spears. Transfer to a plate, sprinkle with a pinch of kosher salt and a squeeze of lemon juice (about 1 tsp/5 mL).

PUTTING IT ALL TOGETHER

Preheat oven to 375°F (190°C).

Spread the cheese mixture evenly on the base of the pastry, add the cooked leeks and top with the grilled asparagus, keeping the spears neatly together (see image). Tent loosely with foil and bake in the preheated oven until the tart is warmed through, about 20 minutes.

Cool on a wire rack and rest for about 20 minutes before serving.

CHERRY TOMATO GALETTES

YIELD

Makes twelve 4-inch (10 cm) mini galettes

PASTRY

1 recipe Flaky Pastry Dough (page 32), divided into 2 portions

1 large egg, lightly beaten, for brushing the pastry

FILLING

2 Tbsp (30 mL) vegetable oil + extra for drizzling

3 cups (750 mL) thinly sliced shallots (about 500 g)

Kosher salt

¾ cup (185 mL) ricotta cheese (about 175 g), strained (see note, page 109)

¾ cup (185 mL) crumbled feta cheese (about 105 g)

¼ cup (60 mL) grated Parmesan (or Gruyère) cheese (about 25 g)

2 anchovies, rinsed and finely chopped, or 1 tsp (5 mL) anchovy paste

1 large egg

Zest from 1 lemon

½ tsp (2.5 mL) finely minced garlic

1 Tbsp (15 mL) fresh thyme leaves (about 6 sprigs) + extra for garnish

¾ lb (375 g) ripe cherry, grape or similar miniature tomatoes, thinly sliced

Fresh basil leaves, for garnish

THESE ADORABLE MINIATURE galettes encase a filling of pan-roasted shallots and a trio of cheeses fragrant with lemon zest and fresh thyme. The tomatoes collapse in the oven, their flavours intensifying with the heat, while the pastry unfurls slightly to expose more filling.

My dear but impatient friend, Carolyn, ditched the galettes after making a few and whipped up a full-sized tart instead—to rave reviews. I'm not encouraging you do the same, but it's good to know you have options.

The ricotta cheese needs to be strained overnight (for at least four hours), so plan accordingly. If you don't care for ricotta, goat cheese is a good substitute.

PASTRY

Prepare the pastry and place one portion of dough onto a sheet of parchment paper dusted with flour. Layer a sheet of plastic wrap over the dough and roll (over the plastic) from the centre toward the pastry's edge in all directions until about ⅛ inch (3 mm) thick. Remove the plastic and cut each portion of dough into six 4½-inch (11 cm) circles using a small bowl as a template, gathering and re-rolling the dough as necessary. Stack the circles of dough between parchment or wax paper, wrap in plastic and refrigerate for at least 20 minutes.

Repeat the process with the remaining portion of dough for a total of 12 circles.

FILLING

Heat the oil in a large skillet and cook the shallots over medium heat in 2 batches, so as not to crowd the pan, until completely soft and starting to brown. Add a pinch of salt (about ¼ tsp/1 mL) to each batch. Transfer to a bowl to cool.

In a medium bowl, combine the cheeses, anchovies, egg, lemon zest, garlic and thyme.

PUTTING IT ALL TOGETHER

Preheat oven to 425°F (220°C).

Working in batches, take 4 circles of dough from the fridge and place them onto a flour-dusted work surface. Spread each with a generous spoonful of the cheese mixture, about 1½ Tbsp (22 mL), leaving a ¼-inch (6 mm) border. Add a generous 1 Tbsp (15+ mL) of the cooled shallots to each and enough tomato slices to cover the cheese mixture, overlapping the tomatoes.

Grasp an edge of the dough with your fingers and fold ¾–1 inch (2–2.5 cm) of the border toward the centre of the galette, overlapping and pleating the dough with your fingers every 1 inch (2.5 cm) or so.

You should have a tidy bundle enclosing the tomatoes. Don't worry if your galettes seem small, they will expand and open somewhat in the oven.

. . . recipe continued

Transfer the galettes to a parchment-lined tray or platter, cover with plastic and refrigerate while assembling the remaining tarts. The galettes need to be chilled until firm, at least 20 minutes. If your pleating is too loose and/or the dough isn't properly chilled before baking, the pastry can unfurl, leaving your galettes looking more like mini pizzas.

When ready to bake, place the chilled tarts on a baking tray lined with parchment or foil, leaving 1–2 inches (2.5–5 cm) between each pastry (you may need 2 baking trays). Brush the dough's edges with beaten egg. Drizzle the exposed tomatoes with a bit of olive oil and sprinkle with a pinch of kosher salt.

Bake in the preheated oven for 10 minutes, then reduce the temperature to 375°F (190°C) and continue to bake until the pastry is browned and cooked through, about 20 minutes. (The more pastries in the oven, the longer the cooking time.) Rotate the pan halfway during baking and tent with foil as necessary to prevent burning.

Transfer the galettes to a wire rack. Just before serving, garnish with additional thyme leaves and freshly torn basil. Best served warm.

STRAINED RICOTTA

To strain ricotta cheese, place a fine-mesh strainer over a bowl, line it with cheesecloth and add the ricotta. Cover and refrigerate a few hours, preferably overnight. Discard any excess liquid.

PAN-SEARED BRUSSELS SPROUTS TART

YIELD

Makes one 9-inch (23 cm) tart

PASTRY

1 recipe Flaky Pastry Dough using the Whole Wheat Flax Variation (page 32), only half the dough needed

¼ cup (60mL) Parmesan cheese (about 25 g)

FILLING

Kosher salt

8 cups (2 L) thinly sliced Brussels sprouts (about 1 kg), tough ends trimmed and discarded

¼ cup + 2 Tbsp (90 mL) vegetable oil

2 Tbsp (30 mL) freshly squeezed lemon juice

1 tsp (5 mL) Dijon-style mustard

2 anchovies, rinsed and finely chopped, or 1 tsp (5 mL) anchovy paste

1 tsp (5 mL) hot sauce, such as Sriracha

3 large eggs, lightly beaten

1 cup (250 mL) whipping cream

¼ cup (60 mL) plain Greek yogurt

Heaping ⅓ cup (80+ mL) crumbled feta cheese (about 60 g)

2 Tbsp (30 mL) pine nuts

SPECIAL EQUIPMENT

9-inch (23 cm) tart pan with a removable base

Pie weights (or beans or rice)

PAN-ROASTED, CARAMELIZED Brussels sprouts are tossed in a lemony dressing and folded into a creamy base in this hearty, savoury tart. Topped with crumbled feta and pine nuts, this unique dish always comes as a pleasant surprise.

A vegetable once loathed for its pungent odour and bitter edge, Brussels sprouts are now celebrated thanks to cooking techniques that coax out their finer qualities. When sprouts are blanched in salted boiling water, then cooked over high heat until nearly charred, they're so delicious you'll want to eat them straight from the pan.

The crust, a hearty whole wheat pastry flecked with flax seeds, lends a nutty nuance. If you prefer a lighter crust, use the standard Flaky Pastry Dough (page 32).

PASTRY

Prepare the pastry and place one portion of dough onto a sheet of parchment paper dusted with flour. Layer a sheet of plastic wrap over the dough and roll (over the plastic) from the centre toward the pastry's edge in all directions until about ⅛ inch (3 mm) thick.

Drape the dough onto a rolling pin and transfer to the tart pan. Press the dough against the fluted edges of the pan and trim the edges. Cover with plastic and refrigerate for at least 40 minutes before baking.

Preheat oven to 375°F (190°C).

Retrieve the tart pan from the fridge and, using a fork, prick the dough in several places (to prevent it from buckling and rising unevenly). Cover with parchment or foil and add the pie weights.

Transfer to a baking tray and bake for 25 minutes, rotating the tray once to promote even browning. Carefully remove the pastry from the oven, discard the foil, remove the pie weights and sprinkle the pastry evenly with the Parmesan cheese. Return to the oven, uncovered, and continue to bake until the Parmesan is golden, about 12 minutes. Cool on a wire rack.

FILLING

Reduce the oven temperature to 350°F (175°C). Place a colander in an empty sink.

Bring a large pot of heavily salted water to a roaring boil (it should taste salty, like seawater; about 2 Tbsp/30 mL kosher salt needed per 12 cups/3 L water).

Tip the sliced Brussels sprouts into the boiling water. Bring to a boil again and blanch for 2 minutes. Pour the Brussels sprouts and water into the colander. Without delay, run cold tap water over the sprouts until cool. Drain well and transfer to a clean tea towel or sturdy paper towel and squeeze dry to remove any excess moisture. (You need the vegetables as dry as possible as they'll be cooked in hot oil.) Transfer to a bowl.

. . . recipe continued

. . . Pan-Seared Brussels Sprouts Tart (cont.)

Heat 2 Tbsp (30 mL) oil in a large skillet until shimmering but not smoking. Working in batches, place about one-third of the blanched Brussels sprouts into the hot skillet and add a small pinch of kosher salt—a mere ⅛ tsp (0.5 mL)—to each batch. Cook until the vegetables have charred around the edges, occasionally stirring the sprouts with a wooden spoon to prevent burning, about 6 minutes per batch. (If using a smaller skillet, you may need to cook an additional batch.) Transfer the sprouts to a medium bowl to cool. Repeat with the remaing oil and Brussels sprouts for a total of 3 batches.

In a small bowl or cup, mix together the lemon juice, mustard, anchovies and hot sauce. Pour the mixture over the cooked Brussels sprouts and mix to combine. Set aside to cool.

In a small bowl or 2-cup (500 mL) measuring jug, combine the eggs, cream, yogurt and 1 tsp (5 mL) kosher salt. Mix well to combine.

PUTTING IT ALL TOGETHER

Spoon half of the cooled Brussels sprouts mixture onto the cooled, baked pastry. Pour half the egg/cream mixture over the sprouts, then layer with the remaining sprouts, followed by the remaining egg/cream mixture. Sprinkle evenly with feta and pine nuts.

Place the tart on a baking tray and bake in the preheated oven for about 40 minutes, or until the centre is nearly firm, rotating the pan halfway through baking. Tent with foil over the tart as necessary to prevent burning.

Cool on a wire rack for at least 40 minutes before serving.

POTATO CHEESE GALETTE

YIELD

Makes two 8-inch (20 cm) galettes

PASTRY

1 recipe Flaky Pastry Dough (page 32), divided into 2 portions

1 large egg, lightly beaten, for brushing the pastry

2 Tbsp (30 mL) grated Parmesan cheese (about 12 g)

POTATO LEEK FILLING

2 Tbsp (30 mL) unsalted butter (about 30 g)

3 lb (1.5 kg) leeks, white part only, washed and thinly sliced (about 5–6 cups/1.25–1.5 L sliced)

Kosher salt

Zest from 1 lemon + 1 Tbsp (15 mL) freshly squeezed lemon juice

¾ cup (185 mL) soft cheese (about 195 g), such as goat cheese or cream cheese

1 cup (250 mL) shredded Gruyère cheese (about 120 g)

1 cup (250 mL) crumbled feta (about 140 g)

2 Tbsp (30 mL) grated Parmesan cheese (about 12 g)

4 anchovies, rinsed and finely minced, or 2 tsp (10 mL) anchovy paste

2 tsp (10 mL) finely minced garlic (about 2 cloves)

1 tsp (5 mL) dried crushed chili flakes (use less if you prefer a tamer galette; this amount packs a punch)

. . . ingredients continued

If you're a pastry novice, consider the galette a gateway pie. With no crimping to master or tart pans to line, a galette is a terrific way to ease into pastry making.

Featuring sweet slow-roasted leeks, savoury cheeses, herbs and thinly sliced potatoes, this galette is as comforting as an oversized sweater on a chilly afternoon.

The galette can be assembled and refrigerated up to 24 hours before baking.

PASTRY

Prepare the pastry and place one portion of dough onto a sheet of parchment paper dusted with flour. Layer a sheet of plastic wrap over the dough and roll (over the plastic) from the centre toward the pastry's edge in all directions until approximately 10½ inches (26 cm) in diameter and ⅛ inch (3 mm) thick.

Repeat the process with the remaining portion of dough to make a second circle.

Stack the 2 circles of dough, with parchment between each, on a parchment-lined tray or platter dusted with flour. Cover with plastic and refrigerate while preparing the filling.

POTATO LEEK FILLING

Preheat oven to 375°F (190°C).

Melt the butter in a large saucepan; add the sliced leeks and ½ tsp (2.5 mL) salt. Cook, covered, over low heat, stirring occasionally until completely soft and tender, about 30 minutes. If the mixture becomes dry and threatens to burn, add a splash of water. Remove the lid for the last 5 minutes of cooking to allow any residual moisture to evaporate. Add the lemon juice. Cool completely.

In a medium bowl, combine the soft cheese, Gruyère, feta, 2 Tbsp (30 mL) Parmesan cheese, anchovies, garlic, chili flakes and lemon zest.

Slice the potatoes as thinly as possible, preferably with a mandolin or vegetable slicer. Place in a medium bowl with 2 Tbsp (30 mL) oil and mix to ensure the potatoes are completely coated. Spread the potatoes onto 2 parchment-lined baking trays in a single layer. Bake in the preheated oven until the potatoes are barely cooked and not yet browned, about 6–8 minutes. Remove the potatoes from the oven.

Increase the oven temperature to 400°F (200°C) and preheat a baking tray. (The preheated tray helps the pastry base firm faster, preventing a soggy crust.)

PUTTING IT ALL TOGETHER

Place each pastry circle and the parchment beneath them on your work surface. (You may have to lift the pastry and add additional flour beneath it to prevent the pastry from sticking to the parchment.) Divide the cheese mixture equally between the pastry circles and spread the mixture evenly on each, leaving a 2-inch (5 cm) border. Divide the rosemary and thyme and scatter evenly over the cheese mixture.

. . . recipe continued

. . . Potato Cheese Galette (cont.)

2 medium red-skinned or yellow-fleshed potatoes, such as Yukon Gold

2 Tbsp (30 mL) vegetable oil

2 tsp (10 mL) fresh rosemary, chopped

2 tsp (10 mL) fresh thyme, chopped

Divide the cooled leeks and spread evenly over the cheese and herbs, leaving a 2-inch (5 cm) border. Finally, divide the cooked potatoes and layer them on top of the leeks, overlapping slightly, leaving a generous 2-inch (5 cm) border. Sprinkle each galette with a pinch of salt.

To crimp/pleat the edges, grasp an edge of the dough with your fingers and fold the border toward the centre of the galette, overlapping and pleating the dough together with your fingers every 1½ inches (4 cm) or so. Galettes are inherently rustic, so you needn't strive for perfection. (If you're not familiar with pleating pastry for a galette, refer to the images on pages 94–95.)

Brush the pastry's edges with beaten egg and sprinkle the exposed pastry with 2 Tbsp (30 mL) Parmesan cheese.

Transfer the galettes and the parchment beneath them to the preheated baking tray using a pizza peel or flat-edged baking tray. Alternatively, carefully remove the baking tray from the oven and transfer the galette, with the parchment paper underneath it, onto the heated tray.

Bake for 15 minutes at 400°F (200°C), reduce the temperature to 375°F (190°C) and continue to bake until the pastry is browned and cooked through, about 30–40 minutes. Rotate the pan halfway through baking and tent with foil as necessary to prevent burning.

Cool on a wire rack without the parchment. Serve at room temperature or rewarm in a low-temperature oven.

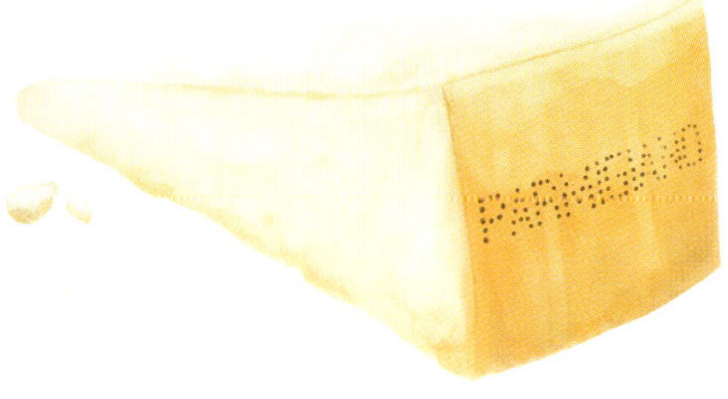

ROASTED VEGETABLE TARTS

YIELD

Makes eight 4-inch (10 cm) tarts

PASTRY

1 lb (450 g) puff pastry, either handcrafted (page 50), rough (page 54) or commercial (frozen)

1 large egg, lightly beaten, for brushing the pastry + more as needed

3 Tbsp (45 mL) grated Parmesan cheese (about 20 g)

FILLING

1 cup (250 mL) ricotta cheese (about 227 g), strained (see note, page 109)

½ cup (125 mL) crumbled feta (about 70 g)

Zest from 1 lemon + 1½ Tbsp (22 mL) lemon juice

Kosher salt

1¾ lb (795 g) vegetables (cauliflower, carrots, tomatoes and/or shallots), or 8 portobello mushrooms, sized to fit neatly in the tarts (see image)

1 Tbsp (15 mL) olive oil + more as needed

1 Tbsp (15 mL) unsalted butter (if using mushrooms; about 14 g) + more as needed

DRESSING

¼ cup (60 mL) white wine vinegar

¼ cup (60 mL) vegetable oil, such as grapeseed (any mild-tasting oil will work)

1 clove garlic, finely minced

1 tsp (5 mL) fresh thyme + extra for garnish

2 anchovies, rinsed, drained and finely minced (optional)

1 tsp (5 mL) capers, roughly chopped

1 tsp (5 mL) Dijon-style mustard

Kosher salt

OVEN-ROASTED VEGETABLES and meaty portobello mushrooms blend with a lemony ricotta filling in these elegant puff pastry tarts. Just before serving, the tarts are brightened with a piquant dressing flecked with tangy capers and fresh thyme.

The tarts are perfectly straightforward, but you'll need to plan ahead, as the ricotta needs to strain for a few hours or, even better, overnight.

PASTRY

Prepare the puff pastry according to the instructions. If using frozen commercial puff pastry, thaw according to the instructions on the package before using.

Working with half the dough (½ lb/227 g) at a time, place the dough onto a flour-dusted work surface (if sticky, place on a sheet of parchment paper dusted with flour instead). Roll the dough into a 10- × 10-inch (25 × 25 cm) square, ⅛ inch (3 mm) thick, then cut into 4 equal squares (5 × 5 inches/12 × 12 cm).

Repeat the process with the remaining pastry for a total of 8 squares.

Brush the border of each square with lightly beaten egg, then fold the edges over about ¾ inch (2 cm) to create an edge. Score the corners of each square with an "x" using the dull side of your knife. Finally, poke holes into the base of each tart (see page 120). If the dough becomes too soft to work with at any time, wrap in plastic and refrigerate until firm.

Place the pastry squares onto a tray or plate lined with parchment paper, cover with plastic wrap and refrigerate for at least 40 minutes. Alternatively, stack the squares of dough between parchment or wax paper, wrap in plastic and refrigerate for at least 40 minutes.

Preheat oven to 400°F (200°C).

Place the chilled squares of dough onto a parchment-lined baking tray (if they're not already on one), leaving 1 inch (2.5 cm) or more between each square. Dust the base of each tart with a rounded teaspoon of Parmesan cheese. Brush the edges with additional beaten egg.

Bake in the preheated oven for 10–15 minutes, or until golden and cooked through, rotating the pan halfway through baking. The pastries will puff in the oven, then settle as they cool. Cool on a wire rack.

CHEESE FILLING

In a small bowl, combine the strained ricotta cheese, crumbled feta, lemon zest and juice and a pinch of kosher salt. Set aside.

. . . recipe continued

. . . Roasted Vegetable Tarts (cont.)

ROASTED VEGETABLES

If using cauliflower, mini carrots, tomatoes and/or shallots, peel, chop and slice your selected vegetables into pieces no larger than 3 inches (8 cm). Spread the vegetables onto a parchment-lined baking tray in a single layer. Drizzle with 1 Tbsp (15 mL) olive oil and sprinkle evenly with a pinch (about ¼ tsp/1 mL) of kosher salt. Roast in the preheated oven for 25–30 minutes, or until tender, rotating the pan to promote even browning. Check the vegetables after 8–10 minutes. If using a combination of vegetables, some will need to be removed earlier than others; alternatively, roast each variety separately to ensure even cooking.

If using portobello mushrooms, clean the mushrooms with a damp cloth and remove and reserve the stems for another use. Heat 1 Tbsp (15 mL) oil and 1 Tbsp (15 mL) butter in a medium skillet (preferably non-stick). Add the mushrooms, without crowding the pan, gills facing down. Cook over medium heat until the caps have softened slightly, they will shrink as they cook. Turn the mushrooms over and sprinkle each with a pinch of kosher salt. Continue to cook, adding additional butter/oil if sticking, until the mushrooms are tender. Reserve any liquid that accumulates (it will be added to the tart).

PUTTING IT ALL TOGETHER

Fill each tart with 2–3 Tbsp (30–45 mL) of the ricotta/feta mixture. Top with your choice of roasted vegetables. If using mushrooms, place the gills facing up and drizzle with the reserved mushroom liquid.

Reheat the tarts in a 400°F (200°C) oven for 10–12 minutes, or until the cheese mixture has warmed through.

DRESSING

In a small container, whisk together the dressing ingredients with a pinch of salt. Taste and add more salt, if desired.

Just before serving, re-whisk the dressing and drizzle over the vegetables. Garnish with thyme leaves.

MUSHROOM & EGGPLANT TURNOVERS

YIELD

Makes about twelve 3½-inch (9 cm) turnovers

PASTRY

1 recipe Flaky Pastry Dough (page 32), divided into 2 portions

1 large egg, lightly beaten, for brushing the pastry + more as needed

FILLING

2 small or 1 medium eggplant (about 375 g total)

¼ cup + 1 Tbsp (75 mL) vegetable oil, divided + more as needed

Kosher salt

1 cup (250 mL) finely chopped onion (about 1 medium onion)*

1 lb (450 g) button mushrooms, cleaned and finely chopped*

1 Tbsp (15 mL) minced garlic (about 3 cloves)

1 tsp (5 mL) crushed dried chili peppers (use less if you prefer a tamer filling)

1 tsp (5 mL) finely chopped fresh thyme

¼ cup (60 mL) finely chopped parsley

Zest from 1 lemon + 2 Tbsp (30 mL) freshly squeezed lemon juice + more as needed

¼ cup (60 mL) freshly grated Parmesan cheese (about 25 g)

¼ cup (60 mL) chopped almonds

---

*It's important to chop the onions and mushrooms finely to achieve the proper texture.

GARLICKY MUSHROOMS AND roasted eggplant blend with fresh herbs, savoury Parmesan and chopped almonds for a filling so tasty you'll want to eat it straight from the bowl. The pastries make a delightful appetizer or snack—and they freeze beautifully.

Select garden-fresh eggplants—ideally from a farmer's market—and cook them straight away. They become more bitter with age, so recently harvested is always best. I don't bother to pre-salt "to extract bitter juices" as some recipes instruct; it's not necessary when using fresh. Choose eggplants that are heavy for their size (pick up a few to gauge the varying weights), with a green stem and a taut, smooth and shiny skin. Lightly press the eggplant with your finger; it should be firm but leave a slight imprint. Smaller eggplants tend to be less bitter with fewer seeds.

It's easy to grab packaged mushrooms on the go, but opt for the loose variety instead so you can select the firmest and plumpest ones. This recipe calls for 1 lb (450 g) of mushrooms, which seems like a lot when you're chopping them, but they shrink as they cook. Be sure to wipe the mushrooms clean with a damp paper towel, or rinse briefly, just before chopping them.

PASTRY

Prepare the pastry and place one portion of dough onto a sheet of parchment paper dusted with flour. Layer a sheet of plastic wrap over the dough and roll (over the plastic) from the centre toward the pastry's edge in all directions until about ⅛ inch (3 mm) thick. Remove the plastic and cut the dough into twelve 3½-inch (9 cm) squares, gathering and re-rolling the dough as necessary. If the dough becomes too soft to work with at any time, wrap in plastic and refrigerate until firm.

Repeat the process with the remaining portion of dough for a total of 24 squares.

Place the squares of dough onto a tray or plate lined with parchment paper and dusted with flour. Cover with plastic wrap and refrigerate for at least 40 minutes. Alternatively, stack the squares of dough between parchment or wax paper, wrap in plastic and refrigerate.

FILLING

Preheat oven to 375°F (190°C).

Using a sharp knife, split the eggplant in half and score the flesh in a crosshatch pattern without piercing the skin. Brush the cut sides with vegetable oil (about 1 Tbsp/15 mL needed) and sprinkle with a pinch (about ¼ tsp/1 mL) of kosher salt. Place the eggplant(s) on a baking tray, cut side up, and bake uncovered until the flesh turns golden, anywhere from 20–40 minutes depending on size. Cover with foil and continue to bake for another 10–15 minutes until completely soft and tender. Set aside to cool.

. . recipe continued

In a large skillet, heat 2 Tbsp (30 mL) oil. Add the onion and ½ tsp (2.5 mL) kosher salt and cook over medium heat, stirring occasionally, until starting to brown, about 5 minutes. Add half the mushrooms and cook until soft, about 5 minutes. Transfer to a medium bowl.

Heat another 2 Tbsp (30 mL) oil in the skillet. Add the remaining mushrooms and another ½ tsp (2.5 mL) salt and cook for another 5 minutes until the mushrooms are soft. Add the garlic and cook until aromatic, about 20 seconds.

Transfer to the cooked onion/mushroom mixture. Add the dried chili peppers, herbs, lemon zest and juice, Parmesan and almonds and mix well.

Scoop the flesh from the eggplant onto a cutting board and chop into small pieces. Add it to the mushroom mixture with a pinch (about ¼ tsp/1 mL) of kosher salt. Taste and season with additional lemon or salt if necessary. Cool completely before using.

PUTTING IT ALL TOGETHER

Working with 8 squares of dough at a time on a floured work surface (keep the balance refrigerated), place a generous heap of filling, about 3 Tbsp (45 mL) each, in the centres of 4 squares. This will seem like a lot of filling, but you want them full for a proper filling-to-pastry ratio.

Brush each pastry's border with lightly beaten egg. Cover the filling with the remaining 4 squares of dough and press the edges together with your fingers. Return to the parchment-lined tray, cover in plastic wrap and refrigerate while you assemble the remaining pastries.

Preheat oven to 425°F (220°C).

Divide the chilled pastries between 2 foil or parchment-lined baking trays (to leave plenty of room between each pastry). Cut an "x" in the centre of each pastry with a sharp knife and crimp the edges with the tines of a fork. Brush the tops with additional beaten egg.

Bake in the preheated oven for 15 minutes, reduce the temperature to 375°F (190°C) and continue baking until the pastry is cooked through, about 5 minutes. Rotate the pan once during baking and tent with foil as necessary to prevent burning.

Cool on a wire rack. Serve warm or at room temperature.

DEEP-DISH VEGETABLE PIE

YIELD

Makes one 9-inch (23 cm) deep-dish pie

PASTRY

1 recipe Flaky Pastry Dough (page 32), divided into 2 portions (one slightly larger for the base and sides)

1 large egg, lightly beaten, or 1 Tbsp (15 mL) dairy-free milk, for brushing the pastry + more as needed

FILLING

6 large orange or yellow bell peppers

3 medium zucchini squash (about 175 g each), thinly sliced horizontally and ¼ inch (6 mm) thick

Vegetable oil

4 large portobello mushrooms

Kosher salt

3 cloves garlic, thinly sliced

6 cups (1.5 L) chopped kale (anywhere from half to a full bunch, depending on the size), stems and cores removed, cut into small bite-sized pieces

½ tsp (2.5 mL) dried crushed chili flakes

½ tsp (2.5 mL) freshly squeezed lemon juice

¾ cup (185 mL) grated Parmesan cheese or shredded dairy-free cheese (about 60 g)

¾ cup (185 mL) grated Gruyère cheese or shredded dairy-free cheese (about 75 g)

10 oz (285 g) smoked or firm tofu, sliced and patted dry

... ingredients continued

LAYERS OF ROASTED zucchini, smoked tofu and peppery kale are paired with sweet roasted peppers and earthy portobello mushrooms for a hearty pie that satisfies meat lovers and vegetarians alike—an enduring challenge when both live under the same roof.

Brightened with a piquant pesto made of sun-dried tomatoes and roasted garlic, as well as a lemony tapenade, this deep-dish pie is intensely flavoured. The filling, an adaptation of my Black Forest Ham Pithivier recipe (page 144), is scaled up for a deep-dish pie, and easily adapted for vegans, too.

Like all layered dishes (think lasagna), this recipe can't be rushed. You'll want to make it when you're happy to tinker in the kitchen without any time restraints. As most of the ingredients need to be precooked, I parse the recipe into manageable chunks and make the filling a day, or several days, in advance. The pastry, too, can be made ahead of time, and the pie can be fully assembled up to 24 hours before baking.

Note that layered dishes must be seasoned throughout to fully develop their intrinsic flavours. To season only the last layer, as an afterthought, is to cheat yourself and your guests out of the recipe's full potential. Season each vegetable layer with a well-distributed but light pinch of kosher salt (a mere ⅛–¼ tsp/ 0.5–1 mL). See "A Salty Note" on page 130 for more information.

PASTRY BASE

Prepare the pastry and place the larger portion of dough onto a sheet of parchment paper dusted with flour. Layer a sheet of plastic wrap over the dough and roll (over the plastic) from the centre toward the pastry's edge in all directions until approximately 14 inches (36 cm) in diameter and about ⅛ inch (3 mm) thick.

Drape the dough onto your rolling pin and transfer to the springform pan, being mindful not to pull or stretch the dough. Gently press the dough into the sides of the pan and trim the edges (you may need to remove some excess pastry from the sides of the pan where the pastry bunches together). Cover in plastic and refrigerate for at least 40 minutes.

PASTRY TOP

Place the remaining portion of dough onto a sheet of parchment paper dusted with flour. Cover the dough with plastic wrap and roll (over the plastic) from the centre toward the pastry's edge in all directions, at least 9 inches (23 cm) in diameter and ⅛ inch (3 mm) thick. Transfer the circle of dough to a tray or plate lined with parchment and dusted with flour, wrap in plastic and refrigerate. If desired, re-roll any excess dough to fashion into a twisted pastry trim (see image). Refrigerate this as well.

... recipe continued

¼ cup (60 mL) Sun-Dried Tomato & Roasted Garlic Pesto (page 303), or store-bought

¼ cup (60 mL) Rustic Tapenade (page 303), or store-bought

Freshly ground black pepper

SPECIAL EQUIPMENT

9-inch (23 cm) springform pan

FILLING

Vegetables should be precooked, cooled and blotted dry before the pie is assembled. The bell peppers and zucchini in particular retain a great deal of moisture and must be *as dry as possible* to prevent the pastry from becoming soggy.

BELL PEPPERS: Place the whole peppers on a parchment- or foil-lined baking tray. Bake in a preheated 375°F (190°C) oven until the peppers have darkened in spots and are starting to collapse, about 45–55 minutes, rotating the pan once during baking. Transfer to a bowl and cover tightly with foil. When cool enough to handle, remove the skin, core and stem, keeping the peppers in large pieces. If not using right away, store on a plate between paper towels, cover and refrigerate. Blot completely dry before using.

ZUCCHINI: Slice the squash horizontally into ¼-inch (6 mm) thick ribbons. Place the ribbons on a baking tray lined with foil or parchment paper, without overlapping. Brush with oil and bake in a preheated 375°F (190°C) oven until soft (zucchini will shrink slightly), about 25 minutes, rotating the tray once during baking. If not using right away, store on a plate between paper towels, cover and refrigerate. Blot completely dry before using.

MUSHROOMS: Wipe clean and slice the portobello mushroom caps horizontally, about ¼ inch (6 mm) thick, so as to increase their surface area. (If using standard button mushrooms, slice them as you normally would.) Reserve the stems for another use. Heat 3 Tbsp (45 mL) oil in a large skillet over medium heat. Working in batches, add the mushrooms in a single layer and cook until browned, about 5 minutes, turning them over once. Add a pinch of salt to each batch and continue to cook until the mushrooms are tender. Cool and blot completely dry before using.

KALE AND GARLIC: Using a slotted spoon within easy reach, heat 3 Tbsp (45 mL) oil in a large skillet over medium-low heat, add the garlic and cook until just starting to brown, about 30 seconds. Remove the garlic with the slotted spoon and reserve. Working in batches, cook the kale in the garlic oil until completely wilted, about 3–4 minutes, turning the greens as necessary to prevent burning. Add a pinch of salt and the chili flakes, lemon juice and the cooked garlic; mix to combine. Cool and blot completely dry before using.

PUTTING IT ALL TOGETHER

Ensure all your vegetables have been blotted *completely dry* before you start layering the ingredients, otherwise your pastry can become soggy.

Place your pastry-lined springform pan and all your ingredients within easy reach. You'll be layering all the ingredients in the pan, but don't worry about the exact order (I've yet to make this in the same order twice). The idea is to have neat layers of well-seasoned vegetables.

. . . recipe continued

A SALTY NOTE

If you shy away from salt, as I once did, consider the wisdom of my chef instructor at culinary school. After tasting one of my dishes he put down his fork solemnly, placed his hands on my shoulders and looked me squarely in the eyes, "If you want to become a great cook, you'll have to overcome your fear of salt."

Chefs prefer kosher salt because the large, irregular crystals are easy to pinch, offering more control when seasoning (and it's usually iodine-free). If using table salt, handle with care—it's easy to oversalt as the crystals are more compact, resulting in more salt per spoonful than kosher.

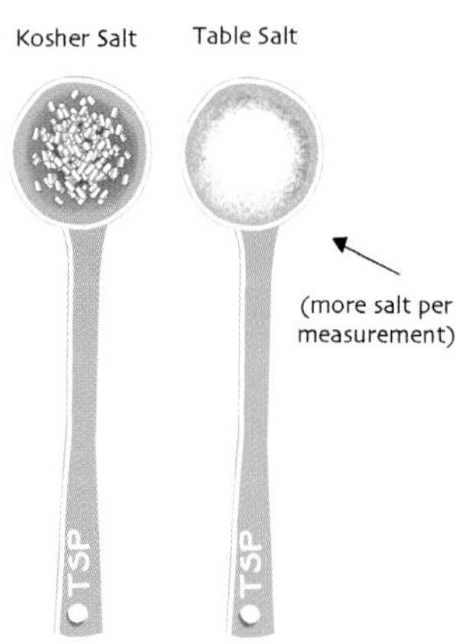

You should have enough ingredients for 2 layers each of the kale, roasted peppers and zucchini, and 1 layer each of the mushrooms and tofu. Start the layering off with ¼ cup (60 mL) each Parmesan and Gruyère, and reserve another ¼ cup (60 mL) of combined cheeses for somewhere in the middle, leaving the remaining ¼ cup (60 mL) for the topping. One layer each of the pesto and the tapenade can fit anywhere in between, just be sure to smooth each layer with a plain or offset spatula.

Finally, be sure to *lightly* season each vegetable layer with a pinch (a mere ⅛ tsp/0.5 mL) of kosher salt and a grind of black pepper. The tapenade and pesto need no seasoning.

Once the springform pan is filled, retrieve the pastry "top" from the fridge. Drape the pastry over the filling, pressing the edges to seal. If you've made a twisted trim from the excess dough, brush the edges with half of the lightly beaten egg (or dairy-free milk) before adding the trim. Gently press the trim in place. Cover the top of the pie with plastic wrap and refrigerate or freeze for at least 20 minutes to firm the pastry.

Preheat a baking tray lined with parchment or foil in a 425°F (220°C) oven. Brush the pastry and trim (if using) with additional beaten egg or dairy-free milk. Cut vents into the pastry to allow steam to escape.

Bake on the preheated baking tray for 20 minutes, rotating the pan once during baking, and cover the edges with foil (or pie shields) as necessary to prevent burning. Reduce the temperature to 375°F (190°C) and continue to bake until the pastry is completely cooked through, about 45–55 minutes, tenting the pastry with foil as necessary to prevent burning.

Cool on a wire rack and wait at least an hour before removing the springform pan. The pie will remain slightly warm, the ideal temperature for serving.

LAND & SEA

AUTHENTIC BEEF PASTIES

YIELD

Makes about seven 6½-inch (16 cm) pasties

PASTRY

1 recipe Flaky Pastry Dough (page 32; replace ½ cup/125 mL white flour with whole wheat flour), divided into 2 portions

1 large egg, lightly beaten, for brushing the pastry

FILLINGS

1 cup (250 mL) thinly sliced shallots (1–2 shallots)

¾ lb (375 g) marbled beef, such as a strip loin grilling steak, trimmed of fat and thinly sliced about 1 or 2 inches (2.5–5 cm) in length

Kosher salt

¾ cup (185 mL) diced new potatoes (½-inch/1 cm cubes; about 1 medium potato)

¾ cup (185 mL) diced turnip (½-inch/1 cm cubes; about half a small turnip)*

1 Tbsp (15 mL) fresh thyme leaves (about 6 sprigs; optional)

Freshly ground black pepper

---

* Cut turnips just before assembling—they tend to turn bitter when cut too far in advance.

THESE FLAVOURFUL PASTIES (pronounced pass-tee) pull at the heartstrings of my dear British friend, Sue. Whenever I whip up a batch, she gets a little misty-eyed for a taste of home.

The British take their pasties very seriously and I've been informed that under no circumstances should they be dressed up with a side salad or a sauce—or made from an expensive cut of meat. I've tried to stay true to a classic pastie recipe but for a pinch of thyme and a somewhat lighter pastry than the original.

PASTRY

Prepare the pastry and place one portion of dough onto a sheet of parchment paper dusted with flour. Layer a sheet of plastic wrap over the dough and roll (over the plastic) from the centre toward the pastry's edge in all directions until approximately ⅛ inch (3 mm) thick. Remove the plastic and, using a saucer or small plate as a guide, cut out 6½-inch (16 cm) circles, gathering and re-rolling the scraps of dough as necessary. Stack the pastry circles between sheets of parchment dusted with flour. Wrap in plastic and refrigerate for at least 40 minutes.

Repeat the process with the remaining portion of dough for a total of 7 circles.

PUTTING IT ALL TOGETHER

Have your prechopped ingredients and a small bowl of water within easy reach.

Working with one pastry circle at a time, scatter half the pastry with 1 Tbsp (15 mL) shallots, leaving a ¾-inch (2 cm) border. Cover with chopped beef (about ¼ cup/60 mL), then season with a small pinch (⅛ tsp/0.5 mL) of kosher salt. Scatter with diced potato and turnip (about 1 Tbsp/15 mL) each. Scatter with a few more slices of shallot, another pinch (⅛ tsp/0.5 mL) of salt, a pinch of thyme and a good grind of black pepper. You should have a generous mound of filling with a ¾-inch (2 cm) border. Moisten the border with a bit of water and cover the filling with the remaining pastry to form a half-circle.

Press the pastry together with your fingers and nudge the filling so you have an even border. Crimp the border to seal, or use the tines of a fork.

Assemble the remaining pasties, wrapping each one in plastic and refrigerating as you go. Refrigerate for at least 20 minutes before baking.

Preheat oven to 425°F (220°C). Line a baking tray with parchment paper or foil.

Brush the chilled pasties with lightly beaten egg. Using a sharp knife, cut vents into each one to allow the steam to escape. Place on the prepared baking tray, leaving 1–2 inches (2.5–5 cm) between each.

Bake in the preheated oven until the pastry is golden, about 30 minutes,

. . . recipe continued

. . . Authentic Beef Pasties (cont.)

rotating the baking tray once to encourage even browning. Tent loosely with foil and continue to bake about 10 minutes longer, monitoring now and again to ensure the pasties don't burn. Turn off the oven and leave the pasties inside for another 10 minutes, leaving the foil intact.

Cool on a wire rack. Serve warm or at room temperature.

CORNISH PASTIES

Traditionally a peasant food, Cornish pasties are perhaps best known for providing sustenance to the men and boys who worked the tin mines of Cornwall. The hearty pasties were designed to provide a sturdy, self-contained meal, each with the miners' initials etched in the pastry for easy identification. The pasties' signature rope-like seam, the story goes, was used to grasp the pastry and later discarded, as the miners' blackened hands were thought to be contaminated with arsenic.

Today Cornish pasties enjoy a protected status awarded by the European commission: Only pasties made in Cornwall, using the traditional recipe, can be labelled "Cornish pasties," much like other protected foods such as Champagne and Parmesan cheese.

BEEF POT PIES

YIELD

Makes eight 1-cup (250 mL) pies or six 1¼-cup (310 mL) pies

PASTRY

1 recipe Flaky Pastry Dough (page 32), only half the dough needed

1 large egg, lightly beaten, for brushing the pastry + more as needed

BRAISED BEEF MIXTURE

3 lb (1.5 kg) well-marbled chuck roast, trimmed of excess fat and cut into 1½- to 2-inch (3.5–5 cm) cubes

2 tsp (10 mL) ground cumin

2 tsp (10 mL) ground coriander seeds

2 tsp (10 mL) kosher salt

1 tsp (5 mL) ground black pepper

About ¼ cup (60 mL) vegetable oil, such as grapeseed or corn oil, divided

2¾ cups (685 mL) robust red wine, such as Côtes du Rhône, divided

1 medium onion, peeled and roughly chopped

2 medium carrots, peeled and roughly chopped

4 cloves garlic, peeled and roughly chopped

½ cup (125 mL) pitted prunes, roughly chopped

3 anchovies, rinsed and chopped

2 Tbsp (30 mL) tomato paste

... ingredients continued

FEW DISHES PROVIDE the comfort of a pot pie brimming with vegetables and fork-tender beef bound in a robust wine sauce.

A good pot pie calls for the best of stews, and I've included my favourite recipe—a richly flavoured beef stew adapted from my first cookbook, *British Columbia from Scratch*. It includes a few unexpected ingredients—prunes, anchovies and hot chili peppers. Although not discernible in the final dish, they create a deeply balanced sauce.

Select a good hearty wine for this recipe (one you enjoy drinking) and a rich stock, ideally homemade. A good roasted chicken stock can fill in for beef stock—and made-from-scratch always yields more flavourful results (see page 306).

The stew takes time to prepare, and is even better after it has melded in the fridge for a few days. The pastry, too, can be made ahead. Plan to make this over a few days when the weather is gloomy and you're happy to putter in the kitchen. The pies can be assembled up to 24 hours before baking, or prebaked and reheated.

PASTRY

Prepare the pastry and place the dough onto a sheet of parchment paper dusted with flour. Layer a sheet of plastic wrap over the dough and roll (over the plastic) from the centre toward the pastry's edge in all directions until about ⅛ inch (3 mm) thick. Remove the plastic and cut the pastry into rounds about ½ inch (1 cm) larger than the ramekins. Stack the pastry rounds between layers of parchment dusted with flour. Wrap in plastic and refrigerate or freeze until ready to use.

BRAISED BEEF MIXTURE

Preheat oven to 300°F (150°C).

Pat the beef dry with a paper towel and season with the cumin, coriander, salt and pepper.

Heat about 1 Tbsp (15 mL) oil in a large skillet over medium-high heat until it shimmers. Sear the seasoned beef in batches until well-browned, being mindful not to crowd the pan. Transfer the seared beef to a bowl (to accumulate the juices). Repeat with additional oil and the remaining beef.

Drain the excess fat from the skillet and discard, reheat the pan to medium-high and add a splash of red wine, scraping the bottom of the pan to dislodge any bits of meat. Pour this liquid into the bowl of seared beef.

Heat about 1 Tbsp (15 mL) oil in the large casserole or Dutch oven, add the onion and 2 medium carrots and cook on medium heat, stirring occasionally, until the onion softens and starts to brown. Add the garlic, prunes, anchovies and tomato paste, stirring constantly until the ingredients are just coated in the tomato paste. Add a splash of wine if the mixture sticks to the bottom of the pot. Add the seared beef, accumulated juices, chilies, bouquet garni and remaining wine. Add enough stock to surround (but not completely cover) the meat.

... recipe continued

CÔTES DU RHÔNE
750 ml
PRODUIT DE FRANCE
Alc 12.5% by vol

Bring to a simmer, then cover tightly and transfer to the preheated oven for about 2½ hours or until the beef is tender enough to cut with a fork. Check the meat after 20 minutes to ensure the cooking liquids are bubbling at a slow, steady simmer; you may need to adjust the heat.

Using a pair of tongs, remove the cooked beef from the casserole. Strain the braising liquid into a clean container, pressing the solids against the strainer to extract as much liquid as possible; discard the solids. Add the beef to the strained braising liquid and cool at room temperature; cover and refrigerate overnight.

The next day, remove the solidified fat from the braising liquid. Warm the beef and braising liquid (which will be gelatinous at this stage) in a medium saucepan over low heat. When it has returned to a liquid state, remove the beef from the braising liquid to a clean bowl with a slotted spoon and set aside.

ROUX

Melt ⅓ cup (80 mL) unsalted butter in a small saucepan over medium heat; add the flour and stir constantly, for a few minutes, until golden and aromatic.

Whisk the flour mixture into the saucepan of braising liquid, over medium heat, until the sauce thickens enough to lightly coat the back of a spoon. Add the red wine vinegar, taste and season with a pinch of salt or a few additional drops of vinegar, if desired. Return the beef to the thickened sauce, off the heat, while preparing the vegetables.

MUSHROOMS AND VEGETABLES

Heat 1 Tbsp (15 mL) butter and 1 Tbsp (15 mL) oil in a large skillet and cook the mushrooms in batches until well browned, being mindful not to crowd the pan (otherwise the mushrooms will steam instead of brown). Add a pinch of salt to each batch.

After all the mushrooms have cooked, return them to the skillet, add the wine and cook on medium heat until the wine has all but evaporated. Add the stock and continue to simmer until the liquid has evaporated and the mushrooms are glazed. Set aside.

Heat the remaining 1 Tbsp (15 mL) butter in a skillet with a tight-fitting lid; add the carrots, a pinch of salt and ¼ cup (60 mL) water. Bring to a gentle simmer, cover and cook on low heat until the carrots are just tender when pierced with the tip of the knife, about 5 minutes. Discard the liquid.

Add the cooked mushrooms, drained carrots and cooked peas to the beef stew mixture. Taste the mixture to check for seasoning, adding additional salt or vinegar if necessary. Cover and refrigerate until ready to use.

. . . recipe continued

2 red Thai chili peppers, cut lengthwise, seeds removed

Bouquet garni (thumb-sized bunch parsley with stems included, 2 bay leaves and 4 sprigs thyme, tied together with kitchen string)

2–3 cups (500–750 mL) beef or dark roasted chicken stock, preferably homemade

ROUX

⅓ cup (80 mL) unsalted butter (about 75 g)

⅓ cup (80 mL) all-purpose flour

1 tsp (5 mL) red wine vinegar (not balsamic) + more as needed

Kosher salt (optional)

MUSHROOMS AND VEGETABLES

2 Tbsp (30 mL) unsalted butter (about 30 g), divided

1 Tbsp (15 mL) vegetable oil, such as grapeseed or corn oil

8 oz (230 g) button mushrooms, wiped clean and quartered

Kosher salt

About ¼ cup (60 mL) robust red wine, such as Côtes du Rhône

About ¼ cup (60 mL) beef or dark roasted chicken stock

1 cup (250 mL) carrots, peeled and sliced into uniform, bite-sized pieces

¾ cup (185 mL) cooked peas (thawed if frozen)

SPECIAL EQUIPMENT

Eight 1-cup (250 mL) or six 1¼-cup (310 mL) ramekins or other ovenproof containers

5.5-quart (5.2 L) casserole pot or Dutch oven, for braising the beef

. . . Beef Pot Pies (cont.)

PUTTING IT ALL TOGETHER

Preheat oven to 375°F (190°C).

Place the ramekins on a baking tray and fill them with the chilled stew. (A chilled filling prevents the pastry from seeping into the filling and getting soggy.)

Retrieve the precut pastry from the fridge. Brush the rims of the ramekins with beaten egg. Place the pastry rounds on top of the stew and secure the pastry to the ramekins by pressing the edges down with your fingers, crimping the pastry over the edge. Cut vents into the pastry and brush the top of the dough with additional beaten egg.

Bake the pot pies in the preheated oven for 30–40 minutes until the pastry has browned and the stew bubbles from the pastry vents.

Allow the pies to cool a few minutes before serving, as the filling is piping hot.

Beef pies can be prebaked and reheated in a 325°F (160°C) oven loosely tented with foil until warmed through, about 15–20 minutes. Insert a paring knife through one of the pastries and into the filling to check the temperature before taking the pies out of the oven.

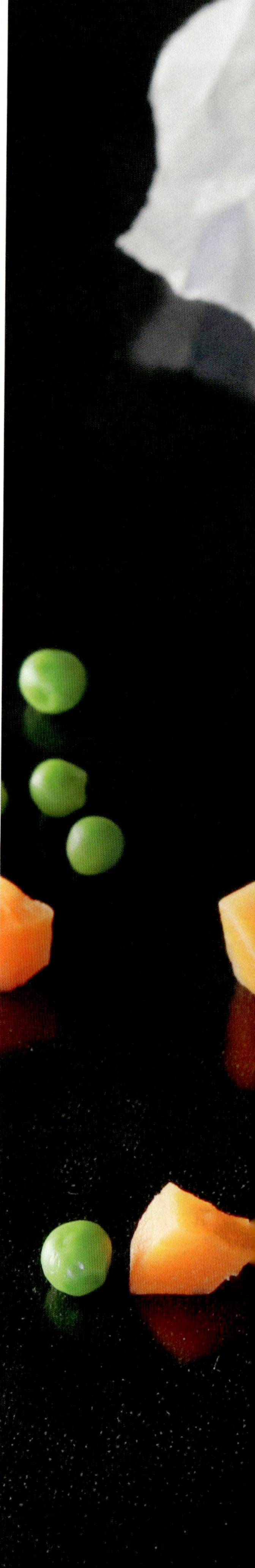

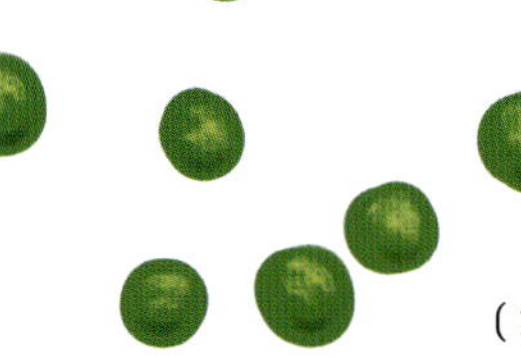

BLACK FOREST HAM PITHIVIER

YIELD

Makes 6 servings

PASTRY

1¼ lb (625 g) puff pastry, either handcrafted (page 50), rough (page 54) or commercial (frozen)

1 large egg yolk

1 Tbsp (15 mL) whipping cream

FILLING

2 large orange or yellow bell peppers

1 medium zucchini squash

Vegetable oil

3 large portobello mushrooms

Kosher salt

3 cloves garlic, thinly sliced

5½ cups (1.3 L) chopped kale (about 1 bunch), stems and cores removed, cut into bite-sized pieces

½ tsp (2.5 mL) dried crushed chili flakes

½ tsp (2.5 mL) freshly squeezed lemon juice

½ cup (125 mL) grated Parmesan cheese (about 50 g)

½ cup (125 mL) grated Gruyère cheese (about 60 g)

Freshly ground black pepper

8 oz (230 g) Black Forest ham (about 12–14 slices)

2 tsp (10 mL) Dijon-style mustard

2 Tbsp (30 mL) Sun-Dried Tomato & Roasted Garlic Pesto (page 303), or store-bought

THIS ELEGANT PASTRY (pronounced pee-tee-VYAY) encloses layers of sweet roasted vegetables, portobello mushrooms, sun-dried tomatoes and Black Forest ham. It also includes just enough Parmesan and Gruyère cheese to lend a savoury note to each splendid bite.

Don't be daunted by the length of the recipe—the step-by-step pictures will walk you through the process. Store-bought puff pastry works fine in this recipe, but there are no shortcuts in making the precooked filling. Each component, however, can be prepared a day or several days in advance, at your leisure.

The pastry is baked (without a pan) directly on a parchment-lined baking tray. I use the fluted edges of a 9½-inch (24 cm) tart pan like a cookie cutter to cut the dough and create the tart's distinctive edges. If you don't have one of these, use a similar-sized plate, or a saucepan lid works well.

PASTRY

If making handcrafted or rough puff pastry, prepare the pastry according to the instructions. If using frozen commercial puff pastry, thaw according to the instructions on the package.

FILLING

The vegetables need to be precooked, cooled and blotted dry before the pie is assembled. The bell peppers and zucchini in particular retain a great deal of moisture and must be as dry as possible to prevent the pastry from becoming soggy.

BELL PEPPERS: Place the whole peppers on a parchment- or foil-lined baking tray. Bake in a preheated 375°F (190°C) oven until the peppers have darkened in spots and are starting to collapse, about 45–55 minutes, rotating the pan once during baking. Transfer to a bowl and cover tightly with foil or plastic wrap. When cool enough to handle, remove the skins, cores and stems, keeping the peppers in large pieces. If not using right away, store on a plate between paper towels, cover and refrigerate. Blot completely dry before using.

ZUCCHINI: Slice the zucchini squash horizontally into ¼-inch (6 mm) thick ribbons (see image, page 146). Place the ribbons on a baking tray lined with foil or parchment paper, without overlapping. Brush with oil and bake in a preheated 375°F (190°C) oven until soft (zucchini will shrink slightly), about 25 minutes, rotating the tray once during baking. If not using right away, store between paper towels, cover and refrigerate. Blot completely dry before using.

. . . recipe continued

. . . Black Forest Ham Pithivier (cont.)

MUSHROOMS: Wipe clean and slice the mushroom caps horizontally, about ¼ inch (6 mm) thick, so as to increase the surface area. Reserve the stems for another use. Heat 3 Tbsp (45 mL) oil in a large skillet over medium heat. Working in batches, adding a pinch of salt to each batch, add the mushrooms in a single layer and cook until the mushrooms have browned, about 5 minutes, turning them over once. Continue to cook until the mushrooms are tender. Cool and blot completely dry before using.

KALE AND GARLIC: Using a slotted spoon within easy reach, heat 3 Tbsp (45 mL) oil in a large skillet over medium-low heat, add the garlic and cook until just starting to brown, about 30 seconds. Remove the garlic with the slotted spoon and reserve. Working in batches, cook the kale in the garlic oil until completely wilted, about 3–4 minutes, turning the greens as necessary to prevent burning. Add a pinch of salt, chili flakes, lemon juice and the cooked garlic and mix to combine. Cool and blot completely dry before using.

PASTRY TOP

Roll the puff pastry onto a flour-dusted work surface (or if it's sticky, onto a sheet of parchment paper dusted with flour) and into a circle about ¼ inch (6 mm) thick. Using a 9½-inch (24 cm) fluted tart pan, if you have one, cut the pastry to form a fluted edge. Alternatively, use a 9½-inch (24 cm) plate or a saucepan lid as a template to cut a circle. (The pastry will be re-rolled later to ⅛ inch/3 mm to create a slightly larger top to accommodate the filling.) Wrap in plastic, label "top" and refrigerate.

PASTRY BASE

Gather and re-roll the remaining pastry into another circle 9½ inches (24 cm) in diameter and ⅛ inch (3 mm) thick, as directed above. Wrap in plastic, label "base" and refrigerate.

. . . recipe continued

. . . Black Forest Ham Pithivier (cont.)

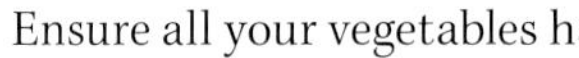

PITHIVIERS

This uniquely shaped pastry is named for the town Pithiviers in north-central France, where it's believed to have originated. Traditionally made with a sweet almond-based filling, pithiviers can be made large or small, sweet or savoury. Once you've assembled one, you'll want to experiment with different fillings.

PUTTING IT ALL TOGETHER

Ensure all your vegetables have been blotted *completely dry* before you start layering the ingredients, otherwise your pastry can become soggy. You'll want to assemble the pithivier on a parchment-lined baking tray (or any flat kitchen tray) that can easily fit in your fridge, as the pastry is chilled before baking. It's easier to maneuver the pastry with a tray underneath it.

Retrieve the pastry "base" from the fridge. Sprinkle with half of both the Parmesan and the Gruyère, leaving a 1-inch (2.5 cm) border. Neatly layer the ingredients, maintaining a 1-inch (2.5 cm) border throughout. Don't worry about the exact order of ingredients, the idea is to have neat layers. And don't forget to add a small but well-distributed pinch (a mere ⅛–¼ tsp/0.5–1 mL) of kosher salt to *each* layer of vegetables. (If using table salt you'll need even less, as the crystals are more compact and lend a saltier punch.)

As a guide, spread half the kale over the cheese with a grind of pepper, then add half the ham spread with half the mustard. Add a layer of roasted pepper, then the mushrooms, and spread with the roasted tomato pesto to form an even layer. Layer with the remaining cheeses and ham and spread with the remaining mustard. Top with the remaining kale and a grind of pepper. Follow with the zucchini and a pinch of salt. You should have a neat, well-seasoned stack of ingredients with a clean 1-inch (2.5 cm) pastry border.

Mix together the egg yolk and whipping cream and brush the border with some of the mixture, setting the rest aside.

Retrieve the pastry "top" from the fridge. Roll the pastry lightly to create a slightly larger circle (about ⅛ inch/3 mm) thick, being mindful to retain the fluted edge (if you have one).

Place the pastry neatly over the stack of ingredients, smoothing the pastry with your hands to form a neat mound with a flat 1-inch (2.5 cm) border. Wrap in plastic and refrigerate (with the parchment and tray beneath) or freeze for at least 20 minutes to firm the pastry.

Preheat a parchment- or foil-lined baking tray in a 425°F (220°C) oven.

Brush the pastry with more of the the yolk/cream mixture, being mindful to cover the entire pastry. Score the (firmed) pastry with a sharp knife, starting from the centre and moving toward the edges in ¼-inch (6 mm) increments (see image, page 146).

Transfer the pithivier, and the parchment beneath it, to the preheated baking tray using a pizza peel or flat-edged baking tray. Alternatively, carefully remove the baking tray from the oven and transfer the pastry, with the parchment underneath it, onto the heated tray.

Bake for 20 minutes, rotating the pan once during baking. Cover loosely with foil, reduce the temperature to 375°F (190°C) and continue to bake until the pastry is completely cooked through, about 15–20 minutes more.

Cool on a wire rack, removing the parchment beneath the pastry. Cool for at least 45 minutes before slicing. Best served slightly warm or at room temperature.

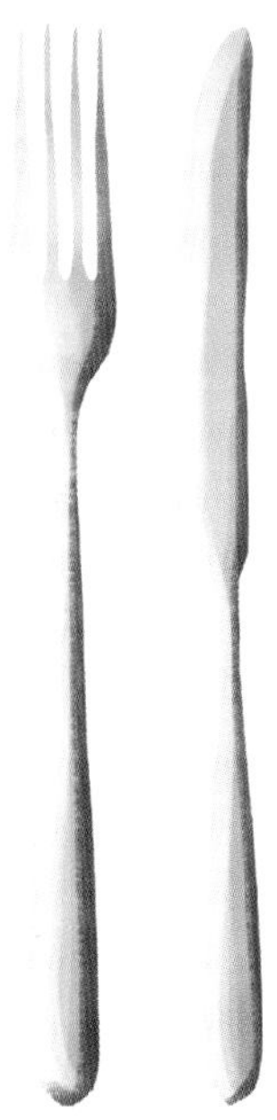

DEEP-DISH CHICKEN PIE

YIELD

Makes 4-6 servings

PASTRY

1 recipe Flaky Pastry Dough (page 32), only half the dough needed

1 large egg, lightly beaten, for brushing the pastry + more as needed

SAUCE

⅓ cup (80 mL) unsalted butter (about 75 g) + more as needed

⅓ cup (80 mL) all-purpose flour

2¼ cups (530 mL) chicken stock, preferably homemade (see page 306)

1 cup (250 mL) whole or 2% milk

½ cup (125 mL) whipping cream

¼ cup (60 mL) lemon juice, freshly squeezed + more as needed

½ cup (125 mL) freshly grated Parmesan cheese (about 50 g)

½ Tbsp (7.5 mL) kosher salt

½ tsp (2.5 mL) hot red pepper flakes

FILLING

3 Tbsp (45 mL) unsalted butter (about 45 g), divided

1 medium onion, diced

2 celery stalks, peeled and diced into ¼-inch (6 mm) pieces

¼ tsp (1 mL) kosher salt, divided + more as needed

3 medium carrots, peeled and diced into ¼-inch (6 mm) pieces

. . . ingredients continued

ROASTED CHICKEN, FRESH herbs and vegetables blend together in a creamy lemony sauce in one of my popular signature dishes. My first cookbook, *British Columbia from Scratch,* featured chicken pot pies in individual ramekins, and they are refashioned here, family style, in a baking dish. This book wouldn't be complete without this recipe.

The creamed chicken filling is refrigerated and firmed in its baking dish *before* the pastry is added, so the pastry doesn't sink into the filling. As with most stews, the creamed chicken tastes even better after a few days in the fridge, so plan ahead. The pastry, too, can be prepared days in advance.

PASTRY

Prepare the pastry and place the dough onto a sheet of parchment paper dusted with flour. Layer a sheet of plastic wrap over the dough and roll (over the plastic) from the centre toward the pastry's edge in all directions until about ⅛ inch (3 mm) thick. Remove the plastic and cut the dough ½ inch (1 cm) wider and ½ inch (1 cm) longer than the baking dish. Gather and re-roll any excess dough for a decorative braid or trim, if desired. Transfer the dough onto a plate or tray lined with parchment and dusted with flour. Cover with plastic wrap and refrigerate for at least 40 minutes.

SAUCE

Ideally, prepare in advance and refrigerate until firm before adding the pastry top.

Prepare a roux (a thickener for your sauce) by melting ⅓ cup (80 mL) butter in a medium saucepan over medium-low heat. I prefer a light, rather than heavy sauce; however, if you prefer a firmer sauce, add an additional 1 Tbsp (15 mL) each of butter and flour to the roux.

Whisk in the flour and cook for about 4–5 minutes, stirring constantly, until the flour and butter are golden in colour. Add the chicken stock, milk and cream to the roux and whisk until thickened and free of lumps, about 8–10 minutes. The sauce should be just thick enough to lightly coat the back of a spoon. Reduce the heat and add the lemon juice, Parmesan cheese, salt and red pepper flakes. Taste the sauce and season with additional salt or red pepper flakes if desired. If the sauce appears too thick, thin it with additional stock.

. . . recipe continued

The Illustrated
Library of Herbs
Bay Leaf
Oregano
Chives
Rosemary
Parsley
Thyme
Tarragon
Dill

FILLING

⅔ cup (160 mL) frozen peas, thawed

3 cups (750 mL) roasted or poached chicken, diced or shredded into bite-sized pieces (a 2½ lb/1.13 kg roast chicken will give you more than enough meat)

3 Tbsp (45 mL) fresh herbs, finely minced (use a single variety or a combination of parsley, dill, chives and tarragon)

Heat 2 Tbsp (30 mL) butter in a large saucepan over medium heat. Add the onion, celery and a pinch of salt. Cook until the onion is tender, about 5 minutes, then transfer to a small bowl. In the same pan, melt 1 Tbsp (15 mL) butter and cook the carrots with a pinch of salt until just tender, taking care not to overcook. Tip the carrots into the bowl with the onions and celery. The frozen peas do not need to be cooked.

Add the cooked vegetables, thawed peas, cooked chicken and herbs to the sauce and stir to combine. Taste and season with additional salt or lemon juice, if desired.

Cool to room temperature then ladle the filling into the baking dish. Cover with plastic and refrigerate until completely chilled and firm (it's easier to add the pastry when the filling is solid). If you don't have time to chill the filling, it can still be cooked straight away, but the pastry may slump a bit during baking.

SPECIAL EQUIPMENT

7-cup (1.75 L) rectangular baking dish

PUTTING IT ALL TOGETHER

Preheat oven to 375°F (190°C). Place the filled baking dish on a parchment- or foil-lined baking tray for easy cleanup. Brush the rim of the baking dish with lightly beaten egg.

Place the precut dough over the firmed creamed chicken mixture. Crimp the pastry at the baking dish's edges. Brush the dough with additional beaten egg and add a decorative braid or trim, if desired. Cut vents into the pastry.

Bake for 30–40 minutes, rotating the baking tray once, until the pastry has browned and the filling bubbles from the pastry vents. Tent with foil as necessary to prevent burning.

Allow to cool for a few minutes before serving, as the filling will be piping hot.

TOURTIÈRE WITH DUCK CONFIT

YIELD

Makes one 9-inch (23 cm) deep-dish pie

PASTRY

1 recipe Flaky Pastry Dough (page 32), divided into 2 portions

1 large egg, lightly beaten, for brushing the pastry + more as needed

FILLING

2 Tbsp (30 mL) vegetable oil

2 large onions, diced

4 cloves garlic, minced

3 Tbsp (45 mL) all-purpose flour

1 cup (250 mL) chicken stock, preferably homemade (see page 306)

1 lb (450 g) lean ground pork

1 lb (450 g) ground chicken thighs or beef (do not use turkey breast, it's too dry)

1 cup (250 mL) diced new potatoes, such as red, white or Yukon Gold (about 1 medium potato), cut into ½-inch (1 cm) cubes as uniformly as possible

2½ tsp (12.5 mL) kosher salt, or 2 tsp (10 mL) table salt + more as needed

¾ tsp (4 mL) ground nutmeg + more as needed

¼ tsp (1 mL) ground cloves + more as needed

½ tsp (2.5 mL) ground black pepper

2 duck confit legs, shredded meat only, skin removed

3 Tbsp (45 mL) breadcrumbs

. . . ingredients continued

TOURTIÈRE, A RUSTIC meat pie, is a sentimental favourite. My beloved French Canadian aunt Aline used to make tourtière whenever my family and I visited her in Montreal.

Customarily served after Midnight Mass on Christmas Eve, tourtière is a Quebécois tradition. My father recalled travelling with his siblings by horse and sleigh through the midnight snow as a child in Gaspé—anticipating tourtière all the way home from church.

Today, some families serve it year-round, often with a side of ketchup, while others reserve it for special occasions. My French Canadian husband, Claude, would eat it every day if offered.

Each family has their own rendition—some including wild game. My version includes ground pork, chicken (or beef) and meltingly tender duck confit (seasoned duck legs slowly poached in fat). Duck confit is available in the freezer section of well-stocked grocers and specialty delicatessens.

Serve tourtière with Red Onion Relish (page 305). Or, just pass the ketchup.

PASTRY

Prepare the pastry and place one portion of dough onto a sheet of parchment paper dusted with flour. Layer a sheet of plastic wrap over the dough and roll (over the plastic) from the centre toward the pastry's edge in all directions until about ⅛ inch (3 mm) thick. Remove the plastic and cut a circle approximately 11½ inches (29 cm) in diameter and ⅛ inch (3 mm) thick for your pastry top. Transfer to a plate or tray lined with parchment and dusted with flour. Cover with plastic wrap and refrigerate for at least 40 minutes.

Place the remaining portion of dough on a sheet of parchment paper dusted with flour. Roll into a circle approximately 14 inches (36 cm) in diameter and ⅛ inch (3 mm) thick. Drape the dough onto your rolling pin and transfer it to the pie (or cake) plate, being mindful not to pull or stretch the dough. Gently press the dough into the sides of the pie plate and trim the edges. Cover in plastic and refrigerate for at least 40 minutes.

FILLING

Heat the oil in a large heavy-bottomed saucepan and cook the onions until they start to brown. Add the garlic and cook until just aromatic, about 20 seconds. Add the flour and stir continuously for about a minute, then add the stock, scraping the bottom of the pan as you do so. Add the pork, chicken (or beef), potatoes, salt and spices and mix thoroughly.

. . . recipe continued

Cook over medium heat, partially covered and stirring occasionally, until the potatoes are just done and the meat is cooked through, about 20 minutes. The amount of liquid will vary depending on the meat used. The filling is meant to be moist, but if the liquid seems excessive, tilt the pan and use a spoon to discard the excess moisture.

Add the shredded duck confit to the meat mixture and stir to combine. Taste to check the seasoning and add additional salt, nutmeg or cloves, if desired. Cool the mixture completely.

SPECIAL EQUIPMENT

Deep-dish pie plate (9½ inches/24 cm in diameter and 2 inches/5 cm deep). If you don't have a deep-dish pie plate, use a standard 9-inch (23 cm) pie plate or 8-inch (20 cm) cake pan instead. You'll have enough leftover filling/pastry for a mini pie.

PUTTING IT ALL TOGETHER

Retrieve the dough-lined pie (or cake) plate and scatter the pastry base with breadcrumbs. Top with the divided, cooled meat mixture. Brush the rim of the exposed pastry with beaten egg.

Drape the pastry top over a rolling pin and transfer to the filled pie, loosely covering the filling. Pinch the edges together with your fingers. Cover with plastic wrap and firm in the fridge, or freezer, for 20 minutes.

Preheat a foil- or parchment-lined baking tray in a 425°F (220°C) oven.

Retrieve the tourtière, cut vents into the pastry lid and brush the top with additional beaten egg. Transfer to the preheated tray and bake for 20 minutes, then reduce the temperature to 375°F (190°C) and continue to bake for another 30–40 minutes, or until the pastry is golden and a knife inserted into the centre comes out warm. Rotate the baking tray once during baking and tent with foil as necessary to prevent burning.

Cool on a wire rack for at least an hour before serving.

FREEZING

Tourtière can assembled and frozen (unbaked) up to 2 months. Bake the frozen tourtière, without thawing, as per the instructions above, or until the pastry is golden and a knife inserted into the centre comes out warm.

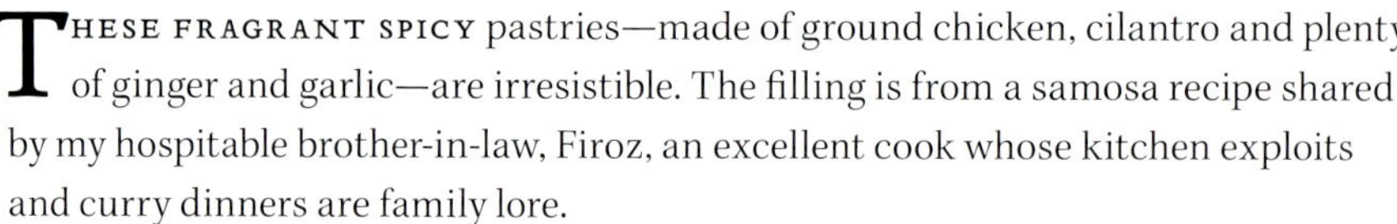

INDIAN-SPICED TURNOVERS

YIELD

Makes twelve to fourteen 4½-inch (11 cm) turnovers

PASTRY

1 recipe Flaky Pastry Dough (page 32), divided into 2 portions

1 large egg, lightly beaten, for brushing the pastry + more as needed

FILLING

1 Tbsp (15 mL) vegetable oil

1 lb (450 g) ground chicken thighs (or ground beef)

1 tsp (5 mL) kosher salt + more as needed

2 Tbsp (30 mL) peeled and minced ginger*

1 Tbsp (15 mL) minced garlic

1 Tbsp (15 mL) garam masala (for homemade, recipe follows)

Freshly ground black pepper

1 onion, finely diced

4–6 spring onions, finely diced

1 cup (250 mL) finely chopped cilantro

¾ cup (185 mL) finely chopped green cabbage

1 Tbsp (15 mL) freshly squeezed lemon juice + more as needed

---

* To peel ginger easily, scrape the skin off with the tip of a spoon.

THESE FRAGRANT SPICY pastries—made of ground chicken, cilantro and plenty of ginger and garlic—are irresistible. The filling is from a samosa recipe shared by my hospitable brother-in-law, Firoz, an excellent cook whose kitchen exploits and curry dinners are family lore.

A key ingredient in this dish, and many Indian recipes, is garam masala, a warm aromatic spice mixture made of cinnamon, cardamom, cloves and fennel. Although readily available in the spice aisle of most grocers, store-bought doesn't offer the fragrant intensity of homemade. It takes little effort to grind whole spices with a mortar and pestle, even less time using a spice grinder, and the results are outstanding. If you love Indian food, you'll love having it on hand.

I find a microplane zester handy for mincing the considerable amount of ginger and garlic used in this recipe. It not only minces finely but it teases out a bit of flavourful juice from the ginger. Be sure to chop the onions and cabbage finely, as they are added to the filling raw.

PASTRY

Prepare the pastry and place one portion of dough onto a sheet of parchment paper dusted with flour. Layer a sheet of plastic wrap over the dough and roll (over the plastic) from the centre toward the pastry's edge in all directions until about ⅛ inch (3 mm) thick. Remove the plastic and cut each portion of dough into six to seven 4½-inch (11 cm) squares, gathering and re-rolling the dough as necessary. Transfer the pastry squares to a parchment-lined tray or platter dusted with flour. Alternatively, stack the squares of dough between parchment or wax paper. Cover with plastic wrap and refrigerate for at least 40 minutes.

Repeat the process with the remaining portion of dough for a total of 12–14 circles.

FILLING

Heat the oil in a large skillet over medium heat. Add the chicken (or beef) and ¼ tsp (1 mL) kosher salt. Cook until no longer pink, stirring occasionally to prevent burning. Drain any excess oil. Add the ginger, garlic and garam masala and cook just until fragrant, about a minute.

Transfer the mixture to a medium bowl to cool. Add ½ tsp (2.5 mL) kosher salt, a generous grind of black pepper and the remaining filling ingredients. Mix together and taste, adjusting the mixture with more salt or lemon if desired. Cover and refrigerate. The mixture must be completely cool before using.

. . . recipe continued

PUTTING IT ALL TOGETHER

Working with 6 squares of dough at a time on a sheet of parchment dusted with flour, place a generous heap (about ¼ cup/60 mL) of the cooled filling on each square and spread the filling so that it covers half the tart diagonally.

Brush the edges of the pastry with beaten egg. Fold the pastry over the filling to form a triangle and pinch the edges together. If you find it easier, hold the pastry in one hand and pinch the edges together with the other. Crimp the edges with a fork.

Place the turnovers on a parchment-lined tray or plate dusted with flour. Cover with plastic wrap and refrigerate while preparing the remaining turnovers. The pastry must be chilled at least 20 minutes before baking.

Preheat oven to 425°F (220°C).

Retrieve the chilled turnovers from the fridge and divide them between 2 parchment- or foil-lined baking trays, leaving plenty of room between each. Alternatively, bake one tray at a time. Using a sharp knife, cut a vent into the centre of each turnover. Brush each with additional beaten egg.

Bake in the preheated oven for 15 minutes. Reduce heat to 375°F (190°C) and continue to bake another 20 minutes, or until the pastry is golden and cooked through. Rotate the baking tray once during baking and tent with foil as necessary to prevent burning.

Cool on a wire rack.

Homemade Garam Masala | Makes about ¼ cup (60 mL)

There are many recipes for this traditional Indian spice mixture, but this is my favourite. You'll get the most flavour if you start with whole spices and grind them yourself (I use a clean electric spice/coffee grinder). Grind whole spices before measuring them.

Combine the spices together. Store in a small container with a tight-fitting lid.

INGREDIENTS

2½ tsp (12.5 mL) ground cinnamon sticks*

2½ tsp (12.5 mL) ground green cardamom seeds**

2½ tsp (12.5 mL) ground coriander

2½ tsp (12.5 mL) ground cumin

1 tsp (5 mL) ground black peppercorns

1 tsp (5 mL) ground cloves

¼ tsp (1 mL) ground nutmeg

---

* Break the cinnamon sticks into smaller pieces before placing in a grinder.

** Lightly crush the cardamom pods and discard the outer pods before grinding the seeds.

FISH POT PIES

YIELD

Makes six to eight 6–8 oz (175–230 g) pies

PASTRY

1 recipe Flaky Pastry Dough (page 32), only half the dough needed

1 large egg, lightly beaten, for brushing the pastry + more as needed

SAUCE

⅓ cup (80 mL) unsalted butter (about 75 g)

⅓ cup (80 mL) all-purpose flour

2¼ cups (530 mL) fish or low-sodium chicken stock, preferably homemade (see page 306) + more as needed

1 cup (250 mL) whole or 2% milk

½ cup (125 mL) whipping cream

¼ cup + 2 Tbsp (90 mL) Parmesan cheese (about 35 g), freshly grated

Kosher salt

FILLING

2 Tbsp (30 mL) unsalted butter (about 30 g)

6 cups (1.5 L) sliced leeks, white part only (about 750 g)

3 cups (750 mL) diced fennel bulb (about 500 g, or 1 medium bulb)

Kosher salt

2 Tbsp (30 mL) Pernod

¼ cup (60 mL) freshly squeezed lemon juice + more as needed

½ tsp (2.5 mL) dried red pepper flakes

. . . ingredients continued

SLOW-COOKED LEEKS and aromatic fennel meld together in a lemony cream sauce for these sumptuous fish pies. A splash of Pernod—a liquorice-flavoured liqueur—accentuates the inherent sweetness of the fish. The seafood is added to the sauce raw, preventing the fish from becoming overcooked in the oven.

The pastry and sauce can be made days in advance. You'll want to purchase the fish/seafood from an outlet with a high turnover—though if it's not recently caught, frozen-at-sea is a good choice too.

PASTRY

Prepare the pastry and place the dough onto a sheet of parchment paper dusted with flour. Layer a sheet of plastic wrap over the dough and roll (over the plastic) from the centre toward the pastry's edge in all directions until about ⅛ inch (3 mm) thick. Remove the plastic and cut the pastry into 6 (or 8, depending on the number of ramekins) circles that are about ½ inch (1 cm) larger than your ramekins, gathering and re-rolling the dough as necessary. Leftover dough can be cut into fish shapes to decorate the pastry tops, if desired.

Place the pastry circles onto a tray or plate lined with parchment paper and dusted with flour, wrap in plastic and refrigerate for at least 40 minutes. Alternatively, stack the circles between parchment or wax paper, wrap in plastic and refrigerate for at least 40 minutes.

SAUCE

Melt ⅓ cup (80 mL) butter in a medium saucepan over medium-low heat. Whisk in the flour and cook, stirring constantly, until the flour and butter are golden, about 4–5 minutes. Add the stock, milk and whipping cream and whisk until thickened and free of lumps. The sauce should be just thick enough to lightly coat the back of a spoon. Reduce the heat, add the cheese and 1 tsp (5 mL) kosher salt and mix until smooth. Taste the sauce and season with additional salt or lemon juice if desired. If the sauce is too thick, thin it with additional stock. Set aside while preparing the filling.

FILLING

Melt 2 Tbsp (30 mL) butter in a large pot or Dutch oven over medium heat. Add the leeks, fennel and 1 tsp (5 mL) kosher salt. Cook, partially covered, over medium-low heat, stirring occasionally until the vegetables are soft and tender, about 25 minutes. Increase the heat, add the Pernod and stir until the alcohol has evaporated. Turn off the heat and add the lemon juice and red pepper flakes.

Pour the leek/fennel mixture into the sauce, stirring to combine. Taste and season with additional salt or lemon juice, if desired.

. . . recipe continued

. . . Fish Pot Pies (cont.)

Season the fish evenly with a pinch of kosher salt. Cut into large, bite-sized pieces (the fish will shrink as it cooks) and add it to the cream/vegetable mixture. Add the fresh herbs and mix until combined.

1½ lb (680 g) fresh fish (salmon, cod, snapper, scallops, etc.), skin and pin bones removed

¼ cup (60 mL) fresh herbs, finely minced (single variety or a mixture of parsley, dill, chives and tarragon)

PUTTING IT ALL TOGETHER

Preheat oven to 375°F (190°C).

Place your ramekins on a baking tray lined with foil or parchment. Ladle the creamed fish mixture into each ramekin. Brush the rims of the ramekins with beaten egg.

Retrieve the pastry circles from the fridge. Place them on top of the ramekins and press the edges down with your fingers, crimping the pastry over the edge. Cut vents into the pastry and brush the dough with additional egg. Decorate with pastry fish shapes, if desired, brushing them with any remaining egg.

Bake the pies in the preheated oven, leaving space between each, for 30–40 minutes or until the pastry has browned and the filling bubbles from the pastry vents.

Allow the pies to cool for a few minutes before serving as the filling will be piping hot.

SPECIAL EQUIPMENT

Eight 6 oz (175 g) or six 8 oz (230 g) ramekins or other ovenproof containers

SALMON COULIBIAC

YIELD

Makes 3–4 servings

PASTRY

1 lb (450 g) puff pastry, either handcrafted (page 50), rough (page 54) or commercial (frozen)

2 Tbsp (30 mL) whipping cream

1 large egg yolk

FILLING

1 lb (450 g) salmon fillet

2 Tbsp (30 mL) unsalted butter (about 30 g)

1½ cups (375 mL) finely minced button mushrooms

¾ cup (185 mL) finely minced onions (about half a large onion)

Kosher salt

1 Tbsp (15 mL) vegetable oil

4 cups (1 L) finely chopped kale (anywhere from half to a whole bunch), washed and dried

⅛ tsp (0.5 mL) dried chili flakes (more if you enjoy spice)

1 tsp (5 mL) freshly squeezed lemon juice or white wine vinegar

3 Tbsp (45 mL) breadcrumbs

2 Tbsp (30 mL) roughly chopped fresh dill

PRONOUNCED koo-lee-BYAHK, I was first introduced to this old-world dish at culinary school. It's a French adaptation of a Russian dish (kulebiaka) often made with chopped eggs and a brioche dough crust. In this variation, salmon sits on a bed of finely chopped mushrooms and pan-roasted kale and is enclosed in puff pastry.

It's an elegant way to serve salmon but not too fancy-pants to enjoy whenever you're in the mood for something special. The Tangy Dill Sauce (page 304) is a simple but delicious accompaniment.

Coulibiac can be assembled a day in advance.

PASTRY

If making handcrafted or rough puff pastry, prepare the pastry according to the instructions. If using frozen commercial puff pastry, thaw according to the instructions on the package.

Roll the dough onto a floured work surface (or if the pastry is sticky, a sheet of parchment dusted with flour) until ⅛ inch (3 mm) thick. Remove the plastic and cut the dough into an 8- × 10-inch (20 × 25 cm) rectangle for the pastry top. Gather and re-roll the dough and cut it into a 5- × 10-inch (13 × 25 cm) rectangle for the base. Place the pastry rectangles on a parchment-lined plate or tray dusted with flour; cover with plastic and refrigerate for 40 minutes.

FILLING

Remove the skin and pin bones from the salmon. Using the thickest portion of the salmon, trim the fish to a neat rectangle 7½ × 3 inches (19 × 8 cm). You want the salmon as uniform as possible so that it cooks evenly throughout. (Reserve the trim for another use, such as Salmon Rillettes, recipe follows.) Wrap the salmon in plastic and bring to room temperature.

Melt the butter in a large skillet. Add the mushrooms, onions and ½ tsp (2.5 mL) kosher salt and cook over medium-low heat until the onions are soft, about 5 minutes, stirring occasionally to prevent burning. Taste and season with additional salt if necessary. Transfer to a wide shallow container to cool (the wider the surface, the faster the mixture cools).

In the same skillet in which the onions and mushrooms were cooked, heat 1 Tbsp (15 mL) vegetable oil. Carefully add the kale (if it's still damp, the oil will sputter). Cook the kale with ¼ tsp (1 mL) kosher salt and a pinch (⅛ tsp/0.5 mL) of chili flakes for about 4–5 minutes, stirring occasionally until wilted and crispy in some spots. Transfer to another wide shallow container, add the lemon juice or vinegar and stir to combine. Set aside to cool completely before using.

. . . recipe continued

PUTTING IT ALL TOGETHER

Combine the whipping cream and egg yolk in a small bowl and mix together.

Place the chilled pastry base (the smaller portion) onto a sheet of parchment dusted with flour. Leave the larger portion covered in the fridge while working.

Place an even layer of breadcrumbs on the pastry, followed by the cooled onions and mushrooms, leaving a ¾-inch (2 cm) border. Top with an even layer of cooled kale, leaving a ¾-inch (2 cm) border. Top with the skinned fish. Season evenly with a pinch of kosher salt and the chopped dill. Brush the pastry border with some of the whipping cream/egg mixture. Cover with the (chilled) pastry top and press the edges along the border to seal. Trim the edges to create a neat rectangle.

With the parchment beneath it, transfer to a plate or tray; cover the pastry with plastic wrap and refrigerate for at least 20 minutes to firm.

Preheat a baking tray in a 425°F (220°C) oven.

Retrieve the coulibiac from the fridge and brush the entire pastry with the remaining whipping cream/egg mixture. Score the top and border at even intervals.

Using a pizza peel or flat-edged baking tray, transfer the pastry, and the parchment beneath it, to the preheated baking tray. Alternatively, carefully remove the baking tray from the oven and transfer the coulibiac, with the parchment paper underneath it, onto the heated tray.

Bake until the pastry is golden and cooked through, about 20 minutes, rotating the baking tray once.

Transfer to a cooling rack and remove the parchment. Allow to rest for 10–15 minutes before serving. The salmon continues to cook during this resting period.

Salmon Rillettes | Makes as much as you have on hand

Rillettes, a savoury pâté, are an excellent use of salmon scraps, and delicious on toast or crackers. I haven't provided exact measurements as your amount of salmon trim will vary. Your best guide is to taste as you mix.

INGREDIENTS

Salmon trim (see Salmon Coulibiac recipe, above)

Kosher salt

Whipping Cream

Lemon juice, freshly squeezed

Capers, chopped

Smoked salmon, chopped (optional)

Bake the salmon trim (skin and pin bones removed) in a 300°F (150°C) oven until barely cooked (I use my toaster oven for such a small amount of fish). Add a pinch of kosher salt and drizzle with a bit of whipping cream to form a paste, much like the texture of a rustic pâté. Season with freshly squeezed lemon juice and chopped capers. If desired, add a bit of chopped smoked salmon to the mix.

CRAB & TARRAGON QUICHE

YIELD

Makes one 9½-inch (24 cm) quiche

PASTRY

1 recipe Flaky Pastry Dough (page 32), only half the dough needed

1 large egg yolk, lightly beaten, for brushing the pastry

3 Tbsp (45mL) freshly grated Parmesan cheese (about 35 g)

FILLING

1 Tbsp (15 mL) vegetable oil

½ cup (125 mL) finely diced onion (about half an onion)

½ cup (125 mL) finely diced red bell pepper (about half a pepper)

Kosher salt

1 large clove garlic, finely chopped

¼ tsp (1 mL) dried chili flakes

1 tsp (5 mL) white wine vinegar or freshly squeezed lemon juice

2 oz (60 g) Black Forest ham (about 2 slices deli ham), finely chopped

4 oz (115 g) cooked crab, shelled and picked over

4 tsp (20 mL) freshly chopped tarragon + extra for garnish

5 large eggs, room temperature, lightly beaten

1 cup (250 mL) whole milk, room temperature

. . . ingredients continued

THIS ELEGANT CRAB quiche, flecked with tarragon and sweet pepper, is made of a custard so delicate and luxurious you'll want to slow down and savour each bite.

A great quiche is a baking paradox—the custard needs to be baked at a low temperature, while the pastry requires high heat. The solution is to precook the pastry in a hot oven, then add the custard and bake at low heat. The resulting twice-baked pastry, unexpectedly, turns out perfectly. It's a clever baking technique I gleaned from *Bouchon*, chef Thomas Keller's exceptional French bistro cookbook.

The quiche is baked in a cake pan (lined with parchment for easy removal) and comes out of the oven slightly jiggly in the centre. Once cooled, it should be refrigerated for at least six hours, ideally overnight, to set the custard. It takes a little planning, but once you try it you'll find it's worth the effort.

PASTRY

Grease the cake pan with a bit of butter (it helps the parchment to stick), then line the pan with parchment paper with a generous overhang (for a visual reference, see page 182). This allows you to remove the entire quiche in one go.

Prepare the pastry and place the dough onto a sheet of parchment paper dusted with flour. Layer a sheet of plastic wrap over the dough and roll (over the plastic) from the centre toward the pastry's edge in all directions until about ⅛ inch (3 mm) thick.

Drape the dough over your rolling pin and transfer it to the parchment-lined pan. Do not trim the excess pastry; this will be done after it's baked. (This method ensures your pastry doesn't sink into the pan during baking, see the unbaked pastry image on page 173.)

Use your fingers to gently press the dough along the pan's base and sides to maintain its shape. Cover the pastry with plastic wrap and refrigerate for 40 minutes.

Preheat oven to 425°F (220°C).

Retrieve the pastry-lined pan from the fridge and replace the plastic wrap with parchment paper or foil, then fill the pan to the top with pie weights.

Bake in the preheated oven for 20 minutes, reduce the temperature to 375°F (190°C) and cook for another 5 minutes. Remove the parchment (or foil) and pie weights and prick the base with a fork to prevent the pastry from buckling, then brush the base with beaten egg yolk and sprinkle with 3 Tbsp (45 mL) Parmesan cheese. Bake until the pastry is golden and cooked through, about 10 minutes longer, covering the edges with foil if necessary to prevent burning

Cool completely in the pan. Using a serrated knife, trim the excess pastry from the pan.

. . . recipe continued

1¾ cups (435 mL) whipping cream, room temperature

½ cup (125 mL) grated Gruyère cheese (about 60 g)

3 Tbsp (45 mL) freshly grated Parmesan cheese (about 35 g)

SPECIAL EQUIPMENT

9½-inch (24 cm) cake pan

Pie weights (or beans or rice)

FILLING

Heat the oil in a large skillet and add the onion, bell pepper and ½ tsp (2.5 mL) kosher salt. Cook over medium heat until the vegetables have softened, about 5 minutes, stirring the mixture occasionally to prevent burning. Add the garlic and stir until aromatic, about 30 seconds. Transfer the mixture to a medium bowl and add the chili flakes, white wine vinegar (or lemon juice), ham, crab and tarragon. Mix to combine and set aside to cool completely.

In a medium bowl or large measuring cup, combine the eggs, milk and whipping cream with 1¼ tsp (6 mL) kosher salt. Mix until well combined.

PUTTING IT ALL TOGETHER

Preheat oven to 325°F (160°C).

Place the cooled prebaked pastry shell (still in its parchment-lined cake pan) on a baking tray lined with foil or parchment paper for easy cleanup.

To ensure the ingredients are evenly dispersed throughout the custard, the filling is layered as follows: Spread half the cooled vegetable/crab mixture along the base of the tart. Sprinkle with half the Gruyère and 3 Tbsp (45 mL) Parmesan cheese. Pour half the cream/egg mixture on top. Add the remaining vegetable/crab mixture, followed by the remaining cream/egg mixture and remaining Gruyère. Scatter with additional tarragon leaves, if desired.

Bake in the preheated oven until the custard has softly set and is still slightly jiggly in the centre, anywhere from 70–90 minutes, depending on your oven. Rotate the pan once during baking and tent with foil when the top is well browned.

Cool on a wire rack and refrigerate (still in the parchment-lined cake pan) for several hours, ideally overnight. When completely cooled, lift the quiche from the cake pan by grabbing hold of the parchment edges. Bring to room temperature or rewarm in a 275°F (135°C) oven for about 20 minutes, or until a knife inserted in the centre comes out warm. Do not overheat, as the delicate custard will overcook.

APPLE

CLASSIC TARTE TATIN

YIELD

Makes one 8-inch (20 cm) tart

PASTRY

6½ oz (185 g) puff pastry, either handcrafted (page 50), rough (page 54) or commercial (frozen)

1 large egg, lightly beaten, for brushing the pastry + more as needed

FILLING

4 medium Granny Smith apples

1 Tbsp (15 mL) freshly squeezed lemon juice

½ cup (125 mL) granulated sugar + extra for the pastry

¼ cup (60 mL) unsalted butter (about 60 g)

SPECIAL EQUIPMENT

8-inch (20 cm) cast iron skillet (measured from the inside), or a heavy-bottomed ovenproof skillet

TARTE TATIN IS a French pastry that will appeal to the minimalists in the kitchen. It contains but a few ingredients and a scrap of pastry, yet produces the most extraordinary dessert. The tart is baked with a layer of pastry on top and served upside-down to showcase caramel-soaked apples so tender they melt in your mouth.

Like most recipes that contain only a handful of ingredients, the key to success is in the technique. I've made enough tartes Tatin to know they can be tricky and, although scrumptious, they don't always turn out picture perfect the first (or second) time around. One side of the tart might be more caramelized than the other, for example . . . although it's nothing a dollop of ice cream can't hide.

Traditionally made with puff pastry, the tart can also be made with Flaky Pastry Dough (page 32) or Buttermilk Shortcrust Dough (page 36). Given the small amount of dough needed, it's an ideal recipe for using up leftover pastry.

You'll want to read the instructions through to the end before you start. (Any recipe involving cooked sugar requires your full attention.) Tarte Tatin is delicious with Handcrafted Vanilla Ice Cream (page 300), Crème Anglaise (page 299) or Whipped Labneh (page 300).

PASTRY

If making handcrafted or rough puff pastry, prepare the pastry according to the instructions. If using frozen commercial puff pastry, thaw according to the instructions on the package.

Roll the pastry out onto a floured work surface or a sheet of parchment dusted with flour until about ⅛ inch (3 mm) thick. Remove the plastic and cut the pastry into a 9-inch (23 cm) circle about 1 inch (2.5 cm) wider than the rim of the skillet. Transfer the circle to a plate or tray lined with parchment and dusted with flour. Wrap in plastic and refrigerate until ready to use.

FILLING

Peel, core and halve the apples. Place in a large bowl, toss with lemon juice and set aside.

Place the sugar in an 8-inch (20 cm) cast iron skillet and moisten with 3 Tbsp (45 mL) water. Stir until the sugar is evenly moist, adding another teaspoon of water if necessary. Cook over medium heat until the sugar melts and turns a light caramel colour, about 5–8 minutes, tilting and rotating the pan as the sugar colours to help keep it uniform (the edges darken faster than the centre). Stir in the butter, off of the heat. If at any time the caramel becomes grainy just be patient, it will eventually become liquid again.

Carefully add the apple halves to the melted sugar, cut side up. You may have to trim the apples *slightly,* but expect them to be bunched together rather awkwardly—they will not lie flat at this stage. They shrink as they bake and will eventually fit together snugly.

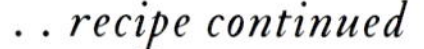

. . . recipe continued

. . . Classic Tarte Tatin (cont.)

PUTTING IT ALL TOGETHER

Preheat oven to 425°F (220°C).

Cover the apples with the chilled pastry and tuck the edges into the skillet so there is no overhang. (As the apples are not lying flat, the pastry will appear lumpy.) Prick the pastry in several places with a knife or skewer to create small vents. Brush with lightly beaten egg and dust with about 1½ Tbsp (22 mL) sugar.

Place the skillet in the preheated oven and reduce the temperature to 400°F (200°C). Bake for 20–30 minutes or until the pastry is golden and puffed and the apples are soft when pierced with a paring knife. Carefully return the tart to the stovetop. Let the tart sit for at least 30 minutes before unmolding. The pastry will deflate during the resting period and the apples will absorb the apple juices and caramel.

Using an offset knife or butter knife, lift a small corner of the pastry to check the amount of caramel/apple liquid in the pan. If your apples are still swimming in excess liquid, as sometimes happens, cook the apples over a burner on low heat for a few minutes, just until the liquid bubbles and some of the liquid evaporates. The idea is to have a moist, not runny tart.

To unmold, draw a knife around the edges of the skillet to ensure the apples and pastry aren't sticking. Place a plate over the skillet and invert the pastry onto the plate in one swift motion. Serve warm or at room temperature.

TARTIN SISTERS

This pastry pays tribute to the Tartin sisters who brought the dessert to fame at their restaurant/hotel in Lamotte-Beuvron, France at the turn of the 20th century.

PURE & SIMPLE APPLE PIE

YIELD

Makes one 9-inch (23 cm) pie

PASTRY

1 recipe Buttermilk Shortcrust Dough (page 36) or Flaky Pastry Dough (page 32), divided into 2 portions

2–3 Tbsp (30–45 mL) whipping cream, for brushing the pastry

FILLING

10 large Granny Smith apples

2 tsp (10 mL) freshly squeezed lemon juice

¼ cup (60 mL) unsalted butter (about 60 g), divided + extra for greasing the pan

¼ cup + 2 Tbsp (90 mL) granulated sugar + extra for the pastry

½ tsp (2.5 mL) cinnamon

¼ cup (60 mL) chopped walnuts

SPECIAL EQUIPMENT

9-inch (23 cm) cake pan (1½ inches/ 4 cm deep)*

---

* If you opt to use a larger or deeper container, you'll have to adjust the filling ingredients and baking time accordingly.

THIS BELOVED APPLE pie is baked into a cake pan rather than a pie dish, for a classic dessert that turns out beautifully every time. The apples are precooked and cooled before they're enclosed in the pastry, ensuring they're never over- or undercooked.

If you've never made a lattice topping, follow the simple step-by-step photos on the following page. Apple pie is especially delicious served with Handcrafted Vanilla Ice Cream (page 300), a simple but luxurious Caramel Sauce (page 302) or, if you're indecisive, both!

If you wish to remove the entire pie from the pan as pictured, you'll need to first line the pan with parchment paper. Removing the pan not only looks beautiful but it makes slicing the pie much easier. (You can, of course, omit the parchment and serve the pie directly from the cake pan.)

PASTRY

Grease the cake pan with a bit of butter (the butter helps the parchment to stick), then line the pan with parchment paper with a generous overhang (see image, page 182). If you prefer to serve the pie in the pan, you can omit the parchment.

PASTRY BASE: Prepare the pastry and place one portion of dough onto a sheet of parchment paper dusted with flour. Layer a sheet of plastic wrap over the dough and roll (over the plastic) from the centre toward the pastry's edge in all directions until approximately 12 inches (30 cm) in diameter and about ⅛ inch (3 mm) thick.

Drape the pastry onto a rolling pin and transfer to the parchment-lined cake pan, using your fingers to gently press the dough along the pan's base and sides to maintain its shape. Trim the pastry edges but leave the parchment intact for easy removal. Cover the lined pan with plastic wrap and refrigerate for at least 40 minutes.

LATTICE TOP: Place the remaining portion of dough and any excess pastry onto a sheet of parchment paper dusted with flour. Re-roll and cut the pastry into twelve 1½-inch (4 cm) wide strips, the length of your cake pan.

Place the pastry strips and the parchment beneath them onto a tray, cover with plastic wrap and refrigerate for at least 40 minutes.

FILLING

Peel, core and slice the apples (about 1 inch/2.5 cm at the widest point). Place in a large bowl and toss with the lemon juice.

. . . recipe continued

. . . Pure & Simple Apple Pie (cont.)

Working in 3 batches (so as not to crowd the pan), melt 1 Tbsp (15 mL) of butter per batch in a large skillet or Dutch oven. Add about one-third of the apples, sugar and cinnamon and cook until the apples are soft and tender, about 15 minutes, stirring occasionally to prevent burning. Some apple slices will turn mushy but most should retain their shape. Repeat with the remaining apples, sugar and cinnamon. Transfer to a baking tray or another wide, shallow container to cool.

PUTTING IT ALL TOGETHER

Spread the chopped walnuts along the bottom of the pastry-lined cake pan. Spread the cooled apples on top. Cut the remaining butter into small pieces and distribute over the apples.

To create the lattice top, place 6 strips of pastry loosely across the pie in one direction. Do not press the dough in place.

To weave in the first pastry strip, gently fold back every other pastry strip to the pastry's edge and lay a perpendicular strip of pastry over the remaining strips. Fold the strips back in place and you'll see you've created your first weave.

Repeat the process with each new strip, pulling back alternating strips of pastry to weave in the strips of dough. When the weaving is complete, trim the excess pastry and tuck the edges of the lattice *into* the cake pan so that when the cake pan is removed the topping stays intact.

Cover lightly with plastic wrap and refrigerate or freeze for about 20 minutes to firm.

Preheat a parchment- or foil-lined baking tray in a 425°F (220°C) oven.

Brush the lattice with whipping cream and sprinkle generously with sugar.

Carefully place the pie on the preheated, lined baking tray, and bake for 20 minutes. Reduce heat to 375°F (190°C) and continue baking for another 40 minutes, or until completely cooked through. Rotate once during baking and cover lightly with foil when the pastry has browned.

Allow to cool for at least 3 hours. Lift the parchment to remove the pie from the pan, if desired. Serve at room temperature or rewarmed.

APPLE RAISIN TURNOVERS

YIELD

Makes 12 turnovers

PASTRY

1 recipe Flaky Pastry Dough (page 32), divided into 2 portions

1 large egg, lightly beaten, for brushing the pastry + more as needed

2 Tbsp (30 mL) coarse raw or granulated sugar

FILLING

¼ cup (60 mL) raisins or currants

3 Tbsp (45 mL) rum (optional)

6 medium Granny Smith apples

4 tsp (20 mL) freshly squeezed lemon juice

¼ cup (60 mL) unsalted butter (about 60 g)

¼ cup + 2 Tbsp (90 mL) granulated sugar

½ tsp (2.5 mL) cinnamon

¼ cup (60 mL) roughly chopped walnuts

PLUMP, RUM-SOAKED raisins, chopped walnuts and a hint of cinnamon make these apple turnovers hard to resist. The pastries can be assembled and frozen unbaked, so you can enjoy them fresh from the oven anytime.

PASTRY

Prepare the pastry and place one portion of dough onto a sheet of parchment paper dusted with flour. Layer a sheet of plastic wrap over the dough and roll (over the plastic) from the centre toward the pastry's edge in all directions until about ⅛ inch (3 mm) thick. Remove the plastic and cut the dough into six 4-inch (10 cm) squares, gathering and re-rolling the dough as necessary. Wrap the squares of dough in plastic, with a sheet of parchment or waxed paper between each. Refrigerate for at least 40 minutes before filling.

Repeat the process with the remaining portion of dough for a total of 12 squares.

FILLING

Place the raisins (or currants) in a small bowl and cover with rum, if using, to macerate (soften) them.

Peel, core and chop the apples into small chunks of about ½ inch (1 cm). Place the chopped apples in a large bowl and toss with the lemon juice.

Heat half the butter in a large skillet until it foams. Working in 2 batches, so as not to crowd the pan, add half the chopped apples and mix to coat with the melted butter. Add half the sugar and cinnamon and cook over medium to medium-high heat, stirring frequently, until the apples are soft and golden but still retain their shape, about 10 minutes. Repeat with the remaining apples, butter, sugar and cinnamon.

Transfer the cooked apples to a bowl to cool. Repeat with the remaining apples, sugar and cinnamon. Combine all the cooked apples and add the walnuts and strained raisins (if soaked in rum). The filling must be completely cooled before the turnovers are assembled.

PUTTING IT ALL TOGETHER

Working with 6 squares of dough at a time, place the pastry on a sheet of parchment dusted with flour.

Place a generous heap (about ¼ cup/60 mL) of the cooled filling on each square and spread the filling so that it covers half the square, diagonally. Brush the edges of the pastry with lightly beaten egg. Fold the pastry over the filling, to form a triangle, and pinch the edges together. If you find it easier, hold the pastry in one hand and pinch the edges together with the other hand. Repeat with the remaining pastry.

. . . recipe continued

. . . Apple Raisin Turnovers (cont.)

Place the pastries on a parchment-lined platter or tray, cover with plastic wrap and refrigerate for at least 20 minutes.

Preheat oven to 425°F (220°C).

Retrieve half the pastries from the fridge and crimp the edges with a fork. Using a sharp knife, cut a triangle vent into the centre of each pastry. Use the tip of the knife to slice a small vent about ½ inch (1 cm) long into each side of the turnover (these vents are barely noticeable, but allow additional steam to escape). Brush each turnover with additional beaten egg and sprinkle generously with sugar.

Place the 6 pastries on a baking tray lined with parchment or foil, leaving a space between each. Bake in a preheated oven for 15 minutes. Reduce heat to 375°F (190°C) and continue to bake for another 20 minutes, or until the pastry is golden and cooked through. Rotate the baking tray once during baking and tent with foil as necessary to prevent burning.

While the first batch of pastries is baking, prepare the next batch, as outlined above.

Cool the pastries on a wire rack.

FREEZING

If you wish to freeze the pastries before baking, place them on a plastic wrap–lined tray in a single layer. Cover and freeze just until near-solid, then transfer to a reusable freezer bag. This prevents the pastries from sticking together. Turnovers can be frozen up to 2 months wrapped in plastic.

Bake from frozen in a preheated 425°F (220°C) oven for 15 minutes. Reduce heat to 375°F (190°C) and continue to bake for another 20 minutes, or until the pastry is golden and the filling is warmed through.

FIG-STUFFED APPLE DUMPLINGS

YIELD

Makes 6 dumplings

PASTRY

1 recipe Buttermilk Shortcrust Dough (page 36) or Flaky Pastry Dough (page 32), divided into 2 portions

½ cup (125 mL) coarse raw or granulated sugar

½ cup (125 mL) whipping cream, for brushing the pastry

FILLING

½ cup (125 mL) finely chopped dried figs (about 6 figs)

½ cup (125 mL) almonds or walnuts

½ tsp (2.5 mL) cinnamon

⅓ cup (80 mL) granulated sugar

6 small Granny Smith or Gala apples (if the apples are larger, you'll only have enough pastry to enclose 5 of them)

3 Tbsp (45 mL) unsalted butter (about 45 g)

Slice of lemon

TOPPING

Caramel Sauce (page 302)

I FIRST SAW apple (and pear) dumplings featured decades ago in Martha Stewart's gorgeous *Pies & Tarts* cookbook. The dumplings were artfully displayed on a pine mantle, illuminated with kerosene lamps and antique candlesticks. I was mesmerized by the image but dismissed the pastries as too difficult and beyond my reach. How wrong I was.

If you're an apprehensive baker as I once was, I can assure you these gorgeous dumplings are completely doable, and the step-by-step images will help you along. The apples are stuffed with figs, cinnamon and nuts, then wrapped in pastry and baked until they're tender and fragrant. These homespun sugar-dusted pastries are as memorable as they are delicious.

Serve dumplings warm with a drizzle of Caramel Sauce (page 302) for a dessert worthy of Martha herself.

PASTRY

Prepare the pastry and place one portion of dough onto a sheet of parchment paper dusted with flour. Layer a sheet of plastic wrap over the dough and roll (over the plastic) from the centre toward the pastry's edge in all directions until about ⅛ inch (3 mm) thick. Remove the plastic and, using a sharp knife, cut each circle of dough into three 7-inch (18 cm) squares with four 2-inch (5 cm) notches cut from each square (see page 192 for info).

Use a sharp knife to fashion apple leaves from the excess dough. Stack the pastry squares, with parchment between each, and wrap in plastic. Refrigerate for at least 40 minutes.

Repeat the process with the remaining portion of dough for a total of six 7-inch (18 cm) squares.

FILLING

In a small bowl, combine the figs, nuts, cinnamon and ⅓ cup (80 mL) granulated sugar.

Peel the apples, leaving the stems intact. Starting from the bottom of each apple, carefully scoop out the core with a melon baller. (If the stem comes loose, save it and insert it into the pastry after the dumpling is assembled.)

From the bottom of the apple, push about ½ Tbsp (7.5 mL) butter (with your finger) into the cavity as far as it will go. Then, using a small spoon (or your fingers), pack the apple with as much filling as possible. Rub the surface of each apple with the lemon to prevent it from browning.

. . . recipe continued

... Fig-Stuffed Apple Dumplings (cont.)

PUTTING IT ALL TOGETHER

Working with one apple and one square of pastry at a time, place the base of the apple in the centre of each square. Wrap the apple in pastry, pinching the edges together and trimming any excess pastry with scissors.

Be mindful to pinch the edges together completely, otherwise the pastry will separate when baked. Cover with plastic, refrigerate and repeat with the remaining apples and pastry squares.

Preheat oven to 400°F (200°C) and pour ½ cup (125 mL) coarse raw or granulated sugar into a wide bowl.

Working over a sheet of parchment or waxed paper (for easy cleanup), brush each apple dumpling generously with whipping cream, ensuring the entire surface (except the base) is covered. Gently press the leaves into the top of the dumpling and brush with additional whipping cream.

Hold each dumpling over the bowl of sugar and, using your hands or a spoon, cover the entire dumpling with sugar, rotating the apple to cover it completely.

With the tip of a paring knife, poke 3 short vents lengthwise into the 4 sides of each dumpling. Ensure the seams are well sealed, especially at the top of the apple (otherwise the pastry will separate from the apple during baking).

Place the apples on a parchment- or foil-lined baking tray (for easy cleanup—the sugar makes a mess), spaced well apart, and bake in the preheated oven for 15 minutes. Reduce the heat to 375°F (190°C), rotate the baking tray and bake for another 15 minutes. Tent loosely with foil and bake for another 5–10 minutes until the pastry is golden and the apples are tender. Be careful not to overcook the apples as they can expand or get mushy, causing the pastry to pull away at the seams.

Cool on a wire rack (place a paper towel under the rack to catch the juices).

APPLE RUGELACH

YIELD

Makes twenty-four 4-inch (10 cm) pastries or thirty-six 3-inch (8 cm) pastries

PASTRY

1 recipe Cream Cheese Dough (page 48), divided into 3 portions

1 large egg, lightly beaten, for brushing the pastry + more as needed

2 Tbsp (30 mL) powdered (icing) sugar

FILLING

¼ cup (60 mL) unsalted butter (about 60 g)

6 Granny Smith apples, peeled, cored and finely diced

½ cup (125 mL) granulated sugar, divided + extra for the pastry

1 Tbsp (15 mL) lemon juice

1 cup (250 mL) toasted walnuts, coarsely chopped

½ cup (125 mL) raisins

2 Tbsp (30 mL) firmly packed golden (light) brown sugar

1 tsp (5 mL) cinnamon

4½ oz (125 g) Philadelphia-style cream cheese (half a brick), room temperature

THESE OLD-WORLD pastries could be filed under pie-ish. Rugelach are not quite a turnover, tart or pie, but they're too scrumptious to be excluded from our lineup.

Stuffed with caramelized apples, toasted walnuts and cinnamon sugar, apple rugelach will leave your kitchen fragrant as a bakery. Traditionally filled with preserves or poppy seeds, rugelach come together surprisingly easily. They're so good, your friends will think you bought them at a patisserie.

PASTRY

Prepare the pastry and place one portion of dough onto a sheet of parchment paper dusted with flour. Layer a sheet of plastic wrap over the dough and roll (over the plastic) from the centre toward the pastry's edge in all directions until about ⅛ inch (3 mm) thick. Remove the plastic and cut a 10-inch (25 cm) circle out of the dough (I use a saucepan lid as a template). Transfer the pastry to a parchment-lined plate or tray dusted with flour, cover with plastic wrap and refrigerate until firm, about 40 minutes.

Repeat the process with the remaining portions of dough for a total of three 10-inch (25 cm) circles.

FILLING

Working in 2 batches, melt half the butter in a large skillet. Add half the diced apples and 3 Tbsp (45 mL) sugar. (If you add all the apples at once, they'll steam and yield a mushy texture, rather than caramelize.) Cook the apples on medium-low, turning occasionally, until soft and golden brown, about 15 minutes.

Transfer to a bowl and repeat with the remaining butter, apples and 3 Tbsp (45 mL) sugar. Combine all of the apples, add the lemon juice and refrigerate until chilled.

In a small bowl, combine the walnuts, raisins, brown sugar, ¼ cup (60 mL) granulated sugar and the cinnamon.

. . . recipe continued

. . . Apple Rugelach (cont.)

PUTTING IT ALL TOGETHER

Preheat oven to 375°F (190°C).

Working with one circle of dough at a time, spread a thin layer of cream cheese (about 2½ Tbsp/37 mL) onto the dough, leaving a ½-inch (1 cm) border. Distribute one-third of the *chilled* apple mixture over the cheese. Finally, sprinkle one-third (about ½ cup/125 mL) of the nut mixture over the apples.

Cut each circle of dough into 8 equal wedges (or 12 wedges for smaller pastries), for a total of 24 (or 36) wedges. If the dough is too warm to cut without tearing, place it in the fridge to firm. Starting from the wide end, roll up each wedge as you would a croissant.

Place rugelach on a lined baking tray, spaced 2 inches (5 cm) apart, with the point of each pastry tucked under (so it doesn't unfurl). Brush with beaten egg and sprinkle with granulated sugar. Refrigerate for at least 30 minutes before baking. Repeat with the remaining dough and filling.

Bake in the preheated oven for 20–25 minutes, or until golden brown, rotating the tray halfway during baking. (If baking more than one tray at a time, increase the cooking time slightly.)

Transfer pastries to a wire rack and dust with powdered sugar. Serve warm or at room temperature.

FRUIT & NUT

ALMOND & PLUM TARTS

YIELD

Makes twenty-four 2½-inch (6 cm) tarts or twelve 4-inch (10 cm) tarts

PASTRY

1 recipe Sweet Tart Dough (page 38), divided into 2 portions

ALMOND CREAM FILLING

¼ cup + 2 Tbsp (90 mL) unsalted butter (about 85 g), room temperature

¼ cup + 2 Tbsp (90 mL) granulated sugar

1¼ cups (310 mL) ground almonds

2 large eggs, lightly beaten, room temperature

⅔ cup (160 mL) apricot jam or preserves

TOPPING

½ cup (125 mL) sliced almonds, or 1 lb (450 g) pitted plums, sliced, quartered or halved

¼ cup (60 mL) powdered (icing) sugar (optional)

SPECIAL EQUIPMENT

Twenty-four 2½-inch (6 cm) tart molds, or twelve 4-inch (10 cm) tart molds

24 miniature baking cups or parchment paper, cut to fit the molds

THESE EXQUISITE TARTS are filled with apricot jam and velvety almond cream, a not-too-sweet ground-nut filling often used in French pastries. Topped with toasted sliced almonds or sweet plums, these tarts are made for a cup of tea.

I made these tarts for years without jam until my friend Jonathan mentioned his European mother made a similar pastry with preserves. Not one to ignore a tip from a European baker, I've since added jam, an upgrade worthy of a fine patisserie.

PASTRY

Line the molds with baking cups or parchment cut to size.

Prepare the pastry and place one portion of dough onto a sheet of parchment paper dusted with flour. Layer a sheet of plastic wrap over the dough and roll (over the plastic) from the centre toward the pastry's edge in all directions until about ⅛ inch (3 mm) thick. Remove the plastic and cut circles of dough slightly larger than the tart molds using a cup or small bowl as a template, gathering and re-rolling the dough as necessary. Transfer the dough to the lined molds and press the dough against the parchment baking cups (if the pastry is sticky, use a scrap of plastic to press the pastry into the mold); trim the excess pastry.

Stack the parchment-lined tart molds in manageable bundles and wrap in plastic, so as not to take up too much room in the fridge. Refrigerate for at least 40 minutes.

Repeat the process with the remaining portion of dough for a total of twenty-four 2½-inch (6 cm) or twelve 4-inch (10 cm) tarts.

. . . recipe continued

. . . Almond & Plum Tarts (cont.)

ALMOND CREAM FILLING

Cream together the butter and granulated sugar. Add the ground almonds and eggs and mix until combined. Set aside.

PUTTING IT ALL TOGETHER

Spoon about 2 generous tsp (10+ mL) apricot jam into each small mold, then cover with about 1 Tbsp (15 mL) almond filling. Double the amount of jam and filling if using the larger (4 inch/10 cm) molds.

Sprinkle with sliced almonds or top with sliced, quartered or halved plums. Place on a tray or plate, cover loosely with plastic wrap and refrigerate for 20 minutes.

Preheat oven to 350°F (175°C).

Place the tarts on a baking tray, leaving at least 1–2 inches (2.5–5 cm) between each. Bake in the preheated oven for 15–20 minutes or until edges have browned, rotating the tray once during baking (the larger the tart, the longer the cooking time). The almond cream filling will puff in the oven, then settle as the tarts cool.

Place the tarts on a wire rack to cool. Dust with sifted powdered sugar, if desired, just before serving. Leftover almond filling can be baked in parchment-lined muffin tins and served with custards or ice cream.

PEACH & BERRY GALETTE

YIELD

Makes one 7-inch (18 cm) galette

PASTRY

1 recipe Flaky Pastry Dough (page 32), only half the dough needed

1 large egg, lightly beaten, for brushing the pastry

1–2 Tbsp (15–30 mL) coarse raw or granulated sugar

FRUIT FILLING

2 cups (500 mL) peaches or other stone fruit, peeled

2 cups (500 mL) berries

¼ cup + 3 Tbsp (105 mL) granulated sugar

3 Tbsp (45 mL) cornstarch*

2 tsp (10 mL) unsalted butter (about 15 g), chilled and cut into small pieces

---

* If your berries are especially juicy, or you've used frozen, add another 2 tsp (10 mL) cornstarch.

THIS BREEZY SUMMER galette comes together as easy as pie (it had to be said). I've used a combination of blueberries, raspberries and peaches, but any berries and stone fruits would work.

If you're longing for a taste of summer off-season, you can use frozen fruit (just add a bit more cornstarch). This galette is especially delicious with a scoop of Handcrafted Vanilla Ice Cream (page 300), a dollop of Whipped Labneh (page 300) or a drizzle of Crème Anglaise (page 299).

PASTRY

Prepare the pastry and place the dough onto a sheet of parchment paper dusted with flour. Layer a sheet of plastic wrap over the dough and roll (over the plastic) from the centre in all directions until approximately 11 inches (28 cm) in diameter and about ⅛ inch (3 mm) thick.

Place the circle of dough onto a plate or tray lined with parchment paper and dusted with flour, cover with plastic wrap and refrigerate for at least 20 minutes.

FRUIT FILLING

Slice the peaches about ¾ inch (2 cm) at their widest point. Place the peaches and berries into a large bowl and toss with ¼ cup + 3 Tbsp (105 mL) granulated sugar and the cornstarch. Allow the fruit to sit for 5 minutes and stir before using.

PUTTING IT ALL TOGETHER

Preheat a parchment- or foil-lined rimmed baking tray in a 425°F (220°C) oven.

Retrieve the pastry from the fridge and place it on your work surface (with the parchment beneath it). Scatter the fruit onto the pastry, leaving a 2-inch (5 cm) border, or, if you prefer a wider pastry edge, leave a 3-inch (8 cm) border. Dot the fruit with the butter. Fold the pastry border toward the centre of the galette, pleating the pastry as you fold (see images, page 94). Brush the pastry's edges with lightly beaten egg and sprinkle with sugar.

Transfer the galette to the oven using a rimless baking tray or pizza peel. Alternatively, carefully remove the baking tray and place the galette on the heated tray with the parchment beneath. Bake for 15 minutes, reduce heat to 375°F (190°C) and continue to bake for another 20–30 minutes until the pastry is golden and cooked through. Rotate the pan halfway during baking and tent with foil as necessary to prevent burning.

Cool on a wire rack. Serve at room temperature or rewarmed with ice cream.

SUMMER PLUM PIE

YIELD

Makes one 9-inch (23 cm) pie

PASTRY

1 recipe Flaky Pastry Dough (page 32), divided into 2 portions

1 large egg, lightly beaten, for brushing the pastry + more as needed

2 Tbsp (30 mL) coarse raw or granulated sugar, divided

FILLING

1 cup (250 mL) granulated sugar

¼ cup + 1 Tbsp (75 mL) quick-cooking tapioca, ideally ground in a spice grinder (see page 19 for info)

7½ cups (1.8 mL) ripe damson plums (about 1.25 kg), pitted and quartered*

1 large Granny Smith apple, peeled and cored

2 Tbsp (30 mL) unsalted butter (about 30 g), chilled and cut into small pieces

SPECIAL EQUIPMENT

Shallow 9-inch (23 cm) pie plate (0.75 quart)

Pie weights (or beans or rice)

---

* If your plums aren't yet perfectly ripe, or if you're making this in the early summer, dial back the tapioca by 1 Tbsp (15 mL).

I MAKE THIS flavourful lattice pie, loaded with sweet plummy flavour, when dusty-hued damson plums are at their juiciest peak. Black and red plums are a nice alternative, too.

Plums produce a great deal of juice during baking and, frustratingly (for us bakers), not all plums are created equal. Early summer plums don't produce the same amount of juice as late summer plums. I've had enough soupy-pie fails to know that super-ripe plums need a little more thickener, so consider this a late summer recipe and, when plums are not quite as juicy, dial back the thickener—in this case tapioca.

You'll never have to worry about the dreaded soggy crust with this pie. The bottom crust is prebaked *before* the filling is added, to keep the pastry firm. I've made plenty of plum pies without prebaking the crust, but the extra step lends more consistent results. If you prefer not to prebake the crust, follow the pastry instructions in the Sweet Bing Pie recipe (page 72).

A just-baked pie is hard to resist, but the filling needs a few hours to set and cool before slicing into it.

PASTRY

BASE: Prepare the pastry and place one portion of dough onto a sheet of parchment paper dusted with flour. Layer a sheet of plastic wrap over the dough and roll (over the plastic) from the centre in all directions until about 11 inches (28 cm) in diameter and ⅛ inch (3 mm) thick.

Drape the dough onto your rolling pin and transfer to the pie plate, being mindful not to pull or stretch the dough. Gently press the dough into the sides of the pie plate and trim the edges. Do not bother to crimp the edges. Cover with plastic wrap and refrigerate for at least 20 minutes.

If you've never made a lattice pie, refer to the step-by-step images on page 183.

LATTICE: Place the remaining portion of dough onto a sheet of parchment dusted with flour. Layer a sheet of plastic wrap over the dough and roll (over the plastic) from the centre in all directions until about 11 inches (28 cm) in diameter and ⅛ inch (3 mm) thick. Remove the plastic and cut eight 1-inch (2.5 cm) wide strips and eight ½-inch (1 cm) wide strips for the lattice. You can, of course, use all wide strips, which is also lovely (see Rhubarb Ginger Pie, page 218). Transfer the strips of pastry and the parchment beneath to a platter or tray, cover with plastic wrap and refrigerate for at least 20 minutes.

FILLING

In a large bowl, combine 1 cup (250 mL) granulated sugar and the tapioca and mix well. Add the plums and stir to coat. Grate the peeled apple and add it to the plum mixture, stirring to combine. Leave the mixture for 30 minutes to allow the tapioca to soften. Don't be tempted to rush this step—I learned first-hand that tapioca can ruin a pie if not softened first.

. . . recipe continued

PASTRY CONTINUED . . .

Preheat oven to 425°F (220°C).

Retrieve the pastry base and prick with a fork. Cover with parchment and fill with pie weights.

Bake in the preheated oven for 15 minutes, then transfer to a wire rack to remove the parchment and pie weights. Sprinkle the base with a scant spoonful of granulated sugar and cover the pastry's edges with foil (or pastry shields) to prevent them from further browning. Reduce the temperature to 375°F (190°C) and bake for an additional 10–15 minutes until the pastry is golden and cooked through.

Cool on a wire rack. Using a sharp knife, carefully trim the edges so the pastry lies flat (it's easier to add the lattice when the edges are smooth).

PUTTING IT ALL TOGETHER

Pour the fruit mixture into the cooled pastry shell, mounding the fruit in the middle. Dot with butter.

LATTICE

If you've never made a lattice topping, refer to the images on page 183. Place 8 strips of pastry (of alternating widths) loosely across the pie in one direction, leaving a ½-inch (1 cm) gap between each strip. Do not press the dough in place.

To weave in the first pastry strip, gently fold back every other pastry strip to the pastry's edge and lay a perpendicular strip over the remaining strips. Fold the strips back in place and you'll see you've created your first weave.

Repeat the process with each new strip (of alternating widths), pulling back alternating strips of pastry to weave in the strips of dough, allowing a ½-inch (1 cm) gap between each.

When the weaving is complete, trim the edges and dab a bit of lightly beaten egg onto the spot where the unbaked strip meets the cooked edge. Press very lightly, so as not to break the cooked pastry. Alternatively, if you have the patience, tuck the strips between the cooked pastry and the pie plate by prying the pastry ever-so-slightly away from the plate (by wedging an offset palette knife or standard knife between the crust and plate), just enough to tuck in the strips of pastry. The latter option provides a seamless finish.

Brush the lattice with additional egg and dust with granulated sugar. Cover the pie loosely with plastic wrap and refrigerate or freeze for about 20 minutes to firm the lattice.

Transfer the pie to a parchment- or foil-lined baking tray and bake in a preheated 425°F (220°C) oven for 15 minutes. Reduce heat to 375°F (190°C) and bake for another 30–40 minutes, until the fruit is tender and the juices are bubbling. Rotate the baking tray once during baking and tent with foil as necessary to promote even baking.

Cool on a wire rack and cool for a few hours before serving.

PERFECT PECAN PIE

YIELD

Makes one 9-inch (23 cm) pie

PASTRY

1 recipe Buttermilk Shortcrust Dough (page 36) or Flaky Pastry Dough (page 32), only half the dough needed

1 egg, lightly beaten

FILLING

3 large eggs, lightly beaten, room temperature

1 cup (250 mL) golden (dark) corn syrup

1 cup (250 mL) firmly packed golden (light) brown sugar

¼ cup (60 mL) all-purpose flour

¼ cup (60 mL) unsalted melted butter (about 60 g)

1 tsp (5 mL) vanilla extract

Pinch of salt

1 cup (250 mL) chopped pecans + about ¾ cup (185 mL) pecan halves to decorate the top

SPECIAL EQUIPMENT

Shallow 9-inch (23 cm) pie plate (0.75 quart)

WE CANADIANS HAVE our sugar pie—but south of the border, pecan pie rules. When I wanted an authentic pecan pie for Thanksgiving one year, I knew exactly who to turn to. My friend Gail White, a passionate and skilled cook, was raised by a Floridian mother who knew her way around a Southern pie.

Now you, too, can enjoy this rich, nutty, caramelly pie thanks to Gail, who shared her family's recipe. Delicious served with Whipped Labneh (page 300).

PASTRY

Prepare the pastry and place the dough onto a sheet of parchment paper dusted with flour. Layer a sheet of plastic wrap over the dough and roll (over the plastic) from the centre in all directions until approximately 12 inches (30 cm) in diameter and about ⅛ inch (3 mm) thick.

Drape the dough onto your rolling pin and transfer to the pie plate, being mindful not to pull or stretch the dough. Gently press the dough into the sides of the pie plate, trim the excess and crimp the edges using one of the two methods below:

TWISTED-EDGE CRIMP: Pinch the edge of the dough diagonally between your thumb and bent index finger, all the way around the pie. Don't pinch so tight that the pastry becomes too narrow or flimsy. See page 212 for an image reference.

TRADITIONAL FLUTED EDGE: Place the knuckle or tip of your index finger on the inner edge of the dough and, with your other hand, pinch the dough around the knuckle. See page 212 for an image reference.

The secret to crimping is uniformity. Any style will look good, providing the grooves are the same size.

Cover with plastic wrap and refrigerate for at least 40 minutes.

. . . recipe continued

CRIMPING THE EDGE: Twisted-edge crimp (top); traditional fluted edge (bottom).

. . . Perfect Pecan Pie (cont.)

FILLING

In a medium bowl, combine the eggs, corn syrup, brown sugar, flour, butter, vanilla and salt. Mix well to combine. Fold in the chopped pecans.

PUTTING IT ALL TOGETHER

Preheat a foil- or parchment-lined baking tray in a 425°F (220°C) oven.

Transfer the dough-lined pie plate to your work surface and brush the pastry's edge with the lightly beaten egg. Pour the pecan mixture onto the plate and decorate with the pecan halves.

Place on the preheated tray and bake for 15 minutes, then reduce the temperature to 375°F (190°C) and continue to bake for another 45–50 minutes, or until the filling has firmed and no longer wobbles. Rotate the baking tray once during baking and cover with foil as necessary to prevent burning.

Cool on a wire rack at room temperature for at least 2 hours before serving.

NUTTY PEAR TART

YIELD

Makes one 14- × 4½-inch (36 × 11 cm) rectangular tart, or one 13-inch (33 cm) round tart

PASTRY

1 recipe Chocolate Walnut Dough (page 42)

ALMOND CREAM FILLING

1¼ cups (310 mL) whole raw almonds (not blanched)

½ cup (125 mL) unsalted butter (about 115 g), room temperature

½ cup (125 mL) granulated sugar

2 large eggs, lightly beaten, room temperature

2 tsp (10 mL) finely minced fresh ginger*

TOPPING

½–3 firm but ripe medium pears (Bartlett, Bosc and Anjou are good choices)

1 Tbsp (15 mL) whipping cream, for brushing the pears

1 Tbsp (15 mL) coarse raw or granulated sugar

SPECIAL EQUIPMENT

14- × 4½-inch (36 × 11 cm) tart pan with a removable base, or a 13-inch (33 cm) round pan

Pie weights (or beans or rice)

---

* If you use a microplane to mince the ginger, it will tease out the flavourful juices too, lending even more of a zing.

"THERE ARE ONLY *ten minutes in the life of a pear when it is perfect to eat.*" —Ralph Waldo Emerson

I think of Emerson's quote every time I reach for a pear. It can be challenging to find a perfectly ripe one, but this tart makes foraging worth your while. Bartlett, Bosc and Anjou are all good choices, just make sure they're fragrant and yield to gentle pressure just below the stem. If they're soft elsewhere, they're overripe.

In this chunky nut tart, pear halves are nestled in a gingery almond cream filling. Delightful on its own, it's even better with a drizzle of Caramel Sauce (page 302) and/or a scoop of Handcrafted Vanilla Ice Cream (page 300).

PASTRY

Line the base of the tart pan with parchment paper.

Prepare the pastry and place the dough onto a sheet of parchment paper dusted with flour. Layer a sheet of plastic wrap over the dough and roll (over the plastic) into a rectangle slightly larger than your tart pan, about ¼ inch (6 mm) thick, or thicker for a chunkier crust. (If using a round pan, fashion into a circle.)

Keeping the plastic intact, drape the dough over your rolling pin and transfer to the parchment-lined pan, plastic wrap facing up. Press the dough into the mold, through the plastic wrap, smoothing the edges with your fingers. Refrigerate for 40 minutes to firm the dough.

Preheat oven to 375°F (190°C).

Prick the bottom of the tart with the tines of a fork. Bake in the preheated oven for 10–12 minutes until the pastry is partially set.

The dough is partially baked *before* the parchment (or foil) and pie weights are added. I learned the hard way that some doughs, especially sweet ones, can stick to the parchment, causing the pastry to tear when the parchment is removed.

Remove the partially set tart from the oven, carefully line it with foil or parchment, fill with pie weights and bake for another 20 minutes. Remove the pie weights and cool the tart on a wire rack for at least 30 minutes. Do not remove the tart pan.

ALMOND CREAM FILLING

Pulse the almonds in a food processor until the nuts are mostly fine-textured with some irregular coarse pieces. (I enjoy the crunch of almonds, so I do not process them too finely.)

Combine the butter and ½ cup (125 mL) granulated sugar in either the bowl of a stand mixer (fitted with the paddle attachment) or a medium bowl and mix until the mixture is light. Add the eggs, ginger and ground almonds.

. . . recipe continued

. . . Nutty Pear Tart (cont.)

PUTTING IT ALL TOGETHER

Spread the filling onto the cooled, partially cooked pastry, smoothing the mixture with a spatula.

Peel, core and halve the pears. You may have to trim the pears to sit level in the almond filling. (If one pear half sits higher than the other, for example, trim the cut side so the pears are level and cook evenly). Gently push the pears into the almond filling, cut side down, to nestle them in the mixture. Brush the pears with whipping cream and sprinkle with sugar.

If using a round pan, position the pear halves in a circle with the cut sides down and the narrow ends toward the centre of the tart. Place the tart on a baking tray and cover the edges with foil to prevent burning. Bake until the filling is cooked through and slightly puffed, about 25–30 minutes.

Cool on a wire rack. Do not remove the pan until the tart has completely cooled. Serve at room temperature.

RHUBARB GINGER PIE

YIELD

Makes one 9-inch (23 cm) pie

PASTRY

1 recipe Flaky Pastry Dough (page 32), divided into 2 portions

1 large egg, lightly beaten, for brushing the pastry

1–2 Tbsp (15–30 mL) coarse raw or granulated sugar

FILLING

8 cups (2 L) sliced rhubarb (½-inch/1 cm thick pieces; about 2 lb/910 g)

1½ cups (375 mL) granulated sugar

1½ tsp (7 mL) freshly grated ginger, ideally with a microplane (to extract the juices)

¼ cup + 1 Tbsp (75 mL) quick-cooking tapioca, ideally ground in a spice grinder (see page 19 for info)

¼ tsp (1 mL) table salt

2 Tbsp (30 mL) unsalted butter (about 30 g), chilled and cut into small pieces

SPECIAL EQUIPMENT

Shallow 9-inch (23 cm) pie plate (0.75 quart)

ALTHOUGH WE'VE SNUCK this pie into the fruit section, rhubarb is a perennial vegetable (with leaves that are too toxic to consume). It has been used in pie fillings for as long as pies have been around, and for good reason. Sweetened and baked, rhubarb is transformed from tough stringy stalks to a meltingly tender filling with a distinctive fruity character. A bit of fresh grated ginger lends a warm spicy note.

Step-by-step instructions for a lattice topping are provided on page 183. (You'll find this wide lattice topping even less work than the thinner versions.)

PASTRY

Prepare the pastry and place one portion of dough onto a sheet of parchment paper dusted with flour. Layer a sheet of plastic wrap over the dough and roll (over the plastic) from the centre in all directions until approximately 12 inches (30 cm) in diameter and about ⅛ inch (3 mm) thick.

Drape the dough onto your rolling pin and transfer to the pie plate, being mindful not to pull or stretch the dough. Gently press the dough into the sides of the pie plate and trim the edges. Cover with plastic wrap and refrigerate for at least 40 minutes.

Place the remaining portion of dough onto a sheet of parchment paper dusted with flour. Place a sheet of plastic wrap on top of the dough and roll (over the plastic) from the centre toward the pastry's edge in all directions, making a circle that's approximately 10½ inches (27 cm) in diameter and ⅛ inch (3 mm) thick. Remove the plastic and cut this into 6 strips that are each 2 inches (5 cm) wide. Transfer to a tray or plate with the parchment beneath, wrap in plastic and refrigerate for at least 40 minutes.

FILLING

In a large bowl, combine the sliced rhubarb, 1½ cups (375 mL) granulated sugar, ginger, tapioca and salt in a large bowl and toss to combine. Set aside for 20 minutes to soften the tapioca.

PUTTING IT ALL TOGETHER

Retrieve the dough-lined pie plate from the fridge. Tip the fruit/sugar mixture into the plate and mound the fruit in the centre. Top with any remaining sugar/tapioca mixture left in the bowl. Gently tap the pie plate on your work surface to distribute the fruit and sugar. Dot with butter.

For step-by-step lattice instructions and photos, refer to page 183. Place three 2-inch (5 cm) strips of pastry loosely across the rhubarb in one direction, leaving a ½-inch (1 cm) gap between each strip. Do not press the dough in place.

. . . recipe continued

. . . Rhubarb Ginger Pie (cont.)

To weave in the first pastry strip, gently fold back 2 alternating strips to the pastry's edge and lay a perpendicular strip of pastry over the remaining strips. Fold the strips back in place and you'll see you've created your first weave. Repeat the process with the remaining 2 strips.

Trim the edges and carefully press the lattice into the pastry base with your fingers. Brush the lattice with beaten egg and dust with coarse raw or granulated sugar. Cover loosely with plastic wrap and refrigerate or freeze for about 20 minutes to firm the lattice.

Preheat a foil- or parchment-lined baking tray in a 425°F (220°C) oven.

Bake the pie on the preheated tray for 15 minutes, reduce the temperature to 375°F (190°C) and continue to bake for another 30–40 minutes, or until the pastry is golden and the rhubarb is tender. Rotate the baking tray once during baking and tent with foil as necessary to prevent burning.

Cool on a wire rack. Allow the pie to cool for at least 3 hours at room temperature before serving. Serve at room temperature or rewarm and serve with ice cream.

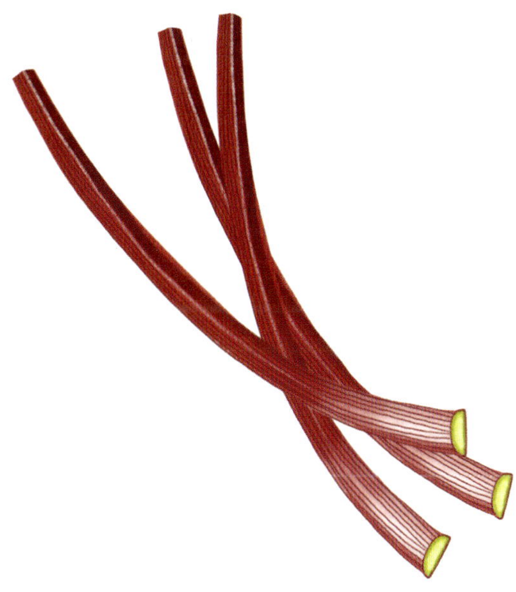

NECTARINE SLAB CRUMBLE

YIELD

Makes 18–20 servings

PASTRY

1 recipe Flaky Pastry Dough using the Whole Wheat Variation (page 32)

1 large egg, lightly beaten, for brushing the pastry + more as needed

FILLING

12 cups (3 L) sliced nectarines, ripe but firm (about 2.2 kg, or 14 nectarines)

¾ cup (185 mL) granulated sugar

1 Tbsp (15 mL) freshly grated ginger (ideally grated with a microplane to extract the juice)

¼ cup + 2 Tbsp (90 mL) quick-cooking tapioca, ideally ground in a spice grinder (see page 19 for info)

CRUMBLE TOPPING

1 cup (250 mL) unsalted butter (about 227 g), chilled and chopped into pea-sized pieces

1 cup (250 mL) large flake oats

1 cup (250 mL) whole wheat flour

1 cup (250 mL) firmly packed golden (light) brown sugar

½ tsp (5 mL) kosher salt

2½ tsp (12.5 mL) ginger powder

SPECIAL EQUIPMENT

14- × 11-inch (36 × 28 cm) baking tray

IF YOU'RE LOOKING for a dessert large enough to feed a crowd, this homespun nectarine crumble with fresh ginger is the answer. Made on a baking tray with whole wheat pastry, this slab pie ensures that every juicy bite is full of crisp, buttery oat topping.

A crumble is only as good as the fruit it contains, so choose nectarines that are somewhat heavy for their size. A light nectarine indicates a disappointingly mealy or cottony-textured fruit that baking won't improve, so don't grab a bag in haste. Choose nectarines that are fragrant and yield to gentle pressure.

Serve with Handcrafted Vanilla Ice Cream (page 300).

PASTRY

Prepare the pastry and place all of the dough onto a sheet of parchment paper dusted with flour. Layer a sheet of plastic wrap over the dough and roll (over the plastic) from the centre to create a rectangle approximately 15 × 12 inches (38 × 30 cm) and about ⅛ inch (3 mm) thick.

Drape the dough onto your rolling pin and transfer to the baking tray, being mindful not to pull or stretch the dough. Gently press the dough into the sides of the baking tray and trim the edges. Cover with plastic wrap and refrigerate for at least 40 minutes.

If desired, gather and re-roll the remaining pastry dough to create a twisted trim (see image). Wrap in plastic and refrigerate for at least 40 minutes.

FILLING

In a large bowl, combine the sliced nectarines and granulated sugar and toss to combine. Add the grated ginger and tapioca and toss to combine. Set aside to macerate (soften) for 15 minutes.

CRUMBLE TOPPING

In a medium bowl, combine the butter, oats, flour, golden brown sugar, salt and ginger powder. Mix together with a fork, or with your hands, until the mixture comes together in clumps.

Preheat oven to 450°F (230°C). Line the bottom oven rack with foil to catch any drippings from the slab pie.

. . . recipe continued

. . . Nectarine Slab Crumble (cont.)

PUTTING IT ALL TOGETHER

Retrieve the chilled pastry from the fridge. If you made a pastry trim, lightly brush the top of the pastry edges with beaten egg. Press the trim onto the moistened edges and brush with more beaten egg.

Fill the pastry shell with the nectarine mixture, reserving the excess juices. (The juices are added just before the pie is baked to keep the pastry crisp.) Smooth the fruit so that it's evenly distributed. Break up the crumble with your hands and distribute it evenly over the fruit.

Carefully drizzle the nectarine juice into a few sections of the pie where there are openings in the crumble, aiming to distribute the juice evenly.

Tent with foil and bake in the preheated oven for 20 minutes; remove the foil and reduce the temperature to 375°F (190°C), then continue to bake for another 30–40 minutes until the pastry is cooked through. Keep an eye on the crumble and rotate the baking tray once during baking; re-cover with foil as necessary to prevent burning.

Cool on a wire rack for at least 2 hours at room temperature before serving. Serve at room temperature or rewarm and serve with ice cream.

POACHED PEAR TARTS

YIELD

Makes 6 miniature ½-inch (6 cm) tarts

PASTRY

8 oz (230 g) your favourite pie or tart dough

FILLING

6 miniature ripe pears, such as Seckel or Forelle, each about 2½–3 inches (6–8 cm) in height

Half a lemon

2 cups (500 mL) granulated sugar

2 cups (500 mL) water

1 lump fresh ginger (about 2½ × 1 inches/6 × 2.5 cm), peeled

3 Tbsp + 1 tsp (50 mL) white wine vinegar

Half a vanilla pod, sliced lengthwise, vanilla seeds scraped out

½ cup (125 mL) apricot preserves

1 Tbsp (15 mL) rum, Grand Marnier or cognac

1 recipe Sweet & Spicy Nuts (page 301), roughly chopped

SPECIAL EQUIPMENT

Six 2½-inch (6 cm) tart molds

12 baking cups or parchment paper, cut to fit the molds

Pie weights (or beans or rice)

THESE CHARMING FALL tarts feature miniature poached pears nestled in pastry cups lined with rum-spiked preserves and edged in spiced nuts. They're the perfect stepping stone to the holiday season.

This recipe involves a number of steps, but each component can be prepared days in advance, at your leisure. The pears soak overnight in a fragrant poaching liquid infused with fresh ginger and pure vanilla. It's an ideal recipe for using up leftover dough, as you only need a small amount for the tart shells.

These tarts are even better drizzled with a bit of Caramel Sauce (page 302) and/or Crème Anglaise (page 299).

POACHED PEARS

Peel the pears, keeping the stems intact. Using an apple corer or a small spoon, carefully remove the cores from the widest ends of the pears, being mindful to keep the pears intact. Rub the surface of each pear with the cut side of the lemon to prevent it from turning brown.

Combine the sugar and water in a saucepan that will fit the pears in a snug single layer. Cut the ginger into 4 pieces and add it to the saucepan along with the white wine vinegar and vanilla pod and seeds. Bring the mixture to a simmer over low heat, stirring occasionally, until the sugar has dissolved.

Add the pears and top with a small plate to keep them submerged in the poaching liquid. Simmer until a knife inserted into the widest part of the pear easily pierces to the centre. This can take anywhere from 10–20 minutes depending on the ripeness of the pears. Remove the pears (to prevent the residual heat from overcooking them). Cool the poaching liquid in a clean container large enough to also fit the pears. When the liquid is no longer warm, add the pears, cover and refrigerate overnight.

Leftover poaching liquid can be frozen solid then scraped with a fork to create a refreshing granita to serve alongside the pears, or for later use (see note, page 229).

PASTRY

Line the tart molds with half the paper baking cups or parchment paper cut to size (the balance of the baking cups/parchment will be used later). The molds need to be *completely* covered with paper, otherwise you won't be able to release the tarts without breaking them (it's fine if your paper overlaps the molds).

. . . recipe continued

Prepare the pastry and place the dough onto a sheet of parchment paper dusted with flour. Layer a sheet of plastic wrap over the dough and roll (over the plastic) from the centre toward the pastry's edge in all directions until about ⅛ inch (3 mm) thick. Remove the plastic and cut the dough into 6 circles slightly larger than your tart molds using a cup or small bowl as a guide. Carefully transfer the circles of dough with a spatula, or your hands, to the paper-lined molds. Cover with plastic wrap and gently press the dough (through the plastic) against the base and edges of each mold, aiming for a uniform thickness. Refrigerate for 40 minutes. Wrap the excess dough in plastic and refrigerate or freeze for another use.

Preheat oven to 375°F (190°C).

Retrieve the tart molds and pierce the base and sides of each pastry with the tines of a fork to prevent it from buckling in the oven. Cover each tart with a baking cup or square of parchment and fill with pie weights to the top of the mold. Place the tarts on a baking tray, leaving plenty of room between each.

Bake 20 minutes in the preheated oven, rotating the baking tray once during baking to ensure that the tarts bake evenly. Remove the tarts from the oven and carefully remove the pie weights and baking cups or parchment. Return the tarts to the oven and continue to bake, uncovered, for another 5–7 minutes, or until the pastry is browned and cooked through. Cool on a baking rack and do not remove the molds until the tarts have completely cooled.

PUTTING IT ALL TOGETHER

Just before serving, place the tart shells on a platter or individual dessert plates.

Thin the apricot preserves with the rum, Grand Marnier or cognac. Fill each shell with about 1 heaping spoonful of the spiked apricot preserves. Remove the pears from their poaching liquid, blot dry and nestle each into a tart shell. Garnish with chopped nuts.

PEAR GRANITA

Granita is a refreshing icy dessert, a cross between a snow cone and sorbet. To make granita, pour the leftover poaching liquid from the Poached Pear Tarts recipe into a wide shallow container and place it in the freezer. When the liquid starts to form ice crystals, drag a fork along the bottom of the container to agitate and turn the mixture. Repeat this every half hour or so until the mixture is icy and fairly uniform. Serve in small (2 oz/60 mL) chilled sherry glasses and spike with vodka, if desired.

CHOCOLATE

TRIPLE-CHOCOLATE TART

YIELD

Makes one 9-inch (23 cm) tart

PASTRY

1 recipe Chocolate Walnut Dough (page 42)

CHOCOLATE MOUSSE

6 oz (175 g) good-quality dark chocolate chips (or chopped), ideally 65%–70% cocoa

1¾ cups (435 mL) whipping cream, divided

GANACHE TOPPING

3 oz (90 g) good-quality dark chocolate chips (or chopped chocolate), ideally 65%–70% cocoa

⅓ cup (80 mL) whipping cream

2 Tbsp (30 mL) clear corn syrup

Candied Hazelnuts (optional; recipe follows)

SPECIAL EQUIPMENT

9-inch (23 cm) square or round tart pan with a removable base*

Pie weights (or beans or rice)

---

* If using a 9½-inch (24 cm) tart pan, you'll need to increase the mousse ingredients to a total of 8 oz (230 g) chocolate and 2⅓ cups (580 mL) whipping cream.

CHOCOLATE MOUSSE IS sandwiched between a nutty chocolate crust and a dark ganache topping in this intensely flavoured triple-chocolate tart. Garnished with crushed candied hazelnuts, this chocolate trifecta is irresistible.

This tart can be prepared in advance of chocolate cravings and it freezes beautifully.

PASTRY

Line the base of the tart pan with parchment paper cut to size. It helps to first brush the pan lightly with butter to make the parchment stick.

Prepare the pastry and place the dough onto a sheet of parchment paper dusted with flour. Layer a sheet of plastic wrap over the dough and roll (over the plastic) into a square (or circle) about 1½ inches (4 cm) larger than your tart pan and about ⅛ inch (3 mm) thick.

Drape the dough over your rolling pin (or use your hands) to transfer the dough to the tart pan, plastic wrap facing up (it's easier to press the dough into the tart mold if you leave the plastic wrap intact). If the pastry breaks, use your hands to press the dough, piecemeal if necessary, into the pan and along the sides. Press the dough into the sides of the tart with your fingers and trim any excess. If desired, use a flat-bottomed cup to level the pastry. Refrigerate for at least 20 minutes.

Preheat oven to 350°F (175°C). The dough is partially baked *before* the parchment (or foil) and pie weights are added. (I learned the hard way that some doughs, especially sweet ones, can stick to the parchment, causing the pastry to tear when the parchment is removed.)

Retrieve the tart pan from the fridge and prick the chilled dough (bottom and sides) with the tines of a fork. Loosely tent the edges with foil (or pastry shields) as the edges tend to burn first.

Transfer to a baking tray and bake in the preheated oven for 15 minutes or just until the dough starts to firm. (The crust will puff slightly in the oven.)

Carefully (as the pan is hot) remove the foil from the tart's edges. Line the partially baked dough with parchment paper or foil and fill with pie weights. Continue to bake for another 15–20 minutes, or until the pastry is cooked through.

Remove the parchment or foil lining and pie weights and cool on a wire rack. Do not remove the tart pan until the pastry has completely cooled.

CHOCOLATE MOUSSE

Place a heat-resistant bowl over a saucepan filled with 1 inch (2.5 cm) of simmering water. The bottom of the bowl should not touch the water. Place 6 oz (175 g) chocolate and ¼ cup (60 mL) of the whipping cream in the bowl. Once the chocolate starts to melt, turn off the heat and continue stirring until all the chocolate has melted. Overheating the chocolate can make it grainy.

. . . recipe continued

In a large bowl, or the bowl of a stand mixer fitted with a wire whisk, add 1½ cups (375 mL) whipping cream and whisk until thickened to a soft peak.

Working quickly, pour the melted chocolate mixture into the whipping cream and mix with a spatula or large whisk until the mousse has thickened and is uniform in colour. Without delay (before the mixture sets), pour the mousse into the cooled tart shell and smooth the top with a palette knife or the back of a spoon. Refrigerate while preparing the ganache topping.

GANACHE TOPPING

Place 3 oz (90 g) chocolate, ⅓ cup (80 mL) whipping cream and the corn syrup in a heat-resistant bowl placed over a saucepan filled with 1 inch (2.5 cm) of simmering water. Heat the chocolate mixture over low heat, stirring, until the chocolate is just melted. Remove from the heat.

Cool the ganache slightly at room temperature so that when you pour it over the tart it doesn't melt the mousse. It will firm as it cools, so stir it now and then to check the texture and temperature. If left too long, the mixture will become too firm to pour. If that happens, you can rewarm the ganache slightly by placing the bowl briefly over a saucepan of simmering water.

PUTTING IT ALL TOGETHER

Pour the slightly cooled ganache over the (slightly firmed) mousse, starting from the centre of the tart. Tip and rotate the mousse slightly to distribute the ganache and smooth with an offset palette knife or spatula. Refrigerate until ready to serve.

Bring to room temperate about an hour before serving and garnish with Candied Hazelnuts, if desired. To freeze, wrap in plastic or place in a reusable freezer bag up to 3 weeks.

Candied Hazelnuts

To prepare this topping, you'll need a non-stick baking mat and a small heavy-bottomed saucepan. As with any recipe involving cooked sugar, read the recipe to the end before you start. Then read it again. Sugar can change from beautiful amber to smoky and charred in a heartbeat. Have your ingredients and equipment in place before you start.

INGREDIENTS

¾ cup (185 mL) whole skinned hazelnuts, lightly toasted in the oven

½ cup (125 mL) granulated sugar

¼ cup (60 mL) water

Pinch cream of tartar

Place a cup of water and a pastry brush near your stove. As the sugar cooks, the pastry brush will be used to brush down any sugar that sputters to the sides of the saucepan. This helps prevent the sugar from crystallizing, which can ruin your caramel.

Spread the hazelnuts onto a baking tray lined with a non-stick baking mat.

Combine the sugar, water and a pinch of cream of tartar in a saucepan and mix to combine. Cook over medium heat for about 4–5 minutes or until the sugar melts and turns amber, brushing down any bits of sugar that splatter onto the sides of the pan with your moistened pastry brush. When the sugar turns amber, carefully and quickly pour the mixture over the hazelnuts.

Cool completely, then roughly chop the caramelized hazelnuts. Use right away or store in a sealed airtight container in the freezer. The sugar will soften and become tacky in the fridge.

WHITE CHOCOLATE MOUSSE TARTS

YIELD

Makes ten 4-inch (10 cm) tarts

PASTRY

1 recipe Sweet Tart Dough (page 38)

FILLING

Heaping ¾ cup (185+ mL) finely chopped good-quality white chocolate (about 140 g)*

¼ cup (60 mL) unsalted butter (about 60 g), softened

2 large egg yolks, room temperature

1 cup (250 mL) whipping cream

1¾ cups (435 mL) strawberry or raspberry jam

GARNISH

2 cups (500 mL) fresh strawberries or raspberries

SPECIAL EQUIPMENT

Ten 4-inch (10 cm) tart molds

20 baking cups or parchment paper, cut to fit the molds

Pie weights (or beans or rice)

---

* Opt for the best white chocolate you can afford with at least 33% cocoa butter (not vegetable shortening).

CHOCOLATE CONNOISSEURS ARE happy to tell you that white chocolate isn't really chocolate—although made from cocoa butter, it doesn't contain any cocoa solids. Still, white chocolate lovers will savour these light mousse tarts with a dollop of jam hidden beneath the frothy, chiffon topping. The pastry comes together as easily as cookie dough.

PASTRY

Line the tart molds with half the paper baking cups or parchment paper cut to size (the balance of the baking cups/parchment will be used later). The molds need to be completely covered with paper, otherwise you won't be able to release the tarts without breaking them (it's fine if your paper overlaps the molds).

Prepare the pastry and place the dough onto a sheet of parchment paper dusted with flour. Layer a sheet of plastic wrap over the dough and roll (over the plastic) until approximately ⅛ inch (3 mm) thick. Remove the plastic and cut the dough into 10 circles slightly larger than your tart molds, gathering and re-rolling any scraps. Use a small bowl as a template, if desired.

Carefully transfer the circles of dough with a spatula, or your hands, to the paper-lined molds. Cover the pastry-lined tart molds with plastic wrap and gently press the dough (through the plastic) against the base and edges of each mold, aiming for a uniform thickness. Refrigerate for 40 minutes.

Preheat oven to 375°F (190°C).

Retrieve the tart molds from the fridge and pierce the base and sides of each pastry with the tines of a fork. Cover each with a baking cup or square of parchment and fill with pie weights to the top of the mold. Place the tarts on a baking tray, leaving plenty of room between each.

Bake for 20 minutes in the preheated oven, rotating the baking tray once during baking to ensure the tarts bake evenly. Remove the tarts from the oven and carefully remove the pie weights and baking cups or parchment. Return the tarts to the oven and continue to bake, uncovered, for another 5–7 minutes, or until each pastry is browned and cooked through. Cool on a wire rack and do not remove the molds until the tarts have cooled completely.

FILLING

Place a heat-resistant bowl over a saucepan filled with 1 inch (2.5 cm) of simmering water. The bottom of the bowl should not touch the water. Place the chocolate and butter in the bowl. Once the chocolate starts to melt, turn off the heat and continue stirring until all the chocolate has melted. Overheating the chocolate can turn it grainy.

Beat the room temperature yolks with an electric mixture in a medium bowl until pale and frothy. In a separate bowl, whip the cream until soft peaks form.

. . . recipe continued

Working quickly, pour the melted chocolate into the yolks and stir to combine. If the mixture separates or clumps, place the bowl over the saucepan of simmering water and gently reheat the mixture briefly, continuously stirring until smooth.

Finally, fold in the whipping cream with a spatula or a balloon whisk until smooth.

PUTTING IT ALL TOGETHER

Spread about 2 Tbsp (30 mL) jam into each cooled tart. Cover each with a generous dollop (about ¼ cup/60 mL) of mousse. Refrigerate until firm.

Garnish with fresh berries just before serving. Leftover mousse can be spooned into small glasses and refrigerated. Mousse tarts can be frozen, without the fresh berries, in a reusable freezer bag up to 3 weeks.

PEANUT BUTTER CHOCOLATE PIE

YIELD

Makes one 9½- to 10-inch (24–25 cm) pie

PASTRY

1 recipe Cookie Crumb Crust (page 46)

FILLING

1 cup (250 mL) chunky-style peanut butter (preferably sugar-free), room temperature

4½ oz (125 g) Philadelphia cream cheese (half a brick), room temperature

½ cup (125 mL) unsalted butter (about 115 g), room temperature

¼ cup + 1 Tbsp (75 mL) powdered (icing) sugar

¾ cup (185 mL) whipping cream, chilled

GANACHE TOPPING

Heaping ⅔ cup (160+ mL) finely chopped good-quality semisweet chocolate (about 120 g)

½ cup (125 mL) whipping cream

Fleur de sel (optional)

SPECIAL EQUIPMENT

9½- to 10-inch (24–25 cm) tart pan with a removable base

I HAVE A weakness for peanut butter and dark chocolate—and cookies. This recipe embraces all three. It's a pie I make and give away immediately, because if it's in the house I'll eat it, slice by slice, until it's gone—even when I bury it deep in the freezer to slow me down. In fact, I quite enjoy it frozen.

The crust is made from crushed cookies—in this instance, gluten-free gingersnaps—which lend a spicy ginger note. But you can use any firm cookie you like.

I've dusted the ganache topping with a little fleur de sel, but chopped nuts would be a fine garnish too.

PASTRY

Prepare the Cookie Crumb Crust and refrigerate.

Preheat oven to 350°F (175°C).

Once the crust has chilled for at least 20 minutes, prick the crust in several places along the base and sides of the tart with a fork. Bake for about 6–10 minutes until slightly firm, watching the crust carefully to ensure it doesn't overcook. If the crust starts to slip down the sides of the tart pan or puff slightly, gently press into place with the tines of a fork. Cool before adding the filling.

FILLING

Place the peanut butter, cream cheese, unsalted butter and powdered sugar in either the bowl of a stand mixer (fitted with the paddle attachment) or a medium bowl and mix until completely smooth.

In a separate bowl, whip ¾ cup (185 mL) whipping cream with a whisk until light and fluffy. Fold the whipped cream into the peanut butter mixture until completely mixed. Transfer to the cooled crust, smoothing the edges. Refrigerate while preparing the ganache.

GANACHE TOPPING

Place the chopped chocolate in a small bowl. Heat ½ cup (125 mL) whipping cream in a small saucepan until just boiling, then pour over the chocolate. Stir until the chocolate is smooth and silky.

Once the mixture has cooled slightly but is still creamy enough to pour, drizzle it evenly over the peanut butter filling and smooth with an offset palette knife or spatula. Refrigerate until ready to serve.

Dust with a pinch of fleur de sel, if desired, before serving. To freeze, firm in the freezer loosely covered, then wrap in plastic or place in a reusable freezer bag with as much air removed as possible.

CHOCOLATE SOUFFLÉ TART

YIELD

Makes two 7½-inch (19 cm) tarts

PASTRY

1 recipe Sweet Tart Dough using the Chocolate Variation (page 40), divided into 2 portions

Powdered (icing) sugar

CUSTARD

1½ cups (375 mL) whole or 2% milk

⅓ cup (80 mL) granulated sugar, divided

3 large egg yolks

3 Tbsp (45 mL) all-purpose flour

CHOCOLATE

1⅓ cups (330 mL) finely chopped good-quality 65%–70% dark chocolate (about 230 g)

MERINGUE

5 large egg whites

¼ tsp (1 mL) cream of tartar

3 Tbsp (45 mL) granulated sugar

SPECIAL EQUIPMENT

Two 7½-inch (19 cm) fluted tart pans with removable bases

Pie weights (or beans or rice).

THIS TART HAS a chocolatey filling so light and delicate it nearly melts in your mouth. Unlike warm soufflés that compel cooks to sprint to the table before they collapse, this tart can stand its ground at room temperature, and it keeps well up to 24 hours. It can also be served straight from the oven, with the filling warm and moist.

Delicious with a side of fresh berries and even better drizzled with Crème Anglaise (page 299). Both the pastry and the custard (for the soufflé filling) can be prepared up to three days in advance.

PASTRY

Prepare the pastry and place one portion of dough onto a sheet of parchment paper dusted with flour. Layer a sheet of plastic wrap over the dough and roll (over the plastic) from the centre toward the pastry's edge in all directions until about ⅛ inch (3 mm) thick.

Drape the dough over your rolling pin (or use your hands) to transfer the dough to one of the tart pans, plastic wrap facing up (it's easier to press the dough into the pan if you leave the plastic wrap intact). If the pastry breaks, use your hands to press the dough, piecemeal if necessary, into the pan and along the sides. Press the dough into the sides of the pan with your fingers and trim any excess dough. If desired, use a flat-bottomed cup to level the pastry. Refrigerate for at least 20 minutes.

Repeat the process with the remaining portion of dough for the second tart.

Preheat oven to 375°F (190°C).

Using a fork, prick the dough of each tart in several places (this prevents the dough from buckling when heated). Cover each tart with parchment paper or foil and fill to the top with pie weights.

Place the tart shells on a baking tray, spaced apart, and bake for 20 minutes in the preheated oven, rotating the baking tray once to promote even browning. Remove the tarts from the oven and remove the parchment (or foil) and pie weights. Bake, uncovered, for another 5–10 minutes, or just until the pastry is cooked through, tenting with foil if necessary to prevent burning.

Cool on a wire rack. Do not remove the tart pans.

CUSTARD

Heat the milk in a medium saucepan and stir in about 2 Tbsp + 1 tsp (40 mL) granulated sugar. Bring to a simmer, then remove the pan from the heat.

Combine the yolks in a small bowl with 2 Tbsp + 1 tsp (40 mL) granulated sugar and whisk until smooth. Add the flour and mix until well incorporated (the mixture will be very thick at this stage). Thin with half the warm milk, mix well, then pour the mixture back into the saucepan.

. . . recipe continued

Stir constantly over medium heat with a small whisk or a wooden spoon; the mixture will thicken as it cooks. When the custard comes to a boil, stir for a continuous minute, then remove from the heat and transfer to a medium bowl large enough to include the whipped egg whites (added later). Once the custard has cooled, cover with plastic wrap and refrigerate.

CHOCOLATE

Place a heat-resistant bowl over a saucepan filled with about 1 inch (2.5 cm) of simmering water. The bottom of the bowl should not touch the water. Place the chocolate in the bowl. Once the chocolate starts to melt, turn off the heat and continue stirring until it has melted completely.

MERINGUE

Preheat oven to 350°F (175°C).

Using an electric mixer, whisk the egg whites with a pinch of cream of tartar at medium speed in a meticulously clean bowl until a network of tiny bubbles has formed, about 1 full minute. Gradually add 3 Tbsp (45 mL) granulated sugar and increase the speed to high, whipping until the whites have expanded and formed firm, billowy, glossy peaks. Be mindful not to overwhip, otherwise the whites will turn grainy and lose their shape.

PUTTING IT ALL TOGETHER

Spread about 2 Tbsp (30 mL) of the melted chocolate over the base of each tart.

Remix the custard with a firm plastic spatula or wooden spoon; the mixture will be thick at this stage. (If you have an emulsion blender, you can use it to mix the custard.) Gently fold the meringue into the bowl of custard in 3–4 batches, mixing until well incorporated. Add the remaining melted chocolate and fold into the mixture until there are no dark streaks.

Divide the mixture between the tart shells and smooth the custard with the back of a spoon. Place the tarts on a baking tray, spaced apart, and bake in the preheated oven for about 30 minutes, or until the filling rises and is cooked through.

Cool on a wire rack and allow to rest for at least 20 minutes before serving. The tarts will deflate slightly as they cool. Serve warm or at room temperature with a dusting of powdered sugar, if desired. If serving warm, the filling will be slightly moist in the centre.

CHOCOLATE LINZER TARTLETS

YIELD

Makes about twelve 3- to 3½-inch (8–9 cm) tarts

PASTRY

1 recipe Chocolate Linzer Dough (page 44), divided into 2 portions

1 large egg yolk

2 Tbsp (30 mL) whipping cream

1 Tbsp (15 mL) powdered (icing) sugar

FILLING

2½ cups (625 mL) raspberry or apricot jam

SPECIAL EQUIPMENT

Twelve 3- to 3½-inch (8–9 cm) tart molds

24 baking cups or parchment paper, cut to fit the molds

Cookie cutter slightly smaller than your tart mold (for the top of the tarts)

Pie weights (or beans or rice)

THESE RICH, NUT-LADEN tarts originate from Linz, Austria, and are considered one of the oldest documented pastries. The fact they're still around is a testament to their widespread appeal.

Traditionally a jam-filled torte with a lattice topping, or a cookie sandwich with a cut-out for the jam to peer though, these tarts have all the goodness of a conventional cinnamon-spiced Linzer torte plus the bonus of grated dark chocolate.

Although reminiscent of holiday flavours, they are to be enjoyed year-round. And they freeze beautifully.

PASTRY

Line the tart molds with half the paper baking cups or parchment paper cut to size (the balance of the baking cups/parchment will be used later). The molds need to be completely covered with paper, otherwise you won't be able to release the tarts without breaking them (it's fine if your paper overlaps the molds).

Prepare the pastry and place one portion of dough onto a sheet of parchment paper dusted with flour. Layer a sheet of plastic wrap over the dough and roll (over the plastic) until it's approximately ¼ inch (6 mm) thick. Remove the plastic and cut the dough into 12 circles slightly larger than your tart molds using a cup or small bowl as a guide. Gather and re-roll the dough as necessary.

Carefully transfer the circles of dough with a spatula, or your hands, to the paper-lined molds. Use a scrap of plastic wrap to gently press the dough (through the plastic) against the base and edges of each mold, aiming for a uniform thickness. Once the tarts are lined with pastry they can be stacked in bundles of four and wrapped in plastic, so as not to take up too much room in the fridge. Refrigerate for at least 40 minutes.

PASTRY TOPS

Place the remaining portion of dough onto a sheet of parchment lightly dusted with flour. Layer plastic wrap over the dough and roll (over the plastic) until it's approximately ½ inch (6 mm) thick.

Stamp out 12 circles of dough (I use a fluted cookie cutter) slightly smaller than the tart molds, so the "lids" fit neatly into the tarts (see image). Stamp a small hole, or cut a vent, in the middle of each circle. If desired, decorate with additional impressions (dots), using a skewer. Place the circles of dough on a plate or platter with the parchment beneath and wrap in plastic. Alternatively, stack with layers of parchment between each circle and wrap in plastic. Refrigerate for 40 minutes.

. . . recipe continued

. . . Chocolate Linzer Tartlets (cont.)

FILLING

Pour the jam into a saucepan and cook over medium-low heat, stirring occasionally, until slightly reduced. The jam should hold its shape somewhat; it should not be loose or runny. Jams vary in consistency, so keep your eye on the saucepan and be mindful that jam can easily burn. You'll need about 1½ cups (375 mL) of thickened jam. Cool completely before using.

PASTRY BOTTOMS

Preheat oven to 350°F (175°C).

Retrieve the pastry-lined molds from the fridge and, using a fork, prick the dough in several places along the base and edges of each tart.

Cover each pastry-lined mold with a baking cup or parchment cut to size and fill with pie weights. Bake in the preheated oven for 15 minutes. Remove from the oven, carefully remove the parchment and pie weights and return to the oven until cooked through, about another 5 minutes.

Cool completely on a wire rack. The tarts will puff slightly from the oven then deflate as they cool. Leave the oven at 350°F (175°C) for the next step.

PUTTING IT ALL TOGETHER

Spread the thickened jam on the base of the cooled, partially baked tarts. You'll need about 2 Tbsp (30 mL) filling for each.

In a small bowl, mix together the egg yolk and whipping cream. Retrieve the 12 circles of dough from the fridge and cover the jam with the pastry "lids." Brush the lids and edges with the yolk/cream mixture. Place the tarts on a platter or tray, cover loosely with plastic wrap and firm in the fridge or freezer for 15 minutes.

Bake half a batch at a time on a parchment- or foil-lined baking tray in the preheated oven for 20–30 minutes or until the pastry is cooked through. Tent loosely with foil and turn the baking tray once during baking.

Cool on a wire rack. Lightly dust with powdered sugar dispensed through a fine-mesh strainer.

If freezing, omit the powdered sugar.

CUSTARD & CREAM

CARAMEL CRÈME BRÛLÉE TARTS

YIELD

Makes twelve 2½-inch (6 cm) tarts or eight 4-inch (10 cm) tarts

PASTRY

1 recipe Sweet Tart Dough (page 38), only half the dough needed

CUSTARD

1½ cups (375 mL) whipping cream

¼ cup (60 mL) granulated sugar + additional sugar for torching

4 large egg yolks

SPECIAL EQUIPMENT

Twelve 2½-inch (6 cm) or eight 4-inch (10 cm) tart molds

24 baking cups or parchment paper, cut to fit the molds (for 12 tarts)*

Pie weights (or beans or rice)

Shallow 2- to 3-cup (500–750 mL) ramekin (use more than one as necessary)

Baking dish deep enough to hold the ramekins

Fine-mesh strainer, fitted over a bowl or jug

Basting brush

Blowtorch (see note, page 255)

---

* If making 8 tarts, you'll need 16 baking cups.

IF YOU LOVE custard, you'll be smitten by these velvety crème brûlée tarts fashioned in buttery pastry shells. The custard is laced with caramel and torched before serving, creating a topping that shatters with every bite.

The tart shells and custard are baked separately and can be prepared up to three days in advance, although you'll want to assemble them just before serving. Recipes with few ingredients are often heavy on technique, but don't let the length of this recipe put you off—the detailed instructions will help you along.

PASTRY

Line the tart molds with half the paper baking cups or parchment paper cut to size (the balance will be used later). The molds need to be *completely* covered with paper, otherwise you won't be able to release the tarts without breaking them (it's fine if your paper overlaps the molds).

Prepare the pastry and place one portion of dough onto a sheet of parchment paper dusted with flour. Layer a sheet of plastic wrap over the dough and roll (over the plastic) until it's approximately ⅛ inch (3 mm) thick. Remove the plastic and cut the dough into circles slightly larger than your tart molds using a cup or small bowl as a guide.

Carefully transfer the circles of dough with a spatula, or your hands, to the paper-lined molds.

Use a scrap of plastic wrap to gently press the dough (through the plastic) against the base and edges of each mold, aiming for a uniform thickness. The tarts need to be refrigerated for at least 20 minutes before baking. Either stack the parchment-lined tart molds in groups of three or four and wrap in plastic, or, if you have the refrigerator space, place them on a baking tray and cover with plastic wrap.

Preheat oven to 375°F (190°C).

Retrieve the tart molds from the fridge and pierce the base and sides of each pastry with the tines of a fork. Cover each with a baking cup or square of parchment and fill with pie weights to the top of the mold. Place the tarts on a baking tray, leaving plenty of room between each.

Bake for 20 minutes in the preheated oven, rotating the baking tray once to ensure the tarts bake evenly. Remove the tarts from the oven and carefully remove the pie weights and baking cups or parchment. Return the tarts to the oven and continue to bake, uncovered, for another 5–7 minutes, or until the pastry is browned and cooked through.

Cool on a baking rack and do not remove the molds until the tarts have completely cooled.

. . . recipe continued

CUSTARD

As custard involves cooked sugar (caramel), you'll want to read the instructions to the end before you start. The custard is baked in a "water bath" to prevent it from cracking or drying in the oven (the water keeps the oven air moist). Line the baking dish with a dish towel to insulate and secure the ramekins.

Heat the whipping cream in a small saucepan, just until it starts to boil, then remove from the heat.

Pour the sugar into a deep saucepan and moisten with 2 Tbsp (30 mL) water. Cook the sugar over medium heat until it melts, bubbles and eventually turns deep golden, about 7–10 minutes. As the sugar boils, you'll notice tiny bits of sugar sticking to the sides of the pan; dip your basting brush in water to remove them and prevent the sugar from crystallizing. When the sugar has turned deep gold, remove the pan from the heat and swiftly and carefully pour the warm cream into the sugar. The mixture will bubble madly; when it subsides, stir the mixture. If bits of caramel stick to the bottom, return the caramel cream to the heat and stir until the caramel has completely dissolved.

In a large bowl, whisk the egg yolks until completely smooth, then add half a cup of warm caramel cream and stir until combined. Add the remaining caramel cream in a narrow stream, whisking until well combined. Strain the custard.

Bring a kettle of water to a boil. Place the ramekins in the prepared baking dish and position near the oven (for easy transport). Pour the strained custard into the ramekins. Pour the hot water into the baking dish around the ramekins, until the water reaches halfway up its sides, being careful not to splash water into the custard (see image at the bottom of the page).

Cover the baking dish with foil, then poke about a dozen scattered holes into the foil with a skewer or knife tip. Carefully transfer the baking dish to the oven and bake for about 25 minutes, rotating the pan halfway during baking. The deeper the ramekin, the longer it takes for the custard to cook. You'll need to check the custard now and again.

Remove the custard from the oven when it's barely set and the centre is ever-so-slightly wobbly. Transfer to a rack to cool before covering with plastic wrap. Chill in the refrigerator for at least 3 hours or up to 3 days.

PUTTING IT ALL TOGETHER

Up to an hour before serving, spoon the chilled custard into the baked tart shells and smooth the tops with the back of a spoon or an offset palette knife.

Just before serving, scatter each custard with a generous spoonful of sugar, enough to cover the entire tart with a fine layer. Tilt the tarts from side to side to disperse the sugar. Using a blowtorch, "burn" the sugar until the top of each custard is nicely browned.

Serve on a platter or individual plates.

BRÛLÉEING

You can find crème brûlée torches at cookware stores, but an all-purpose propane torch (available at hardware stores) does a better job. The idea is to brûlée (burn) the sugar quickly, without melting the custard. For this you need a fast, consistent flame. In a pinch, you can use your oven's broiler, but it's difficult to control the heat. (A BBQ starter will not work.)

Once baked and chilled, crème brûlée can also be portioned into tea cups and torched before serving, as featured on the opposite page.

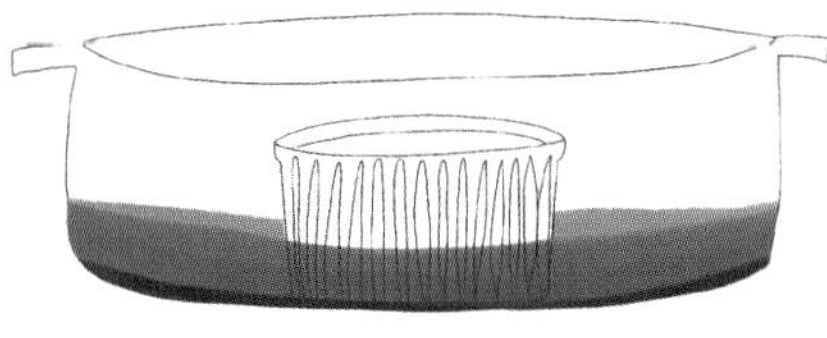

TARTE AU SUCRE

YIELD

Makes one 8-inch (20 cm) pie

PASTRY

1 recipe Flaky Pastry Dough (page 32), divided into 2 portions

FILLING

1 cup (250 mL) firmly packed golden (light) brown sugar

⅓ cup (80 mL) all-purpose flour

½ cup (125 mL) whipping cream + extra to brush the pastry

SPECIAL EQUIPMENT

Shallow 8-inch (20 cm) pie plate or a tart pan with a removable base

TARTE AU SUCRE (or sugar pie) is a French Canadian tradition, much like tourtière. It has a rich, creamy, caramel-like filling that is absolutely habit-forming.

This cherished family recipe, generously shared by Julie Beauchamp (my cousin's wife), has been passed down from generations of Quebécois. My husband, a self-proclaimed sugar pie authority, assures me this version is the finest he's ever tasted.

At one time, tarte au sucre was made exclusively with maple syrup, but many versions, including this one, feature brown sugar.

PASTRY

PASTRY BASE: Prepare the pastry and place one portion of dough onto a sheet of parchment paper dusted with flour. Layer a sheet of plastic wrap over the dough and roll (over the plastic) from the centre toward the pastry's edge in all directions, forming a 10-inch (25 cm) circle about ⅛ inch (3 mm) thick.

Drape the dough onto your rolling pin and transfer to the pie plate, being mindful not to pull or stretch the dough. Gently press the dough into the sides of the pie plate and trim the edges. Cover with plastic wrap and refrigerate for at least 40 minutes.

PASTRY TOP: Place the remaining portion of dough onto a sheet of parchment paper dusted with flour. Place a sheet of plastic wrap over the dough and roll (over the plastic) from the centre toward the pastry's edge in all directions, forming a 10-inch (25 cm) circle about ⅛ inch (3 mm) thick. Using a sharp knife, cut the dough into 9 strips about ¾ inch (2 cm) wide each. Transfer the strips, and the parchment beneath them, to a plate or tray. Cover with plastic and refrigerate for at least 40 minutes.

FILLING

In a medium bowl, mix the sugar, flour and whipping cream to combine.

PUTTING IT ALL TOGETHER

Pour the filling into the (chilled) pastry base. The filling expands as it cooks, so it should not come all the way to the top of the rim. (Otherwise you'll have a mess in the oven.)

Carefully place the pastry strips over the filling, side by side, being mindful not to pull or stretch the dough. Brush the pastry strips with a bit of whipping cream, loosely cover with plastic wrap and firm in the fridge, or freezer, for 15 minutes.

Preheat a foil- or parchment-lined baking tray in a 425°F (220°C) oven. Bake for 15 minutes, reduce the heat to 350°F (175°C) and bake until the pastry is cooked through, about 30 minutes.

Cool on a wire rack. The filling will firm slightly as it cools but will remain soft.

CHEESECAKE TART

YIELD

Makes one 13¾- × 4¼-inch (35 × 12 cm) tart

PASTRY

1 recipe Hazelnut Tart Crust (page 45)

FILLING

One 8½ oz (250 g) brick Philadelphia-style cream cheese (original, not light)

1 cup (250 mL) whipping cream

¼ cup + 3 Tbsp (105 mL) granulated sugar

1½ Tbsp (22 mL) all-purpose flour

¼ tsp (1 mL) table salt

2 large egg yolks

1½ Tbsp (22 mL) freshly squeezed lemon juice

TOPPING

2 cups (500 mL) fresh (or frozen and thawed) berries

Blackberry Coulis (optional; page 298)

SPECIAL EQUIPMENT

13¾- × 4¾-inch (35 × 12 cm) or 11- × 7-inch (28 × 18 cm) tart pan with a removable base

Pie weights (or beans or rice)

A BUTTERY HAZELNUT crust made with whole wheat flour and honey forms the base of this classic cheesecake tart. The cream cheese filling comes together easily and the crust can be made ahead of time.

The baked tart freezes well, although the nutty pastry loses some of its crunch. Some cheesecake lovers (like me) actually prefer a softer, more yielding crust. Either way, this tart never disappoints.

Delicious with fresh berries and a splash of Blackberry Coulis (page 298), Ginger Spiced Peaches (page 297) or Rhubarb Strawberry Compote (page 297).

PASTRY

Prepare the Hazelnut Tart Crust and refrigerate.

Preheat oven to 350°F (175°C).

Once the crust has chilled, prick the pastry in several places using a fork. Cover with parchment or foil and fill with pie weights. Bake for 20 minutes, rotating the pan once during baking, then remove the foil and weights and bake for 5 additional minutes until the tart shell is nearly cooked.

Cool on a wire rack. Do not remove the tart pan.

FILLING

Blend together the cream cheese and whipping cream either in the bowl of a stand mixer (fitted with the paddle attachment) or a medium bowl, scraping down the sides as necessary. Add the sugar, flour and salt and mix until combined. Add the yolks, one at a time, mixing after each addition. Add the lemon juice and mix until combined.

PUTTING IT ALL TOGETHER

Place the baked tart shell onto a baking tray lined with foil or parchment paper. Pour the cheese filling into the shell, nearly to the top of the pastry. Leftover filling can be poured into baking cups and cooked alongside the cheesecake.

Tent the edges of the crust with aluminum foil (or pie shields) to prevent them from burning. Bake until the cheese filling has firmed, about 25 minutes, rotating the pan once during baking.

Cool and refrigerate for at least 4 hours before serving. Serve with fresh berries and, if desired, a Blackberry Coulis on the side.

LABNEH TART

YIELD

Makes one 10½-inch (26 cm) tart

PASTRY

1 recipe Roasted Almond Dough (page 43)

FILLING

2¼ cups (530 mL) labneh (recipe follows)

½ cup (125 mL) honey

3 large eggs, room temperature

½ cup (125 mL) melted unsalted butter (about 115 g), cooled to room temperature

Zest from 1 lemon

TOPPING

Ginger Spiced Peaches (page 297) or Rhubarb Strawberry Compote (page 297)

2 Tbsp (30 mL) shelled pistachios (optional)

SPECIAL EQUIPMENT

10½-inch (26 cm) tart pan with a removable base

Pie weights (or beans or rice)

LABNEH (PRONOUNCED LEB-neigh), strained yogurt, is a revelation to those who've never experienced it. The Middle Eastern staple transforms everyday yogurt into a thick tangy spread with a soft cheese-like texture.

Traditional labneh is made by straining yogurt 36–48 hours with a weight to compress it, or by hanging yogurt in a cotton sack over a bowl to catch the liquid (whey). In this simplified version, yogurt is strained overnight through a fine-mesh strainer lined with cheesecloth.

For this tart, labneh is enriched with eggs and honey and baked in a thick, buttery, roasted almond pastry. Garnished with pistachios and served with Ginger Spiced Peaches (page 297), this tart will transport you to another land.

PASTRY

Prepare the Roasted Almond Dough and refrigerate.

Preheat oven to 350°F (175°C).

Once the dough has chilled, prick the pastry in several places using a fork. Cover with parchment or foil and fill with pie weights. Place the tart on a baking tray and bake for 20 minutes or until lightly browned around the edges. Remove the pie weights and bake for another 20 minutes; tent loosely with foil as necessary to prevent burning. Cool completely on a wire rack.

FILLING

In a medium bowl, whisk together the labneh, honey, eggs, butter and lemon zest until smooth.

PUTTING IT ALL TOGETHER

Place the cooled pastry on a baking tray. Pour in the labneh filling to fill the pastry, smoothing the top with the back of a spoon or spatula.

Bake in the preheated oven until the filling has set, about 30 minutes, rotating the tray once during baking. Tent with foil as necessary to prevent the edges from burning.

Cool completely on a wire rack. Serve at room temperature with Ginger Spiced Peaches or Rhubarb Compote and garnish with pistachios, if desired.

. . . recipe continued

Labneh | Makes about 3½ cups (875 mL)

The Labneh Tart only requires 2¼ cups (560 mL) labneh, but you can use leftover labneh as you would any soft cheese—it's terrific paired with tapenade, oven-roasted tomatoes or drizzled with olive oil and sprinkled with dukkah (an herb, nut and spice mixture). Labneh can be mixed into dips and sauces (see Tangy Dill Sauce, page 304), or combined with cream for a sweet-tart topping (see Whipped Labneh, page 300).

Two 650 mL tubs full-fat 10-11% Greek-style plain yogurt (1.3 L total)

Place a fine-mesh strainer over a bowl so that it rests 2–3 inches (5–8 cm) above the bottom. Line the strainer with a double layer of cheesecloth. Spoon the yogurt into the lined strainer, cover with plastic wrap and refrigerate overnight. Transfer to a lidded container and refrigerate.

NOTE: You'll be left with a fair bit of liquid (whey), but don't discard it. *Yogurt Culture* author Cheryl Sternman Rule suggests adding the nutritious whey to smoothies, bread dough, pancake batter or marinades to help tenderize meats, to name a few.

GRAND MARNIER SOUFFLÉ TART

YIELD

Makes two 7½-inch (19 cm) tarts

PASTRY

1 recipe Sweet Tart Dough (page 38), divided into 2 portions

Powdered (icing) sugar, dispensed through a sieve

ALMOND CREAM

3 Tbsp (45 mL) unsalted butter (about 30 g)

3 Tbsp (45 mL) granulated sugar

¼ cup + 2 Tbsp (90 mL) ground almonds

1 large egg yolk, lightly beaten

2 Tbsp (30 mL) rum, cognac or Grand Marnier

CUSTARD

1½ cups (375 mL) whole or 2% milk

⅓ cup (80 mL) granulated sugar, divided

3 large egg yolks

3 Tbsp (45 mL) all-purpose flour

MERINGUE

5 large egg whites

¼ tsp (1 mL) cream of tartar

3 Tbsp (45 mL) granulated sugar

SPECIAL EQUIPMENT

Two 7½-inch (19 cm) fluted tart pans with removable bases

IF YOU'RE LOOKING for a light and delicate dessert, look no further than this elegant soufflé tart laced with Grand Marnier. The melt-in-your-mouth filling sits atop a buttery cookie-like crust baked with a layer of almond cream (also called frangipane), a sweet nutty filling that's a staple ingredient in French patisseries.

If your tastes veer toward chocolate, check out the Chocolate Soufflé Tart (page 242). I sometimes make one of each, offering guests a taste of both.

Serve with fresh berries and a Blackberry Coulis (page 298), if desired.

ALMOND CREAM

In a small bowl, combine the butter, 3 Tbsp (45 mL) sugar, ground almonds, 1 egg yolk and liquor. Mix well to combine, cover and refrigerate.

PASTRY

Line the bases of the tart pans with parchment paper.

Prepare the pastry and place one portion of dough onto a sheet of parchment paper dusted with flour. Layer a sheet of plastic wrap over the dough and roll (over the plastic) from the centre toward the pastry's edge in all directions until about ⅛ inch (3 mm) thick.

Drape the dough over your rolling pin (or use your hands) to transfer the dough to one of the tart pans, plastic wrap facing up. (It's easier to press the dough into the tart mold if you leave the plastic wrap intact.) If the pastry breaks, use your hands to press the dough, piecemeal if necessary, into the pan and along the sides. Press the dough into the sides of the tart with your fingers and trim any excess dough. If desired, use a flat-bottom cup to level the pastry. Refrigerate for at least 20 minutes.

Repeat the process with the remaining portion of dough for the second tart.

Preheat oven to 375°F (190°C).

Using a fork, prick the each pastry in several places (this prevents the dough from buckling when heated). Divide the almond cream between the tarts and smooth the mixture evenly with a spatula or an offset palette knife.

Place the tarts on a baking tray and bake for 15–20 minutes in the preheated oven, or just until the pastry base is lightly toasted, tenting the foil as necessary to prevent burning. The pastry will puff slightly in the centre but later deflate.

Cool on a wire rack, and turn the oven off. Do not remove the tart molds.

... recipe continued

. . . Grand Marnier Soufflé Tart (cont.)

CUSTARD

Heat the milk in a medium saucepan and stir in about 2 Tbsp + 2 tsp (40 mL) sugar. Bring to a simmer, then remove the pan from the heat.

Combine the yolks in a small bowl with the remaining 2 Tbsp + 2 tsp (40 mL) sugar and whisk until smooth. Add the flour and mix until well incorporated (the mixture will be very thick at this stage). Thin with half the warm milk, mix well, then pour the mixture back into the saucepan.

Stir constantly over medium heat with a small whisk or wooden spoon; the mixture will thicken as it cooks. When the custard comes to a boil, stir for a continuous minute, then remove from the heat and transfer to a bowl. Once the custard has cooled, cover with plastic wrap and refrigerate up to 3 days.

MERINGUE

Whisk the egg whites with the cream of tartar in a meticulously clean bowl at medium speed until a network of tiny bubbles has formed, about 1 full minute. Gradually add 3 Tbsp (45 mL) sugar and increase the speed to high; whip until the whites have expanded and formed billowy, firm, glossy peaks. Be mindful not to overwhip, otherwise the whites will turn grainy and lose their shape.

PUTTING IT ALL TOGETHER

Reheat oven to 350°F (175°C).

Remix the custard in a large bowl with a firm plastic spatula or a wooden spoon spatula; the mixture will be thick at this stage. (If you have an emulsion blender, you can use it to mix the custard.)

Gently fold the meringue mixture into the bowl of custard in 3–4 batches, mixing until well incorporated. Divide the mixture between the tart shells and smooth the custard with the back of a spoon. Place on a baking tray, spaced apart, and bake for about 30 minutes or until the filling has risen and the tops are golden.

Cool on a wire rack and allow to rest at least 30 minutes before serving. The fillings will deflate slightly as they cool. Can be served warm or at room temperature with a dusting of powdered sugar, if desired. If serving warm, the filling will be slightly moist in the centre.

GÂTEAU BASQUE

YIELD

Makes one 9-inch (23 cm) Gâteau Basque

PASTRY

1 recipe Gâteau Pastry Dough (page 49), divided into 2 portions

1 large egg yolk, lightly mixed

2 Tbsp (30 mL) powdered (icing) sugar (optional)

CUSTARD FILLING

1½ cups (375 mL) whole milk

Seeds from 1 vanilla bean, or ½ Tbsp (7.5 mL) vanilla extract

3 large egg yolks, room temperature

⅓ cup (80 mL) granulated sugar

¼ cup (60 mL) all-purpose flour

¼ cup + 2 Tbsp (90 mL) ground almonds

2 Tbsp (30 mL) rum

2 Tbsp (30 mL) unsalted butter (about 30 g)

¾ cup (185 mL) Cranberry Relish (page 298), brandied cherries or your favourite jam or preserve

SPECIAL EQUIPMENT

9-inch (23 cm) cake pan

GÂTEAU BASQUE IS where pie and cake intersect. The sweet egg-enriched dough is mixed like cookie dough, rolled out like a pie dough and cooks up like a cake.

A dessert from the Basque region of France, it is traditionally made with cherry preserves. In this version, a tart cranberry relish enriches the sweet almond custard filling.

Each component—the pastry, custard and relish—can be made up to three days in advance.

PASTRY

Butter the base and sides of the cake pan and line with parchment paper (the butter helps the parchment stick).

BASE: Prepare the pastry and place one portion of dough onto a sheet of parchment paper dusted with flour. Layer a sheet of plastic wrap over the dough and roll (over the plastic) from the centre toward the pastry's edge in all directions, forming a circle about ⅛ inch (3 mm) thick. Remove the plastic and cut the dough into a 9-inch (23 cm) circle using a plate as a template. Drape the dough over a rolling pin and transfer to the cake pan. Gather and re-roll the remaining dough. Cut 3 strips that are each 1½ inches (4 cm) wide, 10 inches (25 cm) long and ⅛ inch (3 mm) thick; if you don't have enough dough, use some from the second portion of dough. Line the sides of the pan with the strips, pressing them into place with your fingers and trimming any excess dough. Cover with plastic wrap and refrigerate for at least 40 minutes.

TOP: Transfer the remaining dough onto a sheet of parchment dusted with flour. Layer plastic wrap over the dough and roll (over the plastic) from the centre toward the pastry's edge in all directions until about ⅛ inch (3 mm) thick. Remove the plastic and cut the dough into another 9-inch (23 cm) circle for the pastry's top. Transfer the circle of dough and the parchment beneath it to a plate or tray. Wrap in plastic and refrigerate for at least 40 minutes.

CUSTARD FILLING

Combine the milk and vanilla bean seeds (or vanilla extract) in a small saucepan. Bring to a simmer, then remove the pan from the heat.

Combine 3 egg yolks and the granulated sugar in a small bowl and whisk until smooth. Add the flour and mix until well incorporated (the mixture will be very thick at this stage). Thin with half the warm milk, mix well and pour the mixture back into the saucepan. Add the ground almonds and rum and mix together. Simmer for 1 minute, mixing continuously. Remove from the heat and whisk in the butter.

Transfer to a bowl and cover with plastic wrap. When the custard has cooled, refrigerate up to 2 days.

. . . recipe continued

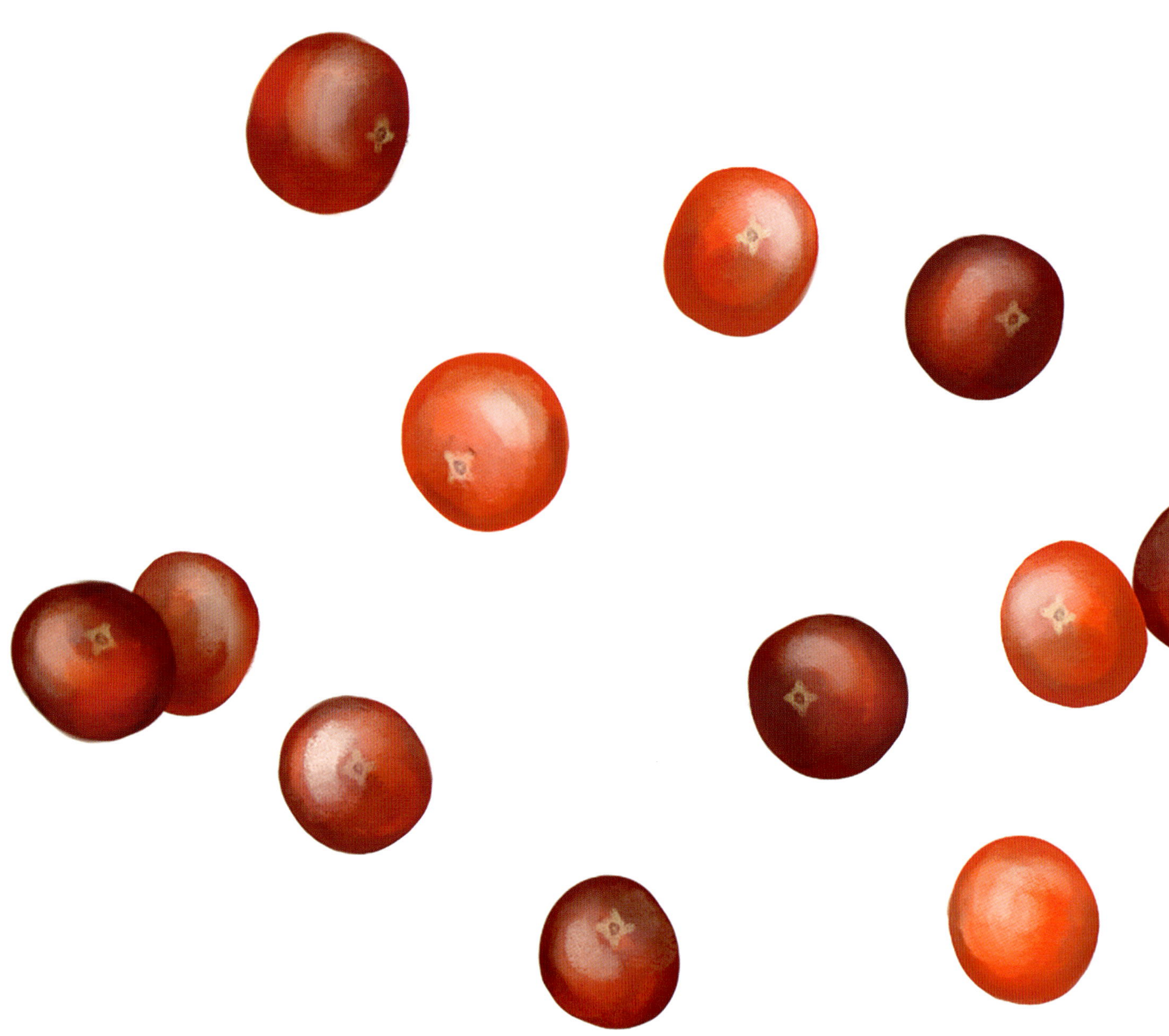

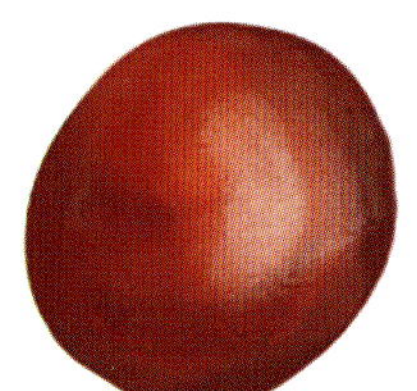

... *Gâteau Basque (cont.)*

PUTTING IT ALL TOGETHER

Retrieve the pastry-lined cake pan from the fridge and fill the pastry with half the chilled custard, smoothing the mixture with an offset spatula so that the custard reaches the edges of the pastry. The custard will be very thick.

Dot the Cranberry Relish (or preferred filling) over the custard, leaving a 1-inch (2.5 cm) border. Top with the remaining custard, smoothing the mixture with an offset spatula so that the custard reaches the edges of the pastry.

If a bit of the pastry that's lining the sides of the pan protrudes above the custard, fold it over the custard—this makes it neater and more level when adding the pastry top. Dab the folded pastry with a bit of egg yolk, which helps the pastry top adhere to it.

Transfer the remaining circle of pastry to the custard, pressing the dough along the edges to seal. Brush the top with the remaining yolk. If desired, etch a cross-hatch pattern into the dough using the tines of a fork. Cover loosely with plastic wrap and firm in the fridge for 40 minutes.

Preheat a baking tray in a 375°F (190°C) oven.

Bake the gâteau on the preheated baking tray for 40–50 minutes until the pastry has risen slightly and cooked through.

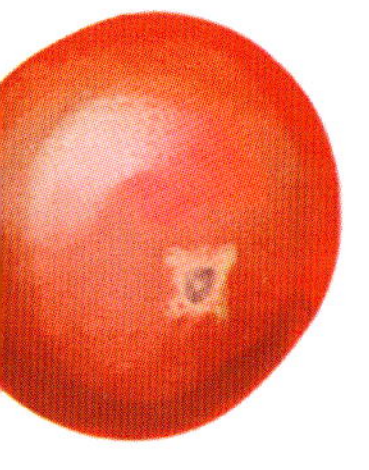

Cool on a wire rack in the cake pan, and don't remove until the gâteau has cooled. It will fall slightly as it cools.

To remove the pan, place a plate on top of the pastry and, using both hands, flip the pastry over so that the bottom of the cake pan is facing up. Carefully remove the cake pan. Top with another plate and flip the pastry again, so the gâteau faces the right side up. Now give yourself a pat on the back.

If desired, dust with powdered sugar before serving.

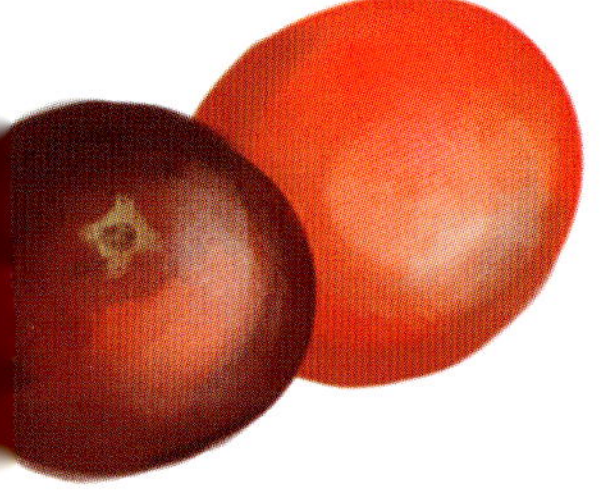

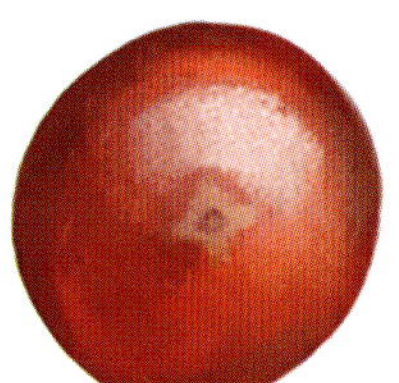

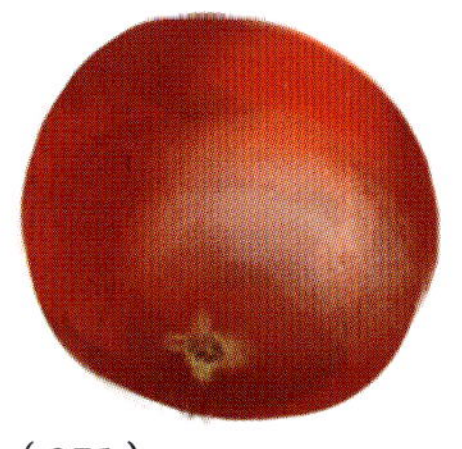

CITRUS

LEMON MERINGUE TARTLETS

YIELD

Makes twelve 4-inch (10 cm) tarts

PASTRY

1 recipe Lemon Almond Dough (page 47)

LEMON CURD

¾ cup (185 mL) freshly squeezed lemon juice (about 3 lemons)

¾ cup (185 mL) granulated sugar

¼ cup + 2 Tbsp (90 mL) unsalted butter (about 85 g), room temperature

7 large egg yolks

MERINGUE

7 large egg whites

1⅓ cups + 2 tsp (340 mL) granulated sugar

¼ tsp (1 mL) table salt

¼ tsp (1 mL) cream of tartar

SPECIAL EQUIPMENT

Twelve 4-inch (10 cm) tart molds

24 baking cups or parchment paper, cut to fit the molds

Pie weights (or beans or rice)

Candy thermometer

Blowtorch*

* You can also toast the meringue under a broiler, but a torch provides more control.

TANGY LEMON CURD and burnished meringue partner with a cookie-like crust in these classic tarts. Made with freshly ground almonds and flecked with lemon zest, the pastry lends a nutty citrus note.

Meringue is easy to prepare but does not behave well in humid conditions—it can turn soft and sticky, so let the weather be your guide.

PASTRY

Line the tart molds with half the paper baking cups or parchment paper cut to size (the balance will be used later). The molds need to be *completely* covered with paper, otherwise you won't be able to release the tarts without breaking them (it's fine if your paper overlaps the molds).

Prepare the pastry and place the dough onto a sheet of parchment paper dusted with flour. Layer a sheet of plastic wrap over the dough and roll (over the plastic) until approximately ⅛ inch (3 mm) thick. Remove the plastic and cut the dough into circles slightly larger than your tart molds using a cup or a small bowl as a guide.

Carefully transfer the circles of dough with a spatula, or your hands, to the paper-lined molds. Use a scrap of plastic wrap to gently press the dough against the base and edges of each mold, aiming for a uniform thickness. The tarts need to be refrigerated for at least 30 minutes before baking. Either stack the parchment-lined tart molds in groups of three or four and wrap in plastic, or, if you have the refrigerator space, place them on a baking tray and cover with plastic wrap.

Preheat oven to 350°F (175°C).

Retrieve the tart molds from the fridge and pierce the base and sides of each pastry with the tines of a fork. Cover each with a baking cup or square of parchment and fill with pie weights to the top of the mold. Place the tarts on a baking tray, leaving plenty of room between each.

Bake for 20 minutes in the preheated oven, rotating the baking tray once during baking to ensure the tarts bake evenly. Remove the tarts from the oven and carefully remove the pie weights and baking cups or parchment. Return to the oven and continue to bake, uncovered, for another 5–7 minutes or until the pastry is browned and cooked through. Cool on a baking rack and do not remove the molds, or peel off the parchment, until the tarts have completely cooled.

LEMON CURD

In a small saucepan, combine the lemon juice, ¾ cup (185 mL) sugar and the butter. Bring to a boil and remove from the heat.

In a medium bowl, whisk the egg yolks. Slowly add the hot lemon juice mixture and whisk to combine. Return the mixture to the saucepan and cook over medium heat until the mixture thickens and comes to a boil, about 2–3 minutes.

. . . recipe continued

. . . Lemon Meringue Tartlets (cont.)

Cool for a few minutes, then distribute evenly among the chilled tart shells. Refrigerate while preparing the meringue.

MERINGUE

Before you start, you'll want to ensure that your mixing bowl and whisk are meticulously clean and perfectly dry. Any residue of fat (traces of yolk, butter or oil) will compromise the meringue.

Place the metal bowl of a stand mixer, or a deep heat-resistant mixing bowl, over a saucepan of simmering water. The water should not touch the bowl. (Have a dry towel or pot holder handy to grasp the hot bowl.) Place the egg whites, 1⅓ cups + 2 tsp (340 mL) sugar and the salt and cream of tartar in the bowl and clip the thermometer onto the side, ensuring it reaches the egg whites. Mix the whites with a spatula, stirring constantly until the mixture reaches 175°F (80°C). (The whites will not expand at this stage.)

Remove the bowl from the heat and whisk with an electric mixer at high speed until billowy and satiny, being mindful not to overwhip the meringue. This can take up to 6 minutes.

Place a generous dollop of meringue onto each tart, using your spoon to spread it to the tart's edge. Create peaks by dipping the spoon into the meringue, then lifting. Use a torch to gently toast the meringue. Alternatively, place the tarts briefly under the broiler, watching them carefully to avoid burning.

Best served the same day they're made.

RED RUBY GRAPEFRUIT TART

YIELD

Makes one 9½-inch (23 cm) tart

PASTRY

1 recipe Sweet Tart Dough (page 38), only half the dough needed

1 large egg yolk, lightly beaten, for brushing the pastry

CUSTARD

1¼ cups (310 mL) freshly squeezed Ruby Red grapefruit juice, strained (about 2 large grapefruits)

½ cup (125 mL) granulated sugar, divided

One 1 Tbsp (15 mL) pkg unflavoured gelatin powder

4 large egg yolks

Juice of 1 lemon (about 3 Tbsp/ 45 mL), strained

½ cup (125 mL) unsalted butter (about 115 g), cut into 1-inch (2.5 cm) pieces

CITRUS JELLY

1¼ cups (310 mL) freshly squeezed Red Ruby grapefruit juice, strained (about 2 large grapefruits)

2 Tbsp (30 mL) granulated sugar

One 1 Tbsp (15 mL) pkg unflavoured gelatin powder

SPECIAL EQUIPMENT

9½-inch (23 cm) fluted tart pan with a removable base

Fine-mesh strainer

Pie weights (or beans or rice)

If you only consider grapefruit a breakfast food, this bracing tart will change your mind. With a silky tangy custard and sparking citrus jelly, grapefruit might become your go-to dessert.

I'm partial to Ruby Red grapefruit—the colour and flavour are more intense than other varieties, and I find them sweeter. Select grapefruits that are heavy for their size—the heavier, the juicier.

This tart holds up especially well in the fridge a day or two after it's baked—except in our house, where it disappears the day it's made. The recipe requires a bit of planning and patience, but if you love grapefruit it's well worth the effort. Be sure to read the entire recipe before you start.

PASTRY

Line the base of the tart pan with parchment paper.

Prepare the pastry and place the dough onto a sheet of parchment paper dusted with flour. Layer a sheet of plastic wrap over the dough and roll (over the plastic) from the centre toward the pastry's edge in all directions until about ⅛ inch (3 mm) thick.

Drape the dough over your rolling pin (or use your hands) to transfer the dough to the tart pan, plastic wrap facing up. (It's easier to press the dough into the pan if you leave the plastic wrap intact.) If the pastry breaks, use your hands to press the dough, piecemeal if necessary, into the pan and along the sides. Press the dough into the sides of the tart with your fingers and trim any excess dough. If desired, use a flat-bottomed cup to level the pastry. Refrigerate for at least 20 minutes.

Preheat oven to 375°F (190°C).

Retrieve the tart from the fridge and, using a fork, prick the dough along the base and sides (this prevents the dough from buckling when heated). Cover with parchment paper or foil and fill to the top with pie weights.

Transfer to a baking tray and bake for 20 minutes in the preheated oven, rotating the tray once to promote even browning. Remove the tart from the oven, remove the parchment or foil and the pie weights and brush the base with egg yolk. Bake uncovered for another 5–10 minutes, or just until the pastry is cooked through, covering with foil if necessary to prevent burning.

Cool on a wire rack. Do not remove the tart pan.

CUSTARD

Heat the grapefruit juice in a small saucepan with ¼ cup (60 mL) sugar and stir until the sugar has dissolved.

Pour 1 Tbsp (15 mL) gelatin powder into a measuring cup or small bowl. Add half the warm juice to the gelatin and stir well with a small whisk or fork until the gelatin has completely dissolved. Pour the gelatin/juice mixture back into the saucepan of grapefruit juice and stir to combine, off of the heat.

. . . recipe continued

. . . Red Ruby Grapefruit Tart (cont.)

In a small bowl, whisk together the 4 yolks with the lemon juice and ¼ cup (60 mL) sugar. Add about half the warmed juice to the yolk mixture to loosen it. Mix well and return the yolk mixture to the saucepan of grapefruit juice.

Bring the mixture to a low steady heat and whisk constantly for a few minutes, allowing the mixture to come to a very mild simmer. The idea is to gently cook the egg yolks without scrambling them. The mixture will thicken slightly (and the gelatin will do the rest of the firming). Remove the custard from the heat and add the butter, two or three pieces at a time, whisking after each addition until completely smooth.

Pour the custard through a fine-mesh strainer into a clean container. Allow to cool about 30 minutes (it should not be piping hot) before pouring the mixture into the baked and *cooled* pastry shell. The custard should form a flat layer. Carefully transfer the tart to the fridge, uncovered, on a shelf with easy access, as the citrus jelly will be poured over the tart while *in the fridge* to avoid any transport mishaps. The custard must be completely chilled and firmed before adding the layer of citrus jelly.

CITRUS JELLY

Heat the grapefruit juice in a small saucepan with 2 Tbsp (30 mL) sugar and stir until dissolved. Once the mixture is hot, turn off the heat.

Pour 1 Tbsp (15 mL) gelatin powder into a measuring cup or small bowl. Add about half of the hot grapefruit juice into the gelatin and stir well with a small whisk or fork until the gelatin is completely dissolved. Pour the gelatin/juice mixture back into the saucepan and stir until well combined.

Transfer to the fridge just long enough for the gelatin mixture to barely thicken. Set a timer at 5 minute intervals to keep an eye on it. If you leave the mixture too long, it will gel and you won't be able to pour it over the custard.

Once the citrus jelly has cooled and slightly thickened, pour it over the chilled and firmed custard while still in the fridge. This avoids having to transfer the not-yet-firmed gelatin from counter to fridge, which can easily spill over and ruin the smooth finish. Refrigerate uncovered for 1–2 hours until completely firm.

Remove the tart mold and serve on chilled plates, if desired.

LEMON CREAM TART

YIELD

Makes one 11-inch (28 cm) tart

PASTRY

1 recipe Sweet Tart Dough using the Lemon Variation (page 40), only half the dough needed

1 large egg yolk, lightly beaten, for brushing the pastry

2 Tbsp (30 mL) powdered (icing) sugar

LEMON CREAM FILLING

4 large eggs + 2 large yolks

¾ cup (185 mL) granulated sugar

¾ cup (185 mL) freshly squeezed lemon juice (about 4 large organic lemons)

¾ cup (185 mL) whipping cream, chilled

SPECIAL EQUIPMENT

One 11-inch (28 cm) tart pan with a removable base

Pie weights (or beans or rice)

THIS IS ONE of the lightest, most lemony tarts imaginable, a perfect blend of sweet cream and tangy citrus. It's a simple recipe with few ingredients, showcasing the sweet edge of lemon in every luscious bite.

PASTRY

Line the base of the tart pan with parchment paper.

Prepare the pastry and place the dough onto a sheet of parchment paper dusted with flour. Layer a sheet of plastic wrap over the dough and roll (over the plastic) from the centre toward the pastry's edge in all directions until about ⅛ inch (3 mm) thick.

Drape the dough over your rolling pin (or use your hands) to transfer the dough to the paper-lined tart pan with the plastic wrap facing up (it's easier to press the dough into the pan if you leave the plastic wrap intact). If the pastry breaks, use your hands to press the dough, piecemeal if necessary, into the pan and along the sides. Press the dough into the sides of the tart with your fingers and trim any excess dough. If desired, use a flat-bottomed cup to level the pastry. Refrigerate for at least 20 minutes.

Preheat oven to 375°F (190°C).

Retrieve the tart from the fridge and, using a fork, prick the dough along the base and sides (this prevents the dough from buckling when heated). Cover with parchment paper or foil and fill to the top with pie weights.

Transfer to a baking tray and bake for 20 minutes in the preheated oven, rotating the tray once to promote even browning. Remove the tart from the oven, remove the parchment or foil and pie weights and brush the base with egg yolk. Bake uncovered for another 5–10 minutes, or just until the pastry is cooked through, covering with foil if necessary to prevent burning.

Cool on a wire rack. Do not remove the tart pan.

LEMON CREAM FILLING

In a medium bowl, whisk together the whole eggs, 2 yolks and granulated sugar. Add the lemon juice and mix to combine.

In a separate medium bowl, whisk the whipping cream to a soft peak. Fold the whipping cream into the lemon mixture in 3 batches, using a spatula or large whisk until no white streaks remain. The whipping cream will deflate somewhat as you mix. Pour the mixture into a spouted container.

. . . recipe continued

. . . Lemon Cream Tart (cont.)

PUTTING IT ALL TOGETHER

Place the cooled baked tart shell on a baking tray lined with foil or parchment, positioned near the oven. Pour the lemon mixture into the tart shell.

Carefully transfer the tart to the preheated oven. Bake for 35–40 minutes until just set and slightly browning. You can tent the pie with foil if necessary once the filling sets, but don't do so beforehand as the filling tends to stick to the foil.

Cool on a wire rack. Serve at room temperate, dusted with powdered sugar, if desired.

TWO TART VARIATION: To make a pair of smaller tarts, divide the dough between two 7½-inch (19 cm) tart pans with removable bases. Follow the same steps as above, reducing the baking time slightly. You'll have a bit of leftover filling, which can be baked on its own in small ramekins.

MARMALADE MINI PIES

YIELD

Makes eight 4-inch (10 cm) tarts

PASTRY

1 recipe Flaky Pastry Dough made with unsalted butter (page 32), divided into 2 portions

1–2 Tbsp (15–30 mL) whipping cream, for brushing the pastry

1–2 Tbsp (15–30 mL) coarse raw or granulated sugar

FILLING

1 large organic lemon

1 large organic orange

¾ cup (185 mL) granulated sugar

2 large eggs

2 Tbsp (30 mL) cornstarch

OPTIONAL GARNISH

Candied Orange (optional; recipe follows)

SPECIAL EQUIPMENT

Eight 4-inch (10 cm) tart molds*

8 baking cups or parchment paper, cut to fit the molds

---

* If you don't have tart molds, use a 12-cup muffin pan with 3-inch (8 cm) wide pockets. Line the muffin pockets with parchment baking cups and cut the pastry to fit the molds.

IF YOU LOVE the sweet and bitter flavour of marmalade, you're sure to fall for these buttery tarts, made with fresh citrus fruit and garnished with candied orange slices.

The candied garnish needs to be prepared a day in advance. They're lovely with the tarts but also make a great cocktail garnish or sweet snack.

PASTRY

Line the tart molds with paper baking cups or parchment paper cut to size. The molds need to be completely covered with paper, otherwise you won't be able to release the tarts without breaking them (it's fine if your paper overlaps the molds).

Prepare the pastry and place the dough on a sheet of parchment dusted with flour. Layer a sheet of plastic wrap over the dough and roll (over the plastic) from the centre toward the pastry's edge in all directions until about ⅛ inch (3 mm) thick. Remove the plastic and cut the dough into 8 circles slightly larger than the tart molds using a small bowl or cup as a template. Transfer the circles to the parchment-lined molds, pressing the dough against the mold with your fingers and trimming the edges. The tarts need to be refrigerated at least 30 minutes before baking. Either stack the parchment-lined tart molds in 2 small bundles and wrap in plastic or, if you have the refrigerator space, place them on a baking tray and cover with plastic wrap.

Gather and re-roll the remaining dough and the second portion of dough and cut another 8 circles, the size of the mold rims, for the pastry tops. Stack between pieces of parchment, cover and refrigerate for at least 40 minutes.

FILLING

Bring a saucepan of water deep enough to cover the lemon and orange to a simmer. Place the fruit in the saucepan and cover with a small plate to keep the fruit submerged and prevent them from bobbing to the top. After 30 minutes, remove the lemon. Simmer the orange for another 30 minutes to tenderize the peel.

When the fruit is cool enough to handle, remove the stem ends with a sharp knife. Quarter the fruit and discard the seeds. Remove the peels from the lemon and orange, and, using a sharp knife, remove and discard the bitter white pith. Slice the peels into thin strips and transfer to a medium bowl. Roughly chop the orange and lemon flesh and add it to the bowl of thinly sliced peels. Add the sugar and mix to combine. Set aside for about 20 minutes to macerate (soften). Add the eggs and cornstarch and mix well.

. . . recipe continued

PUTTING IT ALL TOGETHER

Preheat a foil- or parchment-lined baking tray in a 425°F (220°C) oven. The filling can bubble over, so don't forget to add the foil or parchment.

Retrieve the chilled pastry-lined tart molds and divide the filling between the tarts, first adding the peels and citrus flesh, then spooning in the liquid. Working with one tart at a time, place a chilled pastry circle "lid" onto the filled tart and, using your fingers, press the pastry along each tart's edge; remove any excess dough. If a bit of liquid seeps from the tart's edge, that's fine. Repeat with the remaining tarts.

Brush the tops of the tarts with whipping cream and sprinkle generously with coarse raw sugar, about ½ tsp (2.5 mL) per tart. Place the tarts on a tray or platter, cover with plastic wrap and refrigerate for at least 30 minutes.

Cut vents into the chilled pastry to hold the candied orange in place (see image, page 287). If not using the garnish, you'll still need to cut a vent into each pastry.

Carefully place the tarts on the preheated baking tray, leaving plenty of room between each. (If using a muffin tin mold, this obviously does not apply.) Bake at 425°F (220°C) for 20 minutes, rotating the pan once during baking. Reduce the heat to 375°F (190°C) and bake for another 15–20 minutes, or until the pastry is cooked through. You'll need to tent the tarts loosely with foil once they've browned to prevent them from burning.

Cool the tarts on a wire rack. Remove the molds and parchment once they've cooled. Garnish with candied orange slices tucked into the pastry vents. Serve at room temperature.

NOTE: Leftover filling can be spooned into buttered ramekins and baked until cooked through. It's delicious with cookies and/or ice cream.

Candied Orange Garnish

INGREDIENTS

1 medium organic orange

1 cup (250 mL) granulated sugar + extra for sprinkling

1 cup (250 mL) water

Using a sharp knife, slice the orange into rounds as thin as possible. It helps to firm the orange in the freezer for about 15 minutes before slicing.

Place the sugar and water in a skillet and bring to a simmer, stirring to help dissolve the sugar. Place the sliced oranges in the sugar water, turn off the heat and allow the slices to steep in the syrup for about 40 minutes. Transfer the slices to a wire rack and sprinkle one side with granulated sugar. Reserve the syrup for another use such as cocktails, sorbet or granita (see Pear Granita, page 229).

Dry overnight at room temperature or in a 175°F (80°C) oven until just firmed.

LEMON MOUSSE TART

YIELD

Makes one 9-inch (23 cm) tart

PASTRY

1 recipe Sweet Tart Dough using the Lemon Variation (page 40), only half the dough needed

LEMON MOUSSE

1 cup (250 mL) whipping cream, chilled

½ cup (125 mL) freshly squeezed lemon juice (about 2–3 lemons)

One 1 Tbsp (15 mL) pkg unflavoured gelatin powder

3 large egg whites

Pinch cream of tartar

½ cup + 1 Tbsp (140 mL) granulated sugar

¼ cup (60 mL) water

GARNISH

Candied Lemons (recipe follows)

SPECIAL EQUIPMENT

9-inch (23 cm) tart pan with a removable base

Pie weights (or beans or rice)

Candy thermometer

THIS REFRESHING lemon mousse is so light, you won't need to save room for dessert. With a buttery pastry and a delicate tangy filling, this tart is adorned with a smattering of sweet candied lemons.

This recipe calls for Italian meringue, a process that involves heating the sugar until it liquifies and reaches 230–240°F (110–120°C) before it's added to the egg whites. If you've never cooked sugar before, don't let the idea put you off. The process is straightforward, and the method creates a super-stable and glossy meringue that's ideal for mousse and many other sweets, including macarons and buttercream. If you love desserts, it's a technique worth adding to your repertoire.

This tart can be prepared up to a day before serving.

PASTRY

Line the base of the tart pan with parchment paper.

Prepare the pastry and place the dough onto a sheet of parchment paper dusted with flour. Layer a sheet of plastic wrap over the dough and roll (over the plastic) from the centre toward the pastry's edge in all directions until about ⅛ inch (3 mm) thick.

Drape the dough over your rolling pin (or use your hands) to transfer the dough to the parchment-lined tart pan, plastic wrap facing up. (It's easier to press the dough into the tart mold if you leave the plastic wrap intact.) If the pastry breaks, use your hands to press the dough, piecemeal if necessary, into the pan and along the sides. Press the dough into the sides of the tart pan with your fingers and trim any excess dough. If desired, use a flat-bottomed cup to level the pastry. Refrigerate for at least 20 minutes.

Preheat oven to 375°F (190°C).

Retrieve the tart from the fridge and, using a fork, prick the dough along the base and sides to prevent it from buckling when heated. Cover with parchment paper or foil and fill to the top with pie weights.

Place on a baking tray and bake for 20 minutes in the preheated oven, rotating the tray once to promote even browning. Remove the tart from the oven and remove the parchment or foil and pie weights. Bake uncovered for another 5–10 minutes or until the pastry is just cooked through, covering with foil if necessary to prevent burning.

Cool on a wire rack. Remove the tart pan once the pastry has cooled.

LEMON MOUSSE

To keep the mousse in place and raised above the level of the tart pan (see image), cut a few 1-inch (2.5 cm) strips of parchment long enough to wrap around the mousse. The parchment is added after the mousse is spooned into the pastry shell; it acts as a collar to keep the mousse in place.

. . . recipe continued

Whip the cream in a medium bowl, cover with plastic wrap and refrigerate until ready to use.

The mousse is perfectly straightforward, but as with all recipes involving cooked sugar, you need to pay attention because timing is everything. Pre-measure your ingredients and have your kitchen tools and precooked tart shell within easy reach. Also, you'll want to ensure your mixing bowl and whisk are meticulously clean and perfectly dry. Any residue of fat (traces of yolk, butter or oil) will compromise the meringue.

Pour half the lemon juice into a medium bowl, and the other half into a small saucepan. Heat the saucepan of lemon juice over low heat just until it starts to simmer. Remove from the heat.

Sprinkle the gelatin power over the hot lemon juice (aim to disperse the powder evenly over the juice, rather than dumping it in one spot) and stir until completely dissolved. Pour the hot lemon mixture into the bowl of lemon juice, stir and set aside.

Place the egg whites in the bowl of a stand mixer fitted with a whisk (or use a medium bowl and a hand mixer). Add a pinch of cream of tartar and whip the egg whites just until they start to appear frothy. Do not whip them to soft billows just yet.

Place the sugar and water in a small saucepan and stir. Clip the candy thermometer to the side of the pan and heat the mixture over medium heat until it reaches 230–240°F (110–120°C), the "soft ball" stage.

Working quickly, carefully pour the sugar syrup into the partially beaten egg whites in a thin, steady stream, while at the same time whipping the egg whites at high speed. Continue to whip until stiff glossy peaks have formed (this will take a few minutes).

Fold the lemon juice mixture into the whipped egg whites in 2–3 batches until well incorporated. It takes a minute for the two textures to properly blend, but it will come together. Finally, fold in the whipped cream.

Without delay, before the mixture sets, spoon the mousse directly into the cooled tart shell, adding enough for the mousse to protrude above the pastry by about ¼ inch (6 mm). Press the strips of parchment around the mousse to hold it in place. Smooth the top with a spatula. Loosely cover with plastic wrap and refrigerate until firm.

Just before serving, remove the parchment paper and garnish with Candied Lemons.

NOTE: Leftover mousse can be portioned into small glasses, see image on page 64.

Candied Lemons

Using a sharp knife, slice the lemons into rounds as thin as possible. It helps to firm the lemons in the freezer for about 10 minutes before slicing. Remove any seeds and place a small bowl of ice water near the stove.

Bring a small pot of water to a boil, add the lemon slices and boil for about a minute. Remove the slices with a slotted spoon and plunge them in ice water for a couple minutes. Drain well.

In a medium skillet, combine the sugar and water and bring to a simmer, stirring occasionally until the sugar has dissolved. Add the lemon slices in a single layer and simmer until the rinds are translucent. This can take up to an hour.

Remove and cool on a wire rack. Reserve the syrup for another use, such as cocktails, sorbet or granitas (see Pear Granita, page 229).

INGREDIENTS

2 lemons, washed

Ice water

2 cups (250 mL) granulated sugar

2 cups (250 mL) water

SWEET & SAVOURY COMPANIONS

Pastry Cream

YIELD

Makes 2 cups (500 mL)

INGREDIENTS

One 1 Tbsp (15 mL) pkg unflavoured gelatin powder, divided

1 cup (250 mL) whole or 2% milk

¼ cup (60 mL) granulated sugar, divided

2 large egg yolks

2 Tbsp (30 mL) all-purpose flour

1 Tbsp (15 mL) rum, cognac or Grand Marnier (optional, but worth adding)

1 cup (250 mL) whipping cream, divided

Featured in the Classic Berry Tarts (page 76), this custard is "lightened" with whipping cream and fortified with gelatin for a stable cream that holds up well in any pastry. Pastry Cream is especially good combined with fresh berries and fruit sauces, such as Blackberry Coulis (page 298).

Pour half the gelatin powder into a small bowl or cup and reserve the other half for the whipping cream.

Heat the milk in a medium saucepan with 2 Tbsp (30 mL) sugar. Bring to a simmer, then remove the pan from the heat. Pour about ¼ cup (60 mL) milk into the gelatin and mix vigorously with a fork or small whisk until completely smooth.

Combine the yolks in a small bowl with the remaining sugar and whisk until smooth. Add the flour and mix until well incorporated (the mixture will be very thick at this stage). Thin the mixture with half about half of the saucepan of warm milk, mix well, then pour the mixture back into the saucepan.

Stir constantly over medium heat with a small whisk or wooden spoon; the mixture will thicken as it cooks. When the custard comes to a low boil, stir for a continuous minute, then remove from the heat. Whisk in the gelatin mixture until completely combined. Stir in the alcohol, if using. Transfer to a clean bowl and cover with plastic wrap, so that the plastic touches the custard (this prevents a skin from forming). Once the mixture cools to room temperature, refrigerate until firm.

Pour the remaining gelatin powder in a small bowl or cup. Heat ¼ cup (60 mL) whipping cream in a small saucepan until just warm. Pour the warm whipping cream over the gelatin and mix vigorously with a fork or small whisk until completely smooth.

Pour the remaining whipping cream into a clean bowl and, using an electric mixer, whisk the cream to a soft peak. Once the gelatin/cream mixture has cooled to room temperature, add it to the whipped cream and continue to whip to a stiff peak. Cover with plastic wrap and refrigerate.

Once the custard and the whipped cream are both chilled, re-whip or stir the custard to loosen it (it should be thick and gelatinous). Finally, fold in the chilled whipped cream in 2 or 3 batches, until well combined. Cover with plastic wrap and refrigerate.

Ginger Spiced Peaches

Featured in the Labneh Tart (page 260), these spicy peaches also complement the Cheesecake Tart (page 258) and can be served alongside the Grand Marnier Soufflé Tart (page 264).

Cut the peaches in two and remove the pits. Slice into wedges about 1 inch (2.5 cm) wide.

Heat the honey, ginger, orange juice and zest in a medium skillet over low heat. Add the peaches in a single layer and cook briefly for a minute or two, until they are just slightly softened but still retain their shape.

Transfer the peaches and juice to a serving container and cool to room temperature before using.

YIELD

Makes 3 cups (750 mL)

INGREDIENTS

6 ripe but firm peaches, skinned (see note)

2 Tbsp (30 mL) honey

2 tsp (10 mL) freshly minced ginger

Zest and juice from 2 large oranges

PEELING PEACHES

To easily skin your peaches, first bring a large pot of water to a boil. Score the circumference of each peach with a sharp paring knife, then carefully lower the peaches into the water for about half a minute. Remove the peaches with a slotted spoon and transfer to a bowl of ice cold water. If the peaches are ripe, the skin should easily peel with your fingers or a knife.

Rhubarb Strawberry Compote

This sweet, tart compote complements both the Labneh Tart (page 260) and the Cheesecake Tart (page 258).

Place the rhubarb in a medium saucepan with the sugar and ¼ cup (60 mL) water. Simmer over medium-low heat until the rhubarb has completely softened, about 10 minutes.

Add the strawberries, ginger and balsamic vinegar and mix until well combined.

YIELD

Makes 3½ cups (875 mL)

INGREDIENTS

2 cups (500 mL) chopped rhubarb (about 450 g)

½ cup (125 mL) granulated sugar

¼ cup (60 mL) water

1 lb (450 g) fresh strawberries, quartered and hulled

1 tsp (5 mL) freshly minced ginger

½ tsp (2.5 mL) balsamic vinegar

Cranberry Relish

YIELD

Makes about 2 cups (500 mL)

INGREDIENTS

½ cup (125 mL) granulated sugar

½ cup (125 mL) water

2 cups (500 mL) fresh or frozen cranberries

Featured in the Gâteau Basque recipe (page 268), this sweet-tart relish also complements creamy pastries such as the Cheesecake Tart (page 258) and Labneh Tart (page 260). It's also delicious puréed or used as a tart or cookie filling. This simple relish has loads of flexibility; feel free to add a splash of freshly squeezed orange juice, Grand Marnier or Cointreau.

Heat the sugar and water in a small saucepan over medium heat to dissolve the sugar. Add the cranberries and cook until they have popped, about 5 minutes.

Transfer to a small bowl and cover with plastic wrap. When the mixture has cooled, refrigerate up to 1 week.

Blackberry Coulis

YIELD

Makes about 1¼ cups (310 mL)

INGREDIENTS

⅓ cup (80 mL) granulated sugar + more as needed

⅓ cup (80 mL) water

1¾ cups (435 mL) fresh blackberries (½ lb/250 g)

2 tsp (10 mL) lemon juice

A welcome addition to the Cheesecake Tart (page 258), this berry coulis (pronounced koo-LEE) can be made with any kind of berry. Coulis is also delicious folded into Pastry Cream (page 296) or drizzled over Pavlova (page 66).

Combine the sugar and water in a small saucepan and bring to a simmer, just until the sugar has dissolved.

Process the berries in a blender or food processor until smooth, then press the purée through a fine-mesh strainer into a bowl, using the back of a ladle or large spoon to extract as much liquid as possible; discard the solids. Add the lemon juice and just enough of the sugar mixture so that the mixture is pourable but not too thin. Taste the coulis and if it needs additional sugar, but not additional liquid, add more granulated sugar by the teaspoon. The coulis should be sweet with a slightly tart edge. Transfer to a spouted container. Cover and refrigerate until ready to use.

Crème Anglaise

Crème Anglaise is a dessert cream that adds an elegant finish to fruit pies, galettes and soufflé tarts. And, like ice cream, it pairs especially well with the Classic Tarte Tatin (page 176), Pure & Simple Apple Pie (page 180) and Fig-Stuffed Apple Dumplings (page 190). However, unlike ice cream, it needs no special equipment.

YIELD

Makes 1 cup (250 mL)

INGREDIENTS

1 cup (250 mL) whole milk

¼ cup + 1 Tbsp (75 mL) sugar, divided

3 large egg yolks

You'll need a fine-mesh strainer placed over a spouted jug before you start. If you don't plan to serve immediately, you'll also need a bowl of ice water large enough to accommodate the jug in order to cool the cream quickly before chilling it in the fridge.

Heat the milk with half the sugar in a small saucepan over medium heat. Bring to a boil, then remove from the heat.

Whisk the yolks with the balance of the sugar in a small bowl until smooth. Add about half the warm milk, mix well and return the mixture to the saucepan of milk.

Cook over medium heat without boiling, stirring constantly, until the cream thickens and lightly coats the back of a spoon. Pour the sauce through the strainer, into the jug.

If not serving immediately, nestle the jug in the bowl of ice water. When the cream has cooled, cover and refrigerate up to 3 days. Serve chilled or gently reheated (without boiling).

Handcrafted Vanilla Ice Cream

YIELD

Makes 4 cups (1 L)

INGREDIENTS

1½ cups (375 mL) whole milk

1½ cups (375 mL) whipping cream

Seeds from a vanilla pod, or 1 tsp (5 mL) vanilla extract

8 egg yolks*

¾ cup (185 mL) sugar

*Leftover egg whites can be used to make meringue (see Pavlova recipe, page 66).

Featured alongside the Blueberry Blackberry Galette (page 80), handcrafted ice cream is a welcome companion to just about every sweet pie in this book. You'll need an ice cream maker, but once you've tasted handcrafted, you'll understand why homemade outshines store-bought.

You'll need to plan ahead, as the ice cream canister needs to be frozen at least 24 hours before using.

Heat the milk, cream and vanilla seeds, or extract, in a medium saucepan over medium heat, until the mixture just begins to boil. Remove from the heat.

Whisk together the egg yolks and sugar in a medium bowl. Add about 1 cup (125 mL) of the warm milk and cream to the egg yolks and whisk until the mixture is loosened and well combined. Slowly pour this mixture into the saucepan of milk and cream and bring to a bare simmer, whisking constantly, until the custard thickens and lightly coats the back of a spoon.

Pour the custard through a strainer into a bowl. Cool the custard quickly by placing the bowl into a larger bowl filled with ice. Cover and refrigerate until well chilled.

Pour the chilled custard into a frozen ice cream canister and churn according to the manufacturer's instructions. Transfer to a freezer-safe container and freeze until ready to serve.

Whipped Labneh

YIELD

About 2¼ cups (530 mL)

INGREDIENTS

1 cup (250 mL) whipping cream

4 tsp (20 mL) granulated sugar

½ cup (125 mL) labneh (for homemade, see page 263)

Labneh (strained yogurt) and sweetened whipping cream are combined for a tangy topping that requires no cooking. This recipe pairs especially well with fruit pies and galettes, as well as the Tarte au Sucre (page 256).

You'll need to strain the yogurt overnight (see Labneh recipe, page 263), so plan accordingly.

In a small bowl, whip the cream with the sugar. Whisk the labneh to soften, add to the whipped cream and mix until combined. Serve chilled.

Sweet & Spicy Nuts

Adapted from a *Food & Wine* magazine recipe, these spiced nuts are made for tinkering—try swapping the ginger and cinnamon for cumin and coriander or rosemary and thyme. Or, if you prefer a little more heat, kick up the cayenne and add dried chili flakes.

These addictive fall-spiced nuts, featured in the Poached Pear Tarts (see page 226), can also be served alongside any of the apple recipes in the book. They freeze beautifully.

YIELD

Makes 2 cups (500 mL)

INGREDIENTS

½ cup (125 mL) granulated sugar

½ tsp (2.5 mL) kosher salt

1 tsp (5 mL) cinnamon

½ tsp (2.5 mL) allspice powder

½ tsp (2.5 mL) ground ginger

½ tsp (2.5 mL) cayenne pepper

1 egg white

2 cups (500 mL) assorted salted nuts (walnuts, almonds, hazelnuts, etc.)

Preheat oven to 300°F (150°C).

In a small bowl, combine the sugar, salt, cinnamon, allspice powder, ground ginger and cayenne pepper.

In a medium bowl, whip the egg white until just frothy. Add the nuts and sugar/spice mixture and mix to combine. Spread the mixture onto a baking tray lined with parchment, foil or a non-stick baking mat. Bake for about 30 minutes, rotating the tray once during baking.

Allow the nuts to cool. If they're sticky after baking (rather than crisp), place them back in a 175°F (80°C) oven for another 15 minutes or until they're no longer sticky. Alternatively, if your oven isn't too warm, you can leave them inside with the oven turned off until they're no longer sticky.

Caramel Sauce

YIELD

Makes 1¼ cups (310 mL)

INGREDIENTS

- 1¼ cups (310 mL) whipping cream
- ½ cup (125 mL) granulated sugar
- ¼ cup (60 mL) water
- 2 Tbsp (30 mL) unsalted butter (about 30 g)

Served alongside the Fig-Stuffed Apple Dumplings (page 190), this luscious sauce would also pair beautifully with most of the pastries in the Apple and Chocolate chapters, as well as the pear recipes in the Fruit & Nut chapter.

Caramel sauce is simply caramelized sugar with the addition of cream and butter. Cooking sugar is straightforward, but it demands your full attention, as it can turn from golden to smoking char in a heartbeat. You'll need to read the instructions to the end before starting. Then, read them again. Cooking sugar is all about timing, and everything needs to be in place before you start.

One final caution—sugar can also crystallize as it cooks. To prevent sugar crystals from forming and ruining your caramel, place a cup of water and a silicone brush near your stovetop. As the sugar cooks, brush away bits of sugar that sputter and cling to the sides of your pan.

Heat the whipping cream in a small saucepan just until it simmers. Remove from the heat and keep warm.

In a deep, medium-sized saucepan (the mixture rises as it bubbles) with a heavy bottom, combine the sugar and water and bring the mixture to a boil over medium heat. As the sugar melts and turns to a clear syrup, brush away any bits of sugar that cling to the sides of the pan with your silicone brush dipped in water. Continue to cook the sugar until the mixture turns a deep golden.

Swiftly and carefully pour the warm cream into the sugar, being mindful that the hot caramel will bubble madly with the addition of cream. Add the butter and stir to combine.

Strain the cream through a fine-mesh strainer into a clean jar. Keeps for about a week in the refrigerator.

Rustic Tapenade

Featured in the Deep-Dish Vegetable Pie (page 126) and Savoury Pastry Straws (page 62) recipes, this green and black olive tapenade lends a pleasing briny, tangy punch to everything from cheese to eggs. The olives can be chopped by hand or with a food processor.

YIELD

Makes about 1 cup (250 mL)

INGREDIENTS

½ cup (125 mL) Kalamata olives (about 90 g), finely chopped

½ cup (125 mL) green olives (about 90 g), finely chopped

1 Tbsp (15 mL) capers, rinsed and drained

½ tsp (2.5 mL) finely minced garlic (about 1 small clove)

1 anchovy, rinsed and finely minced (optional)

1 Tbsp (15 mL) lemon juice + more as needed

1½ Tbsp (22 mL) olive oil

Combine all ingredients except for the oil in a small bowl and mix well. Add the olive oil and mix to combine. Taste and season with additional lemon juice, if desired.

Sun-Dried Tomato & Roasted Garlic Pesto

This roasted garlic pesto imparts a sweet and smoky tomato punch to the Deep-Dish Vegetable Pie (page 126) and Savoury Pastry Straws (page 62). This is potent pesto—a little goes a long way.

YIELD

Makes about ½ cup (125 mL)

INGREDIENTS

2 heads garlic

½ cup (125 mL) sun-dried tomatoes packed in oil (about 130 g), drained and finely chopped

2 tsp (10 mL) smoked (not hot) paprika + more as needed

2 tsp (10 mL) freshly squeezed lemon juice + more as needed

Preheat oven to 375°F (190°C).

Cut ¼ inch (6 mm) from the tip of each head of garlic so the cloves are revealed. Wrap the heads in foil and bake for about 30 minutes, or until soft and tender.

In a small bowl, combine the chopped sun-dried tomatoes with the paprika and lemon juice. When the garlic is cool enough to handle, squeeze the cloves from their skins and add them to the tomato mixture. Taste and season, adding additional lemon juice or paprika, if desired.

Tangy Dill Sauce

YIELD

Makes 1½ cups (375 mL)

INGREDIENTS

¾ cup (185 mL) mayonnaise

¾ cup (185 mL) labneh (for homemade, see page 263)

2 tsp (10 mL) freshly squeezed lemon juice + more as needed

½ tsp (2.5 mL) kosher salt + more as needed

2 Tbsp (30 mL) freshly chopped dill

½ Tbsp (7.5 mL) hot sauce, such as Sriracha

Featured alongside the Salmon Coulibiac (page 166), this simple sauce also brightens vegetables and chicken. The labneh, or strained yogurt, gives this sauce a pleasant tangy note.

If you don't have time to make labneh, you can use plain Greek-style yogurt for a thinner sauce.

Combine the ingredients in a small bowl. Taste and add additional lemon or salt, if desired.

Creamy Coleslaw

YIELD

Makes about 8 cups (2 L)

COLESLAW

8 cups (2 L) shredded or thinly sliced cabbage (about half a cabbage)

1 carrot, peeled and shredded or thinly sliced

2 Tbsp (30 mL) finely chopped mint

DRESSING

½ cup + 2 Tbsp (155 mL) mayonnaise

2 tsp (10 mL) granulated sugar

2 Tbsp (30 mL) Dijon-style mustard

2 tsp (10 mL) hot chili sauce, such as Sriracha

3 Tbsp (45 mL) vinegar (white wine, rice or apple cider are all good choices) + more as needed

½ tsp (2.5 mL) kosher salt + more as needed

This old-time salad is never out of style and is especially satisfying with heartier pies like Tourtière with Duck Confit (page 154), Beef Pot Pies (page 138) or Deep-Dish Chicken Pie (page 150).

Toss the cabbage and carrot in a large bowl.

Combine the dressing ingredients in a small bowl or cup and whisk together.

Pour the dressing over the cabbage mixture and mix well. Taste the salad and add additional salt or vinegar, if desired. Just before serving, add the chopped mint and mix well.

Transfer to a serving dish and serve chilled or at room temperature.

Garden Salad

This simple, refreshing salad plays an appetizing support role. It goes especially well with the Crab & Tarragon Quiche (page 170), Salmon Coulibiac (page 166), Fish Pot Pies (page 162) and Black Forest Ham Pithivier (page 144).

YIELD

Makes about 5½ cups (1.3 L)

SALAD

4 cups (1 L) mixed salad greens

2 spring onions, thinly sliced

2 baby cucumbers, peeled and sliced

1 cup (250 mL) snow peas, thinly sliced

1 carrot, thinly sliced

1 handful cilantro (about ⅓ cup/80 mL), roughly chopped

1 handful mint (about ⅓ cup/80 mL), roughly chopped

DRESSING

2 Tbsp (30 mL) white wine vinegar

1 tsp (5 mL) Dijon-style mustard

¼ tsp (1 mL) kosher salt

½ cup (125 mL) neutral-flavoured vegetable oil (grapeseed, canola or safflower are good choices)

GARNISH

¼ cup (60 mL) chopped nuts (peanuts, hazelnuts or almonds), for garnish

Combine all of the salad ingredients together in a large bowl and toss together.

Combine the dressing ingredients in a small jar and whisk together.

Just before serving, drizzle the dressing over the salad, toss and transfer to a salad bowl or individual plates. Garnish with the chopped nuts.

Red Onion Relish

Featured alongside the Tourtière with Duck Confit (page 154), this tart, honeyed relish also pairs well with pâté and cheese.

YIELD

Makes about 2 cups (500 mL)

INGREDIENTS

2 Tbsp (30 mL) vegetable oil

2½ cups (625 mL) sliced red onion (about 2–3 onions)

½ tsp (2.5 mL) kosher salt

½ cup (125 mL) red wine vinegar

2 Tbsp (30 mL) honey

Heat the oil in a large skillet over medium heat; add the onion slices, turning them with a wooden spoon to coat them evenly. Add the salt and cook until the onions soften, about 10–12 minutes, stirring occasionally to prevent burning.

Stir in the vinegar, scraping the bottom of the pan as you do so. Add the honey, reduce the heat and continue simmering until the liquid has evaporated.

Serve warm or at room temperature. Store in the refrigerator up to 2 weeks.

Roasted Chicken Stock

YIELD

Makes 12–15 cups (3–3.5 L)

INGREDIENTS

5 lb (2.2 kg) meaty chicken bones, cut into 2- to 3-inch (5–8 cm) chunks

Water

Bouquet garni (bundled parsley stems, bay leaves and fresh thyme tied with kitchen string)

2 bay leaves

½ tsp (2.5 mL) whole peppercorns

2 small onions, peeled and quartered

3 carrots, peeled and coarsely chopped

1 celery rib, coarsely chopped

Kosher salt

Although it might seem odd to include chicken stock in a book devoted to pies, many of the savoury meat pies rely on a good hearty stock, and although it's easy to grab a box from the grocery store, your pastries will be so much more flavourful if you use homemade.

Many of us were taught to make stock by tossing our leftover chicken or turkey carcasses into a pot of simmering water, along with some chopped onions and celery. While this makes a perfectly acceptable stock, a better way to amp up the flavour is to start with raw, meaty chicken bones and roast them before adding them to the water. When chicken wings (or pieces) are on sale, it's a great time to make stock. Bones themselves impart little flavour.

Do *not* salt your stock, otherwise it will be oversalted when it's reduced. Salt can be added later, when you're cooking with the stock.

Preheat oven to 375°F (190°C).

Scatter the meaty bones in a single layer on a baking tray and roast until browned, turning the bones as necessary to colour them evenly. This can take up to an hour.

When the bones are golden, transfer them to a stock pot. Drain the fat from the roasting pan then place the pan directly on the stove over medium-high heat, straddling multiple burners if necessary. Add just enough water (about ⅓ cup/ 80 mL) to loosen any bits of meat stuck to the bottom of the pan, then scrape the pan clean with a flat-edged wooden spoon or spatula. Pour the liquid into the stock pot, bits and all. Add the bouquet garni and enough cold water to cover the bones by an inch.

Bring the stock to a simmer, uncovered, for 3–4 hours, adjusting the heat as necessary to maintain a bare simmer. Using a ladle or large spoon, skim and discard any foam that rises to the surface of the pot.

Add additional water as necessary to keep the bones covered. The stock should not boil, as this tends to cloud the stock. Add the vegetables to the stock toward the last 40 minutes of simmering.

To test the stock, ladle ¼ cup (60 mL) into a cup, season with a light pinch of salt and taste. If the stock needs more flavour, continue to simmer.

When you are satisfied with the flavour, strain the stock through a colander and discard the bones and vegetables. Pass the liquid again through a strainer lined with cheesecloth into a clean container.

Cool the stock quickly by placing the container in a larger bowl filled with ice water. Once cooled, place in the refrigerator overnight, or long enough for the fat to solidify and form a layer on top.

Remove the solidified fat with a spoon and reserve, if desired, to use as a cooking fat. The stock, now somewhat gelatinous, can be used immediately or portioned into freezer bags and frozen until ready to use.

ACKNOWLEDGMENTS

Behind the scenes are a special group of people who volunteered their time to test recipes. These generous bakers, novices to certified pros, offered helpful suggestions and feedback to help ensure the instructions are clear and the results successful. Their invaluable contributions have helped create a book that is accessible to pie lovers everywhere.

ELLY DRIESSEN

CAROLYN HENSON

KARRI HEYWOOD-SMITH

KATHRYN MUNROE

NANCY PEARSON

LAURI PERRON

CHERYL STERNMAN RULE

KIM TURNER

NICK VERSTEEG

YVETTE WELLS

GAIL WHITE

SPECIAL THANKS

While my shaggy dough of a manuscript took shape there were friends, colleagues and family along the way to lend their support. There's plenty of gratitude to go around.

My first thanks go to my inspired co-partner Deb Garlick, whose playful blend of creativity and whimsy brought life to this book. Deb's photography and artwork created a sense of *joie de vivre*—bringing a fresh look to an old-world craft. I was taken by Deb's commitment to excellence and my ever-present dachshund, Olive, fell hard too (which may explain why Olive has cameo appearances throughout this book).

Deb and I would like to jointly thank Sharon Fitzhenry, CEO, Whitecap Books, for her enthusiasm from the get-go. Receiving Sharon's call the day our proposal landed on her desk was a joy we won't soon forget. Special thanks to Editor Patrick Geraghty for giving the manuscript such meticulous attention. Patrick's suggestions brought order and clarity to all the persnickety details, making the book all the more accessible. And to Andrew Bagatella for designing the book with such thoughtful care.

A heap of thanks to my family, Lucie, Elise, Stephanie, Claudia and Michael for your loving support, near and far. This lovefest includes my rock-steady sibs Brenda, Brian, Robert, Louise and Lorette. And my generous brother-in-law, Firoz, for sharing his standout samosa filling.

Karri Haywood-Smith, dear friend, accomplice at culinary school and go-to gal for all my pastry musings, thank you for the outstanding shortcrust recipe and for testing the lion's share of recipes with such fierce dedication. Who else could I discuss the minutiae of recipes with—and at all hours? I owe you a lifetime supply of pie.

Nancy Pearson, writer and confidant, who never hesitated to review a recipe or food article and found the time to test recipes despite a heartache of a year—thank you for being such a stellar wingman and for lending such thoughtful support no matter how turbulent the skies. You're a cherished friend.

Angela Oakley, and all my Oceanwood neighbours, for boarding the pie train and taste testing my pies at various stages of development. Thanks for feedback and the unexpected treats that showed up at my doorstep in return. From flowers to freshly caught fish and hand-knitted socks, your generosity made this pastry venture an unexpected joy.

Jenni and Nigel Bass, for supplying the perfect pears for a photo shoot and for years of farm fresh eggs. And, for (unwittingly) taste testing many a pie recipe while still in progress.

Carolyn Henson, not only for your hilarious and spot-on recipe testing notes, but for years of friendship, always sharing your latest kitchen tips, recipes and Costco steals.

Sue Pearson, dear friend, who inspired me to include beef pasties in the lineup—and who reminds me that nothing is sweeter than the taste of home.

Chef Natasha Norton, Pacific Institute of Culinary Arts, for helping me to clarify the breakdown of pastry in simple and relatable terms.

Gail White, talented cook and generous friend, for sharing your mother's seriously decadent pecan pie recipe. And for your meticulous and always entertaining recipe testing commentary.

Cheryl Sternman Rule, not only for the professional recipe testing (or the fun of slipping in a quote from your book, *Yogurt Culture*) but for a friendship I cherish even more than pie.

Lora Lonesberry, former pastry chef and dedicated food lover, for the ground tapioca hack (goodbye gelatinous blobs!) and lively food conversations.

Mrs. Galey of Blenkinsop Valley's Galey Farms, for personally picking the most gorgeous berries early one morning to ensure our photo shoot featured the freshest, most beautiful berries possible.

My writing friends: Pamela Tarlow-Calder, Phillipa Sherrill, Courtney Waverick, Jane Miller and Karen Sawatzky, for rallying near the finish line, once again. Heartfelt thanks for brightening our Zoom calls with your long distance laughter, thoughtful suggestions and ever-constructive feedback.

To the generous folks at Everything Old Canada, Brentwood Bay, for lending their gorgeous pastry wares for a photo session. Nothing brings a smile quite like a vintage rolling pin.

Carolyn Bateman for reviewing each recipe with a cook's sensibility, offering suggestions and edits with the kindest touch imaginable.

Julie Beauchamp, for generously sharing her family's outstanding tarte au sucre recipe, passed down from generations of Québécois bakers. Merci beaucoup!

Jenni Hopkyns, mentor and friend, for providing the most perfect apples, fresh off your tree, for an opportune photo shoot.

Michelle Barker for reviewing recipe headers and dishing out comments with her usual wit. And for cracking me up with her memorable apple pie adventure.

Lis Wirsching, the greatest of pie champions, who tried to convince me decades ago to market my pies under her half-baked slogan "Dee's pies are better than 'does pies." Now you have all my pastry secrets and can finally let go of the nectarine pie that got away (a mishap involving a speeding van, a just-baked pie cooling on the passenger seat and a sharp corner).

And finally, my darling Claude, who took on more than a few pounds for this project, taste testing every recipe and cheerfully distributing pie samples throughout our neighbourhood. You've been my biggest supporter, ever since you declared your love for my blueberry pie on our second date. Pie Love You.

NOTE FROM DEB

A thank you to Denise, for inviting me to collaborate on this project. Every shoot day began with an excited, wiggling Olive, Denise's miniature dachshund, and Denise's big smile of welcome.

Denise went to extraordinary lengths to ensure the integrity of every recipe. It was a wonderful experience to work beside her. Her passion for food and flavour, and my passion for illustration and photography, came together like the best kind of recipe. I am delighted to have had this opportunity to create *The Artful Pie Project* with Denise.

And Olive, of course.

INDEX

D

E

F

G

Q

R

S

ABOUT THE AUTHOR & ARTIST/PHOTOGRAPHER

DENISE MARCHESSAULT (AUTHOR)

Denise is a freelance food writer and cooking instructor with a Grand Diplôme from Le Cordon Bleu, Ottawa. Her first cookbook, *British Columbia From Scratch,* is a culinary bear hug to her native home. With a weakness for pies and dachshunds, and a penchant for early morning hikes, Denise enjoys life in Victoria, BC with her husband and twin daughters.

www.denisem.ca

DEB GARLICK (ARTIST AND PHOTOGRAPHER)

Deb is a painter, illustrator, photo stylist and photographer in Victoria, BC. Her art has appeared on book covers, in collaborative projects and part of private collections internationally. When she's not working, she spends her time travelling, running, reading or in the bath. Her home and patio garden, on the top floor of a big, old mansion, on a hill with a view, is a whole creative world.

www.debgarlick.com